More Praise for *First in the Family*

"Jessica Hoppe's *First in the Family* crackles like a bonfire: fierce and wise, bearing light and warmth. I read it in a single sitting, breathless and grateful, spellbound by a voice vibrating with insight, compassion, and candor, and a reckoning unafraid to wrestle fully with the important truths and histories at stake. Like so many American traditions, recovery in the United States has been dominated by whiteness that claims what it did not discover and refuses to listen to what it doesn't want to hear, but Hoppe's stunning book invites us into the next necessary chapter of our collective recovery from our deluded dreams, challenging us to remember James Baldwin's call: 'Everything now, we must assume, is in our hands; we have no right to assume otherwise.' Hoppe does not assume otherwise. Instead, she tells her story and follows it outward into a stunning illumination of American life."
—Leslie Jamison, *New York Times* bestselling author of
The Recovering and *The Empathy Exams*

"A powerful thunderclap of a memoir, Jessica Hoppe's *First in the Family* is a rich excavation of one woman's descent into addiction and the power found in laying it all bare. Hoppe's uncompromising voice doesn't hide behind platitudes but gently unravels damaging legacies tied to the American Dream with a much-needed critique of the recovery movement. A triumphant example of hope where breaking harmful cycles is not found in the individual achievement but in a collective one."
—Lilliam Rivera, award-winning author of *Dealing in Dreams*

"*First in the Family* sings with love and shouts with rage, offering an uplifting account of resilience and recovery even while calling out the seductive dangers of the American Dream. Jessica Hoppe has crafted an important, pathbreaking contribution by distilling the historical stakes of the addiction crisis while simultaneously presenting a wrenching and unique personal narrative. It's an insightful chronicle of the burdens of specialness, the weight of intergenerational trauma, and the stigma of addiction. In the end, it's an inspiring and essential message that there are numerous and diverse pathways of recovery."

—Carl Erik Fisher, MD, author of *The Urge*

"*First in the Family* is a riveting memoir but also a tender guide to overcoming—addiction, trauma, colonialism. It takes a writer with great emotional intelligence and generosity to trace the harrowing moments of her life back to the invisible systems and structures that damage every one of us. Jessica Hoppe has done that and more."

—Alejandro Varela, author of *The Town of Babylon*

"*First in the Family* is the book I've been waiting for: A powerful reckoning combined with an inspiring sense of freedom. Perfect for anyone questioning their relationship with alcohol and looking for an honest account of what it takes to navigate sobriety as a woman of color."

—Lupita Aquino, *Lupita Reads*

FIRST IN THE FAMILY

FIRST IN THE FAMILY

A Story of Survival, Recovery, and the American Dream

———

Jessica Hoppe

FLATIRON
BOOKS

NEW YORK

www.flatironbooks.com

Grateful acknowledgment is made for permission to reproduce from the following: Arundhati Roy, *My Seditious Heart: Collected Nonfiction.* Copyright © 2019 by Arundhati Roy.

Designed by Steven Seighman

Library of Congress Cataloging-in-Publication Data

Names: Hoppe, Jessica, author.
Title: First in the family : a story of survival, recovery, and the American dream / Jessica Hoppe.
Description: First edition. | New York : Flatiron Books, 2024. | Includes bibliographical references.
Identifiers: LCCN 2024000567 | ISBN 9781250865229 (hardcover) | ISBN 9781250865243 (ebook)
Subjects: LCSH: Hoppe, Jessica. | Alcoholics—United States—Biography. | Alcoholics Anonymous. | American Dream. | Racism—United States.
Classification: LCC HV5293.H555 A3 2024 | DDC 362.292092 [B]—dc23/eng/20240326
LC record available at https://lccn.loc.gov/2024000567

Our books may be purchased in bulk for promotional, educational, or business use. Please contact your local bookseller or the Macmillan Corporate and Premium Sales Department at 1-800-221-7945, extension 5442, or by email at MacmillanSpecialMarkets@macmillan.com.

First Edition: 2024

10 9 8 7 6 5 4 3 2 1

To Leo, Bella, Joshua, Emma, Zahir, and Jewel.
Should you ever have to go first, I'll be there for you.

Abby, Maria, and Hans, mis primos queridos,
I love you.
I'm so proud to be your family.

Contents

Come here, fear.
I am alive and you are so afraid of dying.

—Joy Harjo, "I Give You Back"

FIRST IN THE FAMILY

Introduction

I tell this story in fragments because a drunk's memory is fragmented. Because being broken means breaking a narrative spine. A blow I never mended, one split and shattered by alcohol.

Drunks have a reputation for being liars, and I've been called a liar all my life. I never thought of my secrets as lies. Fighting for survival can make a liar out of anyone. But when I got sober I learned that secrets, which are just lies of concealment, are bullshit—believing we must hide the intimate truths that make us human is what makes us sick. *You're only as sick as your secrets*, they say. An elixir far more toxic than any drink, and one I'd been served for as long as I could remember.

I've told this story in fragments because the way we drunks tell our stories matters. The process of recovery is the art of narration. We need the truth to heal. In the rooms, we share snippets of our lives—our lives before, our lives after—in three-minute increments. Slumped in a chair, seated in a circle, each note an echo as strangers speak their truths, our backs straightening with each disclosure. Every story shared brought my own into focus as I stitched my narrative together.

I was not the first in my family to get sick. My family was plagued. The chronic stress of survival inflames the body. Doctors directly correlate chronic stress—particularly racialized trauma—with high blood pressure, diabetes, heart disease, autoimmune disorders, and substance use disorders. My family suffered from all these conditions, though they would never claim such a dubious honor. Addiction was considered not a medical problem but a moral one, especially by the people in my family. To them, addiction wasn't something you got, it was something you did. All you had to do was say no.

Addiction functions like a chronic disease, but it's also a coping strategy. It's how we manage stress and trauma. We tend to think of addiction as hurtling toward death, but it's about wanting to live. It's a primitive search for something higher, holier than the pain of our own reality. We want to find a way to live through the misery.

Coming to terms with myself as an alcoholic, as an addict, was a shock. I felt ashamed and demoralized by my dependency, but more than anything, I was sick of being afraid. Done with being silent. I swore to myself that I would no longer allow anything or anyone to rob me of the right to my story.

I was told the first step was to remove alcohol, and I did. But I also felt that right was never mine in the first place. I knew there was a time when I was whole—I was very young, and the moment was fleeting—but I knew who the fuck I was. And I know that confidence was taken from me. That was why I drank. I was in too much pain to feel, flayed by my own numbness. The pain I felt was the pain of not feeling. I was stripped of the essence of what makes us human.

I've told this story in fragments because it's the closest I can get to the truth. I want to tell you the truth. Trust me. I want you to trust me. And the fact is I wasn't cured with an epiphany, blinded by the white light of a heavenly vision. I didn't dig into scholarly texts or see a doctor—there was no intervention. I stopped reaching outside of myself to be told what I knew best. I sat, I allowed myself to feel, I gave myself time for my instincts to return. I stopped doubting and questioning them. I listened, knowing there was a reason they were here. Instincts exist for a reason.

But I don't have the answers. That's also the truth. In place of answers, I offer you a story—my story, though it's not really about me. No story is ever about one person, and I wasn't interested in a character study. This is a journey study—the embodied experience of a family. A family full of firsts—the first to go to college, the first to own a house, the first to write a book. The first to get sober. Being first in the family is just another way to tell a story about who we are—it's a story we tell ourselves and one we proudly tell others.

But what does it really mean to be first? It can mean ending cycles of generational trauma, yet it can also mean lighting the match that burns fresh blisters. It can mean liberation, it can mean achievement; but such prizes can be burdens, too.

Eventually, every substance stops working—they lose their anesthetizing effect, their energizing power. The tang of the Kool-Aid dulls. If we're lucky, we come to a place of powerlessness. We tell the truth, we tell our story, and we purge the lies from our system. We finally see things as they are.

That's the story, a kind of meta-story, that I most want to share; this story, this dream, was the first drug to seduce me. It's the story we're all told, an addiction we all share. My family's misunderstanding of substance use disorder wasn't due to their ignorance or inclination toward callous judgment, but it was a result of that addictive story—this story is the poison, as powerful as that first hit. This story tells us that we aren't sick; we're bad. That we'll be safe when we arrive. That our threadbare bootstraps can hold. That failure is inadequacy—constitutional incapability. That story is the American Dream. It is the ultimate gateway drug.

Where I got sober, the American Dream was baked into the recovery process. In some ways, it was its founding document. I got clean and I got clear in the rooms of Alcoholics Anonymous, an organization founded by two white men who didn't think much about how people like me—a brown woman in debt, not from drinking but from the failures of a system that propped up people who looked like them—would fit into their program of recovery. Still, it saved my life. And for that, I am grateful. But it was just the beginning.

The longer I stayed, the deeper I reached into the well. My hands found sediment at the base. Coming into awareness meant understanding the root of my pain. That included the harm that can be perpetuated within AA.

I needed to break free of my addiction to drugs and alcohol, but also of my addiction to being first, to being excellent and exceptional, a model minority. Paradoxically, despite my pursuit of this label, and recognizing no one label could define me, it is not what set me free. And all I want, all any of us wants, is to be free. Free from feeling like we're a work in progress. Free from believing that we deserve what we get, that we'll only be worthy when we're out of debt, own a home, or have a kid. Model minority narratives traffic in a mindset that judges our humanity by our output, cataloging brown life in binary columns of good immigrant versus bad hombre, essential versus deportable. Identifying as an addict bestowed upon me a legacy I never wanted. I wanted the exceptional one, the multihyphenate one, the #latinagenius one. Recovery exposed the danger of this seductive message. It is a familiar siren song, a popular narrative among the white-adjacent architects of the Latinx monolith in recruiting racialized youth—one that tells us we are worthy only when we are extraordinary, when we prove our resilience.

I'm writing this book not because I believe my story can save you but because I want you to know: yours will.

———

I never learned the true history of substance use disorder in my family—people just disappeared, a tradition across the Americas as old as colonialism. Many developed dependencies on drugs and alcohol to cope with the pain of their untreated trauma and minoritization in this country—grandparents estranged, uncles deported, cousins dead. Researching their stories was also exploring my own history, retracing my steps, and identifying the traps set out for me, the same set for generations. Eventually, I forgave myself for falling into them, too.

In my recovery I began to turn over the stones of our family secrets. I could no longer stomach secrets. Why did my mother wait until her father's death to admit he was an alcoholic? Could my mother stand shoulder to shoulder with me as a survivor without blaming herself? Would we always deny our homelessness, incarcerations, and deportations? How could I explain that the violence my parents fled was inescapable? Could they acknowledge that it hurt me, too?

I sat at kitchen tables, took long car rides, and spammed the family group chat—all in pursuit of the answers to these questions and others. I collected the pieces of my identity and asked my parents to see *me* when they called out the druggie, la puta, la sinvergüenza. What I found initiated a new chapter for our family to write our story on our terms.

The story of being "first in the family" denies the things of value created by our ancestors, separating us from our inherent worth. It is the blow that shatters us and scatters the pieces. We are set on a path to prove our humanity. Only that path is a dead end. The way out is found inside of us, and the key that unlocks it is love. You must learn to love yourself again. Without conditions. Not with a love that insists we earn a prize to be worthy of it. Not with a love that demands we live up to something, that we climb to the top of a pedestal and sit there alone. A love that is immense, encompassing, and wholehearted enough to ask a mother or a father or a friend: *Will you come with me?* Mending that separation reminds us of who we belong to—that being first in the family is not the responsibility of the individual but the work of the collective. A reclamation in the family name.

Our strategy should be not only to confront empire but to lay siege to it. To deprive it of oxygen. To shame it. To mock it. With our art, our music, our literature, our stubbornness, our joy, our brilliance, our sheer relentlessness—and our ability to tell our own stories. Stories that are different from the ones we're being brainwashed to believe.

—Arundhati Roy, *My Seditious Heart*

1

Dream On

In recovery, they tell you that the day you stop using is called your birthday. As if you've been born again.

I hate that shit.

I was born once, on November 5, in a Catholic hospital in San Antonio, Texas, in front of a bunch of nuns who wouldn't let my father in the room. I know it wasn't his choice or his fault, but I have always resented that he wasn't there to see me come into this world. In my newborn portrait, with my tiny ears already pierced, I am visibly upset, presumably at my father and the nuns, my small hands as coiled as my face, with one digit on my left hand poking straight up—my middle finger, as if flipping off the viewer—and yet no one saw me coming.

——

The most powerful weapon in the American arsenal is the story. The narratives we're spoon-fed from birth. You can be anything you wanna be, anything you put your mind to, if you work hard enough. If you're *good* enough: smart, pretty, rich, or white enough.

There's an unspoken standard. One that has nothing to do with you; it's not made for you, doesn't give a fuck about you. If you aren't naturally good, born into goodness, or destined to acquire it, they promise you'll get there. You can get the degree, land the job, buy the house and put up a white picket fence. You can throw a white wedding on credit, have the two point five kids and smile, always smile, say thank you (en inglés, tiene que ser), lose the accent, keep your head down, cover up, and wash out your hair before you leave the house. You do not want to remind people of where you're really from, who you really are.

When you live your life trying to balance on the width of a tight-rope, no one tells you there is freedom beyond its edge. They tell you that if you slip, nothing will break your fall.

The first margin I ever encountered was a long pink vertical line on the left side of a piece of single-space paper when I opened my notebook on my first day of school. The place I was told marked the starting line of my story. One I never managed to stop trespassing. The last was the windowsill across the hall from the door of the home where I once lived. Five stories high, barely five inches wide. I stepped out on the ledge in a stupor, reached for the pebbled corners of the cement frame, splayed like a starfish and hidden from the police who had been called a second time to remove me from the building. Permanently.

It was not an insatiable drive for danger that propelled me to risk my life. I was trying to escape. I was accustomed to being captive, running for the exit only to fall through a trapdoor. I was so familiar with being marginalized, confined to a box and tossed to the back. Why would I fear what I know?

———

My mother used the term *desalmado* the other day. She was talking about her father, the first addict in our family we ever discussed in this way, meaning we named it, or at least I did. I called him an addict.

I repeated the word, *desalmado*, held it in my mouth, spit it out, and picked it apart. *Alma*, a word like honey, its potency derived from its sweetness, stands raised like a flag between the most curious modifiers. *Alma. Soul.* The whole word, *desalmado*, doesn't mean my grandfather was born soulless. The *des* that dresses *alma* doesn't mean he never had one; it implies that he lost it. Somewhere along the way, his soul was removed from his body.

Desalmado. Look it up in the dictionary and you'll find the English word *fiend*.

The thing my grandfather and I were both addicted to—at least, the thing that got the most attention—was, or perhaps for me still is, alcohol. How I wish I could have talked to him about our shared infatuation, asked him how it began and ended, how much it hurt him, and how he still never gave it up. How instead he lost us, hardly knew us.

I would have told him I drank Mind Erasers in college. That's how the need for alcohol every day started for me. I worked as a waitress at McCormick & Schmick's, an upscale chain restaurant in the Boston Theater District that served seafood to suburbanites in town to catch a show.

In the course of one shift, I'd push a steaming ladle through the gelatinous fat that accumulated at the top of the clam chowder pot hundreds of times. I'd carry dozens of seafood towers as tall as me, pounds and pounds of lobster tail and shrimp scampi so hot and so heavy that the weight bent my wrists until my knuckles touched my forearm. Eventually, I could carry three at a time, one in each hand and another balanced against the inside of my arm, the flat, soft, lighter skin offered up like a platter, my bust reinforcing the precarious placement, the hot plate branding the side of my breast in wine-dark blots. "You're stronger than you look," my manager would remark. I'd already learned to take that as a compliment.

At the end of the night, after taking orders, after burning my hands to fulfill the desires of others, when I could peel the skin of my labor from my callused palms and my bruised feet and reward myself with a drink, it would all be worth it. I'd strip off my damp uniform in the single-user bathroom off the bar. Rinse off the crud of clam chowder gunked onto the sleeves of my white button-down, run the elbows, where butter had pooled into a stain, under hot water and hope I wouldn't have to return to Filene's Basement to get a new one. I'd yank my hair loose from the tight regulation ponytail, scratch my scalp with my nails, and catch a whiff of the stench of fried fish oil. I'd flip my hair back and forth over my knees a couple of times like a headbanger at a metal concert in an attempt to shake out the dank smell, then head straight to the bar. Into a pint glass—the size we used to serve water, lemonade, and sodas—the bartender would pour a dash of Kahlua, a highball's worth of vodka, and a splash of soda. "You have to suck it down in one shot," he said, handing me a straw, the first night I ever tried one. "That's how it works." My coworkers gathered around me and chanted, "Drink, drink, drink!" When I managed it, they cheered like home fans at Fenway. Soon I could do three in a row.

The pain I had suppressed spread—the frame of my person made sturdy as a puddle, the core of me in decay. Alcohol was the solution. It filled my rotten teeth with porcelain, poured marrow into my fragile bones. Booze pumped air into my lungs and blood back into my heart. It was a life force, the can of spinach I could crack open for strength, the only friend I could trust. Alcohol cured the cavity—numbing the nerve of my consciousness and filling the hollow with cement. All I had to do was swallow.

Right after the jerk of my throat came the freedom of oblivion. A mind erased. A body abandoned. A soul removed.

Alcohol undergoes the same process of extraction it performs. Vaporized to strip all adjacent compounds, it is transformed into the purest essence of itself. The vapor released during distillation is believed to be the spirit—the soul—of the liquid and what remains the liquor, a theory believed to originate with Greek philosophers, Franciscan monks, alchemists in the Middle East.

Apart from myths, alcohol serves a practical purpose. Before penetrating the skin with a needle or dressing an injury, a doctor will apply alcohol to sterilize the area or clean an open wound. The point is to disinfect, remove any foreign agent, prevent it from slipping inside and wreaking havoc on our softest, most vulnerable parts. Many cultures believe alcohol, when ingested, is a scavenger, sapping the spirit from our vessels and taking our bodies for a joyride.

The psychologist Bruce Alexander identified a relationship, a cause and effect, between the pain one endures as a result of losing one's soul and one's insatiable need for relief from that pain. His dislocation theory of addiction shifts our lens from the individual—the diseased patient or the sinful antisocial—and calls attention to the environment, one that is psychologically unsustainable for many of us.

"Dislocation, in other words radical social isolation . . . is torture," Alexander said. "Addiction is to some extent a compensation, or we could say it's a substitute for a more complete life."

The isolation of a fractured society, Alexander explained, refers not only to the physical and material consequences of leaving home, the separation from extended family, community, culture, and traditions, but also to the acts of self-betrayal and erasure typical in the requirements of assimilation: so-called progress and upward mobility. Our collective psychospiritual wound can be traced back to our shared dream. Only by regaining consciousness is that so-called dream exposed as the nightmare that costs us dearly. We sacrifice our souls for the dream.

Centuries before Alexander's hypothesis, Handsome Lake, a Seneca chief of the Haudenosaunee Confederacy, intuitively understood this disconnect and the role of alcohol in its perpetuation, and he also knew that it didn't have to be this way. Before the arrival of Europeans, alcoholic beverages were brewed widely by Indigenous people across Central and South America, climbing north into some parts of what would become the United States as early as the sixteenth century. These homemade spirits—balché, tiswin, and pulque—were mainly used for rituals and religious ceremonies. Colonization—the violent dislocation of land and culture—and subsequent generational trauma and poverty mutated the balanced and purposeful use of drugs and alcohol by Indigenous communities into devastation and ruin. While Indigenous people fought for their rightful sovereignty, white settlers introduced distilled liquor, namely whiskey, to countless tribes, which contributed to the theft of Indigenous land and enabled the rapid decline of Native communities across the region. According to historians, this created the first known epidemic of addiction in America—and the first sobriety movement, a story that is rarely told or honored.

By sharing his own heroic journey as well as a series of messages received through visions from the Creator, Handsome Lake became a prophet for holistic sobriety. His teachings, known as Gai'wiio (Good Message), and the tradition of sobriety circles remain the universal bedrock of addiction counseling to this day, though his work is largely erased outside of Native teachings.

—

"No one leaves home unless home is the mouth of a shark," the poet Warsan Shire wrote. "You only run for the border when you see the whole city running as well."

For generations, the United States has parked its car in the garage of the Latin American psyche, shut the door, and turned on the ignition.

By the time my family, my father hailing from Ecuador and my mother from Honduras, made landfall, the United States was practically mythical—a place beyond reproach—and who were they as perceived invaders to be critical? They clung to the propaganda of the American Dream like a life raft. All they had to do was get there. All would be well. Not easy, but better than if they were home.

Although alcohol would become my drug of choice, American exceptionalism was the first drug I ever took—an IV drip fed to me through childhood, ingested in the womb. I believed we were to blame for the unexplained deaths, untreatable diagnoses, unbeatable charges, and irreversible deportations. Once I started using, all the other lies became easier to pick up—the lies we were told and, in turn, told ourselves. The anesthetizing power of the American Dream dulled my senses and blunted the focus of my logic—it worked by design.

The pursuit of the American Dream requires the sacrifice of our physical and mental health. Though marketed as the road to progress, it is the ultimate gateway into substance use disorder. When we inevitably become disillusioned by ever-shifting goalposts and are harmed by capitalist schemes that prioritize profit over people, how are we encouraged to take the edge off? And when we fall off the precipice, who is to blame?

Of course, I blamed myself—ignorant of the direct biological correlation between racialized trauma and oppression and substance use disorder. I had no idea how frequently drugs are used to self-medicate, to treat the debilitating effects of exploitative labor, sexual assault, and abuse. I never considered the role of "adverse childhood experiences" or realized that those who live through them are ten times more likely to abuse drugs.

The great American drug story is one of sin, of the individual falling out of step with society by succumbing to weakness, indulging the taste for the devilish spirit inside us all to the point of degradation. The only result of this wayward path of bad behavior is punishment or redemption. Historically, fatal drug use has risen alongside colonization, industrialization, and times of collective societal pain, such as war and economic depression. We use drugs when we are sad and lonely and hopeless. But this story is not good for American business. Drug use is best framed as a morality tale, one narrated by white supremacy, specific drugs coded to specific groups—cannabis as Mexican locoweed, cocaine ghettoized as crack. Among other forms of oppression, such coding triggers the need to assimilate, align, and aspire to whiteness in order to survive.

In the story of Handsome Lake, I found the root of my ills—a persistent lack of belonging: to a family as an imperfect daughter, to the country as an immigrant, to a community as a wounded misfit, to a partner as an equal. I didn't want to be separated from any of them by a pedestal or by a plague—I sought acceptance, whole and human.

2

Location, Location, Location

My mother had just turned twenty-one, the legal drinking age, when she and my father decided to reinvent themselves by moving south. The United States was headed toward recession, and they'd been in the States for seven years—together for six years. Unemployment skyrocketed throughout 1981 and climbed to 10.8 percent by the time I was born at the end of 1982, the highest it had been since the Second World War. Some friends at the plastics factory where my father worked told him they were headed to Texas, where there were more jobs, cheaper houses, and puro Latinos.

My parents' love story began unconventionally. It was 1975; my father was making $1.50 an hour at the factory and took work anywhere he could. He rented a room in a large house near his mother, Benedicta. He had spent much of his childhood without his mother, and their estrangement had made him desperate for her love. Now that he could control his whereabouts, he vowed to always be near her. Through her example, my father learned that love was best communicated by surrender. After several abusive relationships, including with my grandfather, my grandmother could interpret love only through control. And the only man she was capable of controlling was her son.

My mother, meanwhile, lived in a small apartment with her mother, stepfather, and two brothers. When she gave birth to my sister Karina that year, a social worker was called and signed her up for a program called welfare and WIC (Women, Infants, and Children). Her mother, my grandmother Beatriz, cashed the checks and used the funds to care for her husband and adult sons. She believed men should eat first, even if it was at the expense of a baby girl.

My mother took long walks to get out of the house and find some food, as starved in the land of opportunity as in that of her birth. When she had a dollar, she'd stop at a corner store for a Coke and a bag of chips or a Twinkie. My father, in the neighborhood to visit his mother, noticed her as he drove by one day. Within the small, close-knit pan-Latinx neighborhood, it was easy to gather intel on anyone, and he quickly learned who her family was and where she lived.

Having known Beatriz casually from work for some time, he first asked for my grandmother's permission to date her daughter. When he showed up at her door and asked my mother to grab a bite with him, he might have believed Beatriz had put in a good word for him. But my mother refused his offer. She thought of Karina, who was just six months old, and didn't believe any man could love a child who wasn't his own.

Undeterred and feeling romantic, my father came back the next day with a car seat, a couple of diapers, some bottles, and formula—a baby care package—and asked again. "Trae a tu hija," he said, clarifying that the invite was for her *and* her daughter. Every day he made sure they were fed—the hot meal a simple gesture that opened the door to my mother's trust.

When my mother told her family she was pregnant again, my grandmother kicked her out, and she moved in with my father. Despite all objections, my parents officially began their life together, and my sister

Karla, named after our father, Carlos, was born in October 1980. By this point, my father made $3.50 an hour at the factory and was now the head of the household. He demanded my mother get off government assistance. He didn't want anyone to think he needed help taking care of his family. Under the spell of the American Dream our basic needs were cast as charity.

The American ideal of the nuclear family, one that existed in a patriarchal orbit all its own, appealed to my father, atomized from his extended family as he already was. All he and my mother needed was each other. But my mother, young and headstrong, wasn't content as a housewife. She landed a job in an office doing clerical work, thanks to her high school diploma and fluent English. She hated the work but was determined to make a living with her mind and not her hands. My mother was desperate to go back to school—something the promised move to Texas seemed to offer her. She wanted what she heard the gringos call a higher education.

My parents stuffed whatever they could into an old station wagon and drove for days with one-year-old Karla, five-year-old Karina, and their neon-green pet parakeet, Agi. They stopped often along the way, staying in cheap motels, until they finally made it to San Antonio. Things changed for them in Texas. My parents leveled up from a small apartment to a three-bedroom house at the end of a cul-de-sac and neatly tucked our growing family into the warm blanket of a middle-class neighborhood. My father secured steady paychecks doing maintenance for the city hospital during the day, washing dishes at a Mexican restaurant at night, and working for a catering business over the weekends. Whenever catering gigs were scarce, he painted houses for a contracting company.

But my mother, only twenty-two, felt trapped alone with three children. Along with her two daughters, my stepbrother had also come to live with them. My mother needed an escape, so she convinced a neighbor to watch her kids and snuck out to enroll at the local city college. She could register for only one class, so she picked English literature. She hung around before and after class, eager to mingle. The campus was energized with students of all ages, backgrounds, and interests, the quads thick with booths full of young undergraduates soliciting for their causes, activities, and events. One was giving away a book called *Our Bodies, Ourselves.* They handed my mother a copy and a flyer and told her to come back in a week when Gloria Steinem would be there to give a lecture. My mother didn't know who would watch her kids, but she swore to herself she'd make it.

And she did. She listened, rapt, as Steinem told an auditorium of more than three hundred people at San Antonio College about the wage gap, reproductive freedom, and the democratic family. My mother later described Steinem as "a badass." Even though my mother couldn't identify at all with the particulars of how Steinem—unmarried, childless, famous— lived, she wanted what Steinem had. "She had so much passion," my mom recalled. "I felt like she cared about other women, not like my mother."

Three weeks after hearing the feminist icon preach liberation, three weeks after leaving her baby in my father's arms and walking out against his wishes, three weeks after cheering and pumping her fists and screaming "Fuck our husbands!" in a thunderous chorus of hundreds, right on the brink of radicalizing, she found out she was pregnant. With me.

All my parents' children have been unplanned, which is just a polite way of calling us each a mistake. Our family was an accident, but my father always said having children was something one must do with a bit of spontaneity, or else you'll never do it. My parents envisioned me as an opportunity to get it right and make sure things were better for us than they had been for them. A task my father was determined to fulfill by not beating us and my mother by not abandoning us. These were the primary torments of their pasts, which they swore never to repeat. And they didn't, for the most part. These firsts were the blueprint for many more to come.

But raising multiple children tends to transform spontaneity into mo- notony, depleting resources of all kinds, causing couples to turn on each other—leveraging children for power, converting burden to resource. "Si te vas," my father said whenever my mother motioned toward the door, "te llevas a tus hijas." We were the leash he tied around her neck.

———

My mother is the first in our family to go to college, even though she never graduated. "I still feel ashamed I never finished my degree," she told me, teary-eyed, for the first time. We were parked outside my sister's garage on my fortieth birthday. Our chat began with the story she always tells on my birthday, the one where she was convinced her chronic upset stomach was a reaction to all the Tex-Mex she had started eating. (Could this be why I hated beans as a child? A quirk my mother warned would get my Latina card revoked.) She always claimed never to have thought twice about having me. She also always admitted she was devastated to find out she was pregnant again. She knew what a fourth child at twenty-three meant for her.

That day she also told me about Gloria Steinem, how my father thought *Our Bodies, Ourselves* was pornographic smut and didn't want her to go to the lecture, but she stood up to him and went anyway. When she found out she was pregnant, she knew better than to tell him before deciding what she wanted to do. She went to the local clinic to confirm and hear her options. She sat in the parking lot and asked God what to do. "I just felt like you came for a reason," she sobbed, "and you know what? I never got pregnant again. And you know your father tried."

I wondered if the energy of that rally—the anger and opportunity—penetrated in utero. Had the message written itself into my genetic code, along with the grief and fear and joy of my family's past? Did the rally bequeath some kind of legacy, even if not directly to my mom? Was I the reason it skipped her? Is that why she always believed it was my destiny?

Two years after my birth, my mother was regularly attending classes at the local college, which provided day care services to students, and working a few nights as a hostess at a restaurant. My father always showed up early to pick her up or arrived unannounced to check on her. His surveillance embarrassed her, but she didn't want to quit. They'd finally saved up enough money for a down payment on a house when my father's mother got sick, and he decided we would leave Texas to return to New Jersey. His family blamed my grandmother's worsening health on the stress of their ongoing rift. My father promised my mother once my grandmother got better, they'd come back, so she packed very little and left all they had built behind. My grandmother died of an aneurysm right before we made the move. I never met her. My father didn't get to say goodbye. After the funeral, they never returned to Texas; they stayed in New Jersey, eventually settling in rural Mendham. My years as a Tejana are documented by a single photograph of our family at the River Walk, the only shred of evidence that I ever lived there.

3

Workhorse

In Jersey, my father got a job working for the county as a tree surgeon, the first job in a long career to provide health insurance and secure an affordable rental, a neglected colonial-era schoolhouse. This meant he agreed to be a part-time farmhand for the owners of the large estate, committing himself to a seven-day workweek.

"Camina por la sombrita," my father said, "no te vayas a quemar." I was raised on dichos like these. Clever sayings and phrases, like nursery rhymes, told with a laugh or a solemn nod; my father's wisdom sounded sweet but was deadly serious.

To be a working-class immigrant in America was to live in inhospitable conditions, like walking in the hot sun. You could easily get burned. When the heat beat down on my father's back, he knew to find some shade and follow its path home.

My parents' plan for survival hinged on establishing a refuge, a house of their own, the hallmark of American culture that prized property over people. My parents didn't see it that way—they just needed a respite from the grind, some authority and autonomy.

"En esta casa," they'd begin, a constant prepositional refrain before announcing a command or launching a complaint or a brag. "In this house . . ." a declaration of all their power in this world.

Growing up on a street named after our house made us feel pretty proud, even if we were just renters in a town that boasted a rich Washingtonian history and was officially listed on both the New Jersey and National Registers of Historic Places for its Revolutionary War–era landmarks. According to the town's self-proclaimed founders, we resided where US history began, in what was supposedly a former schoolhouse dating back to the nineteenth century. Hence our address: 1 Union Schoolhouse Road. This myth animated my childhood, transforming the dilapidated farmhouse into legend—a fantastical realm where white children once learned to read and spell and probably used terms like *arithmetic* (a word I felt should never have gone out of style). We were walking the floors of history, which splintered our feet daily. I thought the wood was worn by *our* ancestors, including myself, a newcomer, in this whitewashing pageant.

Outside, our house was a monument to colonial revisionist history; inside, a full-on fritanga. The smell of fried oil, grasa o aceite, se dice, soaked through the walls, which were as bumpy as my papier-mâché projects in preschool. When I started going to Mendham, I learned to avoid the kitchen if I had showered or changed my clothes. The smell of frying oil really had a way of embedding itself into the hair fibers, and we had a lot of hair. Clumps of long, thick, black strands accumulated in the one shower we all shared, a whole family—"cuatro mujeres," as my father would say, "pelos por todos lados." I loved running my wet finger along the basin and up the tiled walls. The strands attached like a magnet, and when I captured them all, I'd twirl and spin them into a spool of yarn. Our family DNA, a tangled little tumbleweed.

The awkward floor plan of the house was justified by its conversion from school to home, which carved the south-facing corner into two misshapen bedrooms. One space, the size of a walk-in closet, went to my oldest sister, Karina, and the larger, L-shaped half was shared by Karla and me. The walls of Karina's room bit into our jurisdiction like teeth through a sandwich, forming blocks down the adjoining wall, which were curiously accessorized by the sharp remnants of wainscot molding. Karla and I constantly banged our elbows, backs, and knees on those edges, and horseplay often brought us dangerously close to concussion. The odd placement of this ornamentation posed such a hazard to small children that one could have easily doubted the origin story of the house, though we never did. Much like the American project, legends superseded facts.

The actual schoolhouse, Union School, built in 1851, was down the road. A five-minute walk, or less than a minute on my bike. The one-room schoolhouse, one of five in the area, was constructed in the age of "common schools," public schools providing free education for, supposedly, all students from 1829 through 1928. *All* meaning, of course, *white*.

When our family arrived in the mid-1980s, the estate consisted of three houses. One, a farmhouse built in 1800, stood beside the stables below a high hill. Our landlords lived at the top, in the main house overlooking the extensive acreage. Ours was built farther up the road at the entrance to the sheep's stalls. It had been and continued to be servants' quarters, a home for the help. In high school, I learned from my boyfriend's parents that maintaining a farm was a common practice among wealthy landowners to minimize their taxes. For the family who owned the property, it made financial sense for them to allow us to live in one of their hovels for a small rent and the weekend services of my father as a farmhand. In fact, it was a steal.

Our house had no front door—just a side door that led directly into the kitchen, with an outer screen on a very tight hinge that often slipped through our fingers and slammed loudly into the doorframe, which was already split from age. With our bedroom directly overhead, the noise would alert Karla and me that our father was headed to the farm at 6 a.m. on a Saturday. We'd try to dress quickly and catch up with him, hopping the wooden fence and racing across a field covered in gray goose droppings to see who could reach him first. He'd smile but never say he was happy to see us or glad we came. He'd remove his gloves, hand one to each of us, and get to work. My father was strong, Herculean. We'd gasp as he hoisted a three-string bale of hay nearly his height over his shoulder, lifting it as if it were light as a feather, the other arm outstretched for balance. He'd dump the hay into a trough, cut the string with a pocketknife, and teach us how to spread it out for all to get an equal share, giving special attention to the pregnant sheep. Animals had power over my father, as he had over them; he understood what they needed, and it made him tender to know he could provide for them. My father, most himself on the land, could tend to the whole farm in about an hour. My sister and I usually split when it was time to head down the hill to feed the cranky and very smelly pig. We'd wash up and wait for Dad to get back and drive us to the bakery in town—all before my mom and Karina had woken up.

As a child, I had no idea we were the help. I bought into the romance of the clawfoot tub, the white picket fence, and accented shutters, the charm of which erased for me the toxic rust inside the bath, the rot of the wood on the fence, and the decay of the shutters that sagged like disjointed limbs. I saw the house in its original glory, though my mother had no appreciation for antiquity, and my father had no time or money for repairs. To them, *vintage* meant old, and old meant dirty, and dirty equaled poor—conditions they'd come here to change.

But the land was unequivocally bucolic—like the illustrations in the storybooks they read me at night come to life. The beauty of that land, the remote location, the stillness and quiet, convinced my parents of its safety, and that was their priority. "Go play outside," they'd reply to our demands for entertainment or when we wanted things the other kids had, passing us off to the outdoors, confident in Mother Nature's pastoral pen. In this town, they let down their guard, no longer the hawks they'd had to be in the places they came from. But even the meadow has its dangers.

4

Shadow Self

My mother always went to the bathroom with the door open. Her muscular stream of urine was often audible from my bedroom across the hall. It was a habit I imagined was born of necessity—a young mother of three small children, two under age three, had barely enough freedom to pee. Or it was the insouciance of someone who said she grew up pissing into a hole in the ground outside their house. No matter the reason, the sight of my mother's shoulders crouched over the edge of her knees atop the toilet bowl was a great comfort to me. It was my mother being herself, undisturbed and relaxed. It meant that while my sisters were at school and my father was at work, I was home alone with a version of my mother who was moored—an adult who could care for me.

A closed door, which happened from time to time, was a foreboding signal.

I don't know how long I would sit outside her bathroom door, but I know it was long enough to get hungry and wish I'd brought a book or a doll to keep me company. I could see my room from where I sat on the thin marble ledge that separated the hardwood floor of her bedroom and the strip of tile in the bathroom, where I caught glimpses of my mother's shadow. I thought about making a run for it, but our family was prone to superstition, so I didn't dare move until she came out.

I've always thought I knew my mother best, was more privy to the intimate details of her life than my sisters. She showed me how much blood she lost during her period when I was small, after I asked. That amount of blood couldn't be right. I feared she was hurt, sick, or dying, but she assured me it was natural, part of a monthly cycle. The same would happen to me one day.

I wasn't old enough to be told what actually happened on the other side of that door, but I could sense it. I began to believe it was up to me to fix it. At five years old, my solution was to trick my mother into coming out by telling her I had a secret. While dangling my tiny fingers under the door for sentimental effect, I told her I couldn't risk saying it through the door, I must whisper it into her ear. Sometimes, I'd beg for a while; other times she'd emerge quickly, always crying.

"Ya no puedo más," she'd say. "If it weren't for you and your sisters . . ."

My mother used that phrase often, *ya no puedo más*, confessing how she felt she lacked the strength to *go on*. But then she always did. Life went on. Little changed. As a child I wondered what it was she felt she could no longer do. *Go on* being my mother? *Go on* being my father's wife? I couldn't conceive at that age that what she meant was that she felt she could not go on with her life. But there I was, on the other side of the bathroom door she hid behind, knowing soon her two other children would be home. Daughters she'd sworn to protect. Lives, unlike her own, she deemed worth living.

That day, my mother told me about the abuse she'd experienced—how she never wanted the same to happen to me. She made me promise to tell her if anyone crossed the line from "good touch" to "bad touch," that if they did, I should fight and yell like her. Silence is the denial of experience, and my mother was a screamer. I admired that. But the world seemed deaf to her voice. Not even her own mother would listen, would take the word of her daughter over her son.

Mine became determined to break a family pattern, one that she thought could be solved with geography, religion, hypervigilance, and a good school system. All the things she wanted and never had her daughters, as US citizens, were guaranteed. On the road to generational progress there was no lane for two victims of the same crime.

As she strived to shield us, my mother's wounds remained agape. Moving back to New Jersey, near her family again, had forced repressed memories to the surface, and she needed someone to believe her. She knew I would. Though the disclosure was not without cost—the violation that robbed my mother's fundamental innocence, had now claimed mine, too. I began to affix the delicate, burgeoning sense of myself to how my mother was feeling, to whether I could alter her mood, lift her spirits.

"La sombrita de la mamá," people would call me, noting our closeness. They must have assumed I clung to her for my protection, but I wanted to protect her. Every time the door of my mother's trauma shut me out, I sprang into action, though I was no match for it. I felt responsible for her. No person is capable of saving another, and each attempt made me feel like a failure.

"Don't worry, mami," I said. "One day I'm gonna take care of you." That's what my mother says I told her that day.

The weight of that responsibility hung heavily on me. I couldn't relate to kids my own age. They seemed to expect the adults to care for their feelings, while I took my mother's feelings upon myself and never felt safe to express my own. It was always my mother I looked to, always her long shadow I stood in.

"Why are you holding your pencil like a monkey?" the girl seated beside me in class said. "Is it 'cause you look like a monkey?"

I glanced down at my hand, balled in the shape of a fist around the thin utensil, my thumb tucked tightly into the curve of my index finger, leaning on the back of the wooden pencil when it was supposed to be suspending it. I adjusted my position repeatedly, smearing graphite skid marks down my long fingers and under my nails. The pressure of my grip yellowed my ruddy fingertips, driving the blood out like the air from my lungs.

My classmate, one of the smartest students, was porcelain skinned. Everyone but me was white, and this girl had the fairest skin and the darkest hair. Her black hair was pin straight and thick. It grew not only on her head but along her cheeks and over the top of her lip like mine. I wanted to rip the prepubescent mustache off her face, but I've never been quick with a comeback. Instead, I started to cry, drawing the attention of our teacher, who knelt down to meet my watery eyes.

"Place the pencil between your index finger and your thumb," she said as she guided my hand with hers. "Yup, just like that. Then you use your middle finger to support your index finger and the pencil, and make sure you hold the pencil close to the tip."

It was so simple, so easy. I nodded and smiled silently to indicate I understood, but I continued to struggle.

I slouched over my desk to block my classmate's view of my work, tucked my furred cheek into the palm of my hand, snug as a baseball in a catcher's mitt, and glared at her through the corner of my eye. She was just as peluda as I was. If I looked like a monkey, so did she. But I was the one who couldn't spell my own name. I was the one with dark skin whose dark-skinned family had just moved to town, whose father didn't even speak English.

At a young age my father taught me there is no official language in the United States, though Spanish was the official language in our home. The name *America* didn't simply refer to the United States, he constantly reminded us, but to the whole of the hemisphere—it was ours just as much as it was theirs. He never responded when strangers demanded he *speak English*. Instead, he'd turn his mouth toward the floor, to us, his daughters, dictate in stern undertones, and we would translate. If my mother was there, she'd tell them off. When we got older, so did we.

My father rarely raised his voice. Maintaining a discreet, even tone that required you lean into him and pay close attention. Dry-humored and quick-witted, he was particular with his words; he always knew exactly what he wanted to say and Spanish allowed him to say it. Why would he twist his tongue for those who couldn't even roll theirs, who lacked the eloquence to comprehend the romance of his expression, upon whom his humor was lost entirely? *Pity for them*, he thought. When he heard mistakes in our diction, he'd interrupt, "¡Qué es eso!" and we'd obediently try again. As I grew up it undoubtedly became a barrier—between us, for him, for his career, but still, I admired my father's defiance, even when it took aim at us.

An autodidact, my father had a brief and violent academic education. He was naturally left-handed, and his teachers labeled him abnormal. They forced him, through corporal punishment, to write the *right* way. My father, who became ambidextrous, told me this story after hearing from my mother the feedback at the parent-teacher conference. My teacher had told her I was bright, bubbly, and creative, but she'd noticed some issues with reading and writing that might indicate dyslexia.

My mother says my father refused my teacher's suggestion that I receive extra help, insisting his child was not stupid. My father says he protected me from being unfairly labeled as he had been and grabbed a pen to show me how he wrote with equal ability with both hands. This was my opportunity to do the same.

I tried my best to hold a pencil properly but needed the support of a four-finger grip to follow the dotted lines of the penmanship lessons. When given the assignment to copy a word without the guide of the dotted pattern, I often omitted letters or inverted them. My handwriting never improved, but save for my trembling hands, I managed to mask my shame. Despite my father's best intentions, the injustice of his experience blocked my path to an equitable education. Neither one of us would get the help we needed. At home, I started asking my sister Karina, who had the most beautiful penmanship I knew, to write for me. I was already failing my mother; I couldn't bear to fail my father, too.

5

Lost in Succession

The first time I went ice skating, I peeled out onto the rink and quickly found myself alone, soaring at top speed. Terrified and unsure what to do, I bent down to slow my skates, slipping my hand underneath the blade and slicing my palm wide open. I hadn't been taught how to pigeon-toe my feet into a snowplow stop or point my skates in a 45-degree angle, allowing one foot to drift behind the other into a T stop. The split-second decision was the result of novice but also desperation.

My father never skated with us; he never learned how. He watched intently and always tied our laces. It was something he took great care and pride in—figuring we'd need firmly stabilized ankles to balance on shoes attached to knives. The thing is, he usually tied them too tight, cutting off circulation, and I hated telling him he was hurting me when he said all he meant to do was protect me.

———

By the time my father got the job as a landscaper at Morris County Shade Tree Commission, he was already a skilled farmer, merchant, manufacturer, and caterer. Still, the only work he remembered fondly was his time as a sailor. Aboard a ship named *Sarita*, my father sailed from the Port of Guayaquil to a refinery in San Nicolas, Aruba, collecting and distributing airline fuel to countries along the Central American isthmus on the way back down to South America.

"Regando combustible por Tela, La Ceiba, El Salvador, Nicaragua, Costa Rica," he'd tell us, animating my mother, who was the first to run down to the docks when men like my father pulled into a slip in La Ceiba. If they had ever crossed paths in my father's sailing days, she would have been a toddler.

Every year, around the time school started, the Morris County Shade Tree Commission planted seeds in bulk throughout the county—new shrubs, flowers, trees. They used a lattice system to transport and overturn huge piles of mulch and fertilizer, after which my father would always collect the leftover pieces of rope. Curious to see if he had retained his seafaring skills, he braided the pieces into a long reusable strap. A superior noticed his handiwork and told him he would need these skills to pass a test required to secure the promotion to climber, a position that paid $7,000 more annually. He passed the test three times, but he never got the promotion.

The fastened rope scraps would become a tire swing, a homemade volleyball net, or a sack to carry my sister's soccer balls. And we, his daughters, despite knowing the pressure of his vise grip, would offer up our tiny ankles to our father and marvel at his skill for tying anything in this world into a knot.

———

Like most children testing out personalities through short-lived obsessions, I quickly lost interest in ice skating competitively when I discovered a talent for voice impersonation. Fascinated with Jaleel White's Steve Urkel, I held my family hostage weekly with my one-woman show. Dressed in suspenders, pants pulled high up to my chest, arms spread wide open, I'd burst into the living room with Urkel's signature "Did I do that?" to uproarious laughter.

My very first high.

After I watched Robin Williams's iconic "I Do Voices" scene in *Mrs. Doubtfire* in 1993, having memorized every line and character, I knew I was destined to be a performer because I, too, could "do voices."

My father disapproved of anything that distracted me from my schoolwork—the only guaranteed road to progress for us in his mind and the reason he made so many sacrifices. But every day when my father came home from work, he'd sit quietly in front of the TV. He'd watch las noticias, sometimes mumbling toward the day's headlines but mostly sitting quietly. Quietness, he required from us—grade-school children desperate for his attention, help with homework, company for reading a book or kicking the soccer ball. As a child, I took his desire for isolation as a sign he loved TV like me, and I was right to an extent.

Eventually, he'd walk into the kitchen where my mother was cooking, where I would always be helping, to tell her what went down at work that day. "Wetback" painted in white letters across the back of his orange uniform. A stick found in his locker labeled "Hoppe's Stick" that his coworkers threatened to shove up his ass. He'd been kicked out of the lunchroom—"No spics allowed," they said, forcibly, physically removing him. Another request for a well-deserved promotion or raise, rejected. "Go back to work, Hoppe," his boss would say.

"Trabajo! Trabajo! Ándele!"

His boss could not do voices, or accents.

My sisters and I—still children—started researching, writing letters, and calling lawyers. But my father, unconvinced, would return to the couch and continue watching TV in silence for hours. Once the novelas began, he'd go to bed. Absorbing the daily death of my father's dignity was not a pain any of us discussed. The pain was his. The duty was ours. An entanglement no one knew how to unravel.

I'd feel uneasy until the sound of my father's singing returned—classic boleros románticos resounding from the shower and all throughout our home. Then, I knew I could beg him to retell how he and his sister had won a radio singing competition as children, and he'd oblige. As I grew up, his undeniable and natural talent, suppressed unfairly by oppressive circumstances, fed my compulsion to perform.

I dove into the pages of the local newspaper, searching for any artistic avenue available. My mother, the quintessential stage mom, indulged me. She chauffeured me to countless auditions and comforted me when every lead role in school or community theater went to white children, with me chronically cast as supporting or background because my look didn't make a believable Annie Warbucks. My mother was determined not to allow our narrow-minded environs to stomp out my wunderkind potential, so we went together to New York City.

Using my vocal skills, I was able to convince someone over the phone that I was calling on behalf of a friend or client, and I secured a meeting with an agent near home who sent kids on auditions in the city. When we met, I told my agent I wanted to focus on television, and she began booking go-sees for me regularly. Behind my father's back, my mother and I conspired on new and creative excuses to get me out of school, until an administrator called home to warn that I had accumulated a dangerous number of absences.

I was undeterred. I needed to get on TV. It was the thing my father loved so much—the thing that got his undivided attention night after night. Once he saw me on-screen, he would understand.

———

Decades later, I wound up on television for being a drunk—well, a sober drunk. Not exactly the trajectory I'd imagined as a child, though I said yes to the producer without a moment's pause.

Until I thought of my father.

Now retired, my father keeps the television on all day. Set to the Spanish-language news channel, the stories rotate, recycling the same salacious headlines. He still talks to the screen—calling the attractive anchor "la madre de mis hijas"—laughing with the hiss of a former smoker even though he never took one puff of anything in his life, glancing across the room to glean a reaction from his wife who never looks up from her phone.

I knew my segment wouldn't appear on the channels he watches. But in the days leading up to the episode airing, I couldn't sleep. I kept picturing him rocking gently in his pink La-Z-Boy, bathed in the blue light of the flatscreen, half-asleep. Awoken by the sound of his daughter's voice, the recognition of his daughter's face. Listening intently to decipher the meaning of the words in English, he mumbles toward the screen: "¿Trauma? ¿Qué trauma?"

I decided it was best to tell him myself first. But when I called, I lied about why I'd been booked for the interview. "Vamos a hablar de salud," I said, glossing over the topic of addiction by calling it "wellness." I expanded, testing his intuition by explaining that many people had begun drinking much more during the pandemic, and they wanted to talk to people who don't drink.

"Eso sí," he agreed without missing an opportunity to talk about how he never drank and bring up my cousin Macho, whose lack of restraint confounded the family. "Es que dicen que no quiere cambiar."

"That's not how it works," I murmured, taking his judgmental comment personally, knowing via FaceTime and in English we'd pretend he didn't hear it.

I couldn't properly explain the mechanism of addiction clinically and politically to my father in Spanish. But the truth is it didn't matter. My father believed children are taught by example. And when did he ever drink in front of me? "Nunca. ¡Jamás!" I'd summoned this demon all on my own.

He knows I quit drinking and is proud of me for that. "Tienes carácter fuerte como yo," he boasts. But the concept of recovery and the term *sobriety* rings hollow to him. In my father's mind, when you say you aren't going to do something, you just don't do it.

I nodded and agreed with him that I was different, better than my family, knowing well I'm just lucky.

"Sí, papi, gracias a Dios que yo soy diferente, como usted."

I sent him a link to the segment. He never mentioned it, and I didn't ask.

6

Humildad

When I was in sixth grade, our dutiful tenure at the so-called schoolhouse in Mendham ended unceremoniously. A makeshift eviction letter slipped under our door—the one that led to the kitchen, which meant my mother was the first to find it and read it. When she told us the news, my sister Karla, still dressed in her soccer uniform, collapsed on the carpeted stairs she loathed to vacuum (her one chore), as hysterical as the day our cat, Leonardo, was hit by a car and found dead on the side of the road. That day, my father had let my sister sob into her pillow without offering any condolence. This time, he ran to her immediately and kissed her forehead. "Ya, mija, ya," I heard him whisper, his heavy hands in her hair. "No te preocupes." He promised her nothing would change.

The property owner's daughter had recently married and decided to move into one of the three family homes on the property, dispossessing us from the only one I ever knew. My father had served as a footman for the horse-and-carriage-drawn procession in the heiress's wedding. We had a framed portrait of the occasion on our mantel as if they were monarchs and we the subjects, blindly taking pride in the indentured relationship.

As another parachute of generational wealth puffed to cushion its descendants comfortably through life's milestones, our entire family was plunged into freefall. What one father could easily bestow, another could never replace. Only by reading the now-vintage wedding announcement in the paper can I understand the astounding pedigree, the truth of what we were up against. Without sufficient notice, the best we could do was hide the fact from our school, pack a lifetime of belongings into a storage facility, and appeal to the kindness of my mother's friends from the Spanish-language church.

My father placed his trust in this land—not just in its soil, which he tended, but in its zoning, in what he thought was fertile ground for an ideal upbringing. My parents gave up their families and community in exchange for a well-funded school system. Like most immigrants, they believed in the American Dream and focused on positioning my sisters and me to achieve what they could not. Yet none of us truly grasped the wealth and privilege of the area, nor the fact that simply living there entitled us to none of it, not even the house we had made our own for nearly a decade. As the eviction notice made clear, we couldn't lay claim even to the roof over our heads.

My last days at Mendham were spent living out of a bedroom in Dover, a neighboring, predominantly Latinx town my racist classmates referred to as Doverico, sharing one bunk bed with my sister Karla, while my mom took the other and my dad slept on the floor. Karina crashed at a friend's place in Mendham. I scavenged through black garbage bags to find my school clothes and was up at 5 a.m. to use the one bathroom at my mother's friend's house before their two sons woke up. My mother never told my school we'd lost the house, that we were homeless. Until summer, she drove us the hour each way in silence.

My father bought groceries for the entire household and offered cash for our occupancy, and though I know he missed it as much as I did, he never dared use their TV. We took our clothing to the local Laundromat on weekends and wandered the mall to give our hosts some space, paranoid that they'd see us as an imposition and kick us out. We'd already been ousted from my aunt's apartment after I used her kitchen to bake a chocolate cake—a simple recipe from the box I'd long mastered. As I crouched to watch the batter leaven into a spongy foam under the cast of the oven light, my aunt stormed into the kitchen with a water bucket full of bleach and a mop that reeked of mold. When she claimed I'd made a mess of her kitchen, my mother, who had opened her home to her cousin on so many occasions without question or judgment, lunged for her. My father had to break up the melee, and we were on the street that night.

After months of displacement, we managed to qualify for a home on the border of the well-funded school district, on a street that marked the cutoff, a place known to house the poorest families in the area. My mother hated the house, more dilapidated than our first and much too small for us. But my father refused to change school districts.

The way the school district was organized, my sisters could continue with their graduating classes without changing schools. Yet I would have to attend Black River Middle School in Chester for two years and then rejoin the kids I'd grown up with in high school, which all four grade schools fed into. Two out of three ain't bad, my dad figured. An assumption I wasn't about to contradict. Not after all he'd been through to keep his promise to my sister.

I never made friends at school easily, especially compared to my sister Karla. Perhaps this was because the first school I went to was the preschool where my mother worked in Morristown. She'd come into the auditorium during nap time, weave quietly around the cots of children pretending to sleep, and put her hand on my back. We'd sneak out for her lunch hour and go to August Moon, our favorite Chinese place, where we shared the lunch special: a choice of entrée with rice, soup, an egg roll, and a can of Coke, all for five bucks. We ate like queens. My mother wasn't shy there, like she was at other restaurants, if she'd even go in. She didn't mumble when the waitress came by. She encouraged me to try the tea—it made me smart, she said—and taught me how to read my fortune cookie. For once, we felt nourished and taken care of—we were welcome there.

Despite the difficulties dyslexia presented, at Mendham I was known as a good student with a well-rounded set of extracurriculars. I was a writer on the school newspaper, I played forward on the junior soccer team, and my artwork had been selected to represent Mendham Township Elementary School in the *Our World—Our Way* exhibit, sponsored by the Art Educators of New Jersey, which would be on display at the local college. My parents received a letter informing them of my achievement, one they remind me of to this day. My English teacher signed my yearbook to a "fine student and a talented girl!"

That changed when I got to Chester. I can't recall one teacher's name from my two years there, nor the names of the principal or guidance counselor. I'd been completely written off. I remember the classrooms were in the front of the building, but I cannot picture a single one. The lunchroom and gymnasium were in the back, a layout I could describe to you in vivid detail, as if these were the only two places where I spent any time.

Two sets of double doors on each end of the hall led into the gymnasium. All four were propped open to reveal stations of activity intended to test our physical fitness according to a national standard developed by the president. I wasn't the athlete in my family, but I was naturally athletic and liked competing. Teachers encouraged me to pursue my athletic potential, thinking this would solve the problem of my future. I couldn't care less about sports, but I wasn't entitled to decide my own interests—it was clear that the way I looked communicated something to them about me, something that inspired little faith in my intellectual or creative potential. But it was assumed I could perform physically, that I would be faster, stronger, my steps worth watching as I darted from ruler to ruler in record time.

Most of us dreaded the fitness tests. We suffered silently, shyly; some boys couldn't bear the feeling, so they forced their discomfort on the rest of us. I surveyed the scene across the lacquered gymnasium floor as the teachers extended the bleachers from the wall like an accordion. The entire seventh-grade class filed in, and students grabbed seats beside their friends, cliques like little nodes. I was the new girl, and being good at this could go either way for me. I wasn't sure how to play it—go hard and try to impress or play small and fly under the radar. I sat alone on the wooden bleachers and tugged regretfully at my new bangs, which flopped in my eyeline, too short to be pulled back into a ponytail. I'd cut my long hair because if I was being forced to change schools right when things were starting to go well for me, then I needed to reinvent myself. To make friends at a new school, I must appear as someone universally adored—hence the Rachel. Jennifer Aniston's famously layered shag required that I wake up hours before school to blow out then flatiron my textured hair. My mother had taken me for a fresh peinado at the Dominican salon for my first week of school, and I knew the fitness tests would sweat it out.

When the whistle blew, assigned groups queued up at their designated stations. I positioned my feet against the red milk crate, reached toward the ruler fastened to the top with a rubber band, and stretched as far as I could. The sit-and-reach was one of my best exercises, and I was leading the scores for the girls. My athleticism caught the attention of one of the school's top athletes, part of a small clique of smart girls who would befriend me. She invited me to join them on the bleachers to wait for the next activity and then to sit with them at their lunch table, a small round one in the far corner that comfortably fit four, but at which they made room for a fifth. Adored by faculty and indifferent to petty popularity contests as they were, I tried to follow their lead, though the same rules did not apply to me. These girls held their standards high.

At a sleepover a few months later, I accidentally stepped on one of the smart girls' glasses while playing near the fireplace at her house, but

I couldn't admit it. I knew how rich white people handled these things. We didn't have the money to replace her frames. I never spoke to them again.

I started to see myself differently. I wasn't like the other kids who were still able to be kids. They didn't have to lie because they couldn't afford to fix their mistakes. When you get in through the service entrance, mistakes aren't a rite of passage; they're proof you don't belong.

7

Traviesa

No one asked us if we wanted to meet our uncle Jaime, a man we had heard so much about but never spoken to. No one even told us where we were going.

I remember that day because it was the day I began collecting art. It was the day I decided what constituted art was beauty. From a very young age, I knew that what spoke to me was beauty. And if I could learn how to create art, my life would be beautiful. Jaime was the first person I'd met who called himself an artist and the only family member to speak of its merit and share his work. He gave me permission to love what I loved and to dream of becoming an artist, too. My eyes brightened as he presented my grandmother with a painted portrait of her. Arms stretched, she held it out as if to focus and furrowed her brow, gathering the muscles around her jaw to smush her lips toward the sweeping portrayal. Finally, she smacked her gums, rejecting his vision of her and the proof of his talent. She was too focused on what she called the reality of the circumstances—how it looked that he was locked up. "¿Qué va a decir la gente?"

He ignored her slight and turned to me.

"¿Te gusta el arte?" he asked, handing me a small sculpture of an abstract object. "Te la regalo."

I wasn't close to any of my aunts or uncles, but Jaime's gift and our shared vision of art gave me hope for a relationship. I kept this wish secret, in a demonstration of loyalty to my mother. I knew my uncle had beaten her as a girl. Once, he had nearly killed her. But that wasn't why he was in prison. We didn't know why.

"Una mujer lo acusó," my grandmother said, urging my mother over the phone to drive her to Northern State Prison, where my uncle was incarcerated after, we were told, being falsely accused. "Pero él no hizo nada, pobrecito."

Despite my uncle's guilty plea, my grandmother maintained his innocence. My mother knew a plea didn't mean shit—especially for a Central American immigrant caught up in the US carceral system—but I could tell my mother didn't believe Beatriz either.

———

I was thirty-six years old when I first saw my mother as a child. She texted my sisters and me an iPhone picture of a photo. While traveling in Florida, she'd been reunited with a friend from her past who'd shared the photo with her. "Hey, girls! Look, it's your mamá en Honduras. Aquí con mi amiga Cristelia paseando por memory lane . . ."

In the photo, she's fifteen; dressed in a short-sleeve western, a color so softly blue it's practically invisible against the sky. Buttoned up high to the neck, the collar cuts a sharp angle under her chin—a serious statement reinforced by a thick brown leather belt and bootcut jeans draped over the heavy soles of her shoes. Parece la muy caballera.

Her look is nearly identical to that of the man standing beside her, though he added spacey-looking shades and a straw campesino hat. Her friend, Cristelia, stands on the other side of the man wearing low-slung bell-bottoms the color of ripe bananas, with shoes to match and a halter top exposing her entire belly, ribs and all, a beaded national emblem necklace dangling off her chest. They were headed to Carnaval. My mother had never been allowed to go before.

I stared at the image in search of myself. Many say I look like my mother, but I couldn't see it. Only the hair—slicked back in a bun, baby hairs glued to the forehead save two long twisted tendrils dangling from each temple—a style I would copy at the same age in the '90s, decades in the future.

All I could see was the before of an after. The person before the irrevocable, the mother I could have had. The woman I want to know.

———

I could have sworn my mother told me she washed clothes in a river as a child, but that must have been my father. My mother didn't live near a river; she lived by the ocean. She washed clothes by hand in a communal pileta—a large cement basin where townspeople would gather to clean their laundry. From a very young age, even before her mother left for the States, she was charged with this chore for the entire household—four brothers, her mother, and herself. She'd kick over a crate or stool, whatever she could find to stand on to reach into the tub with the others. She'd absorb the local gossip, a pleasant distraction from the harsh friction of grating wet denim against a steel washboard until her knuckles were rubbed raw. Indigo dye ran from the thread of the cheap slacks, pooled in her palms, and stained her hands blue for days, a sign of her poverty and position in her home.

It wasn't in my mother's nature to take orders, but she obeyed her mother because she loved her. And she obeyed her brother because she had no choice. Jaime, diagnosed with epilepsy as a boy, was prone to rage. His childhood was scarred by the constant fear of collapse, violent convulsions lasting minutes that no one could explain or stop as large

crowds gathered to stare and snicker. As the eldest son, he was determined to overcome his reputation as an invalid—terrified of being perceived as weak, he preferred to be known as a monster. But he was a
virtuoso with a pencil. He'd use any instrument or canvas to leave his
mark. He drew still-life portraits of the mangoes that sat in a heap on
the kitchen table, a bird in flight outside the window, his dick erect early
in the morning.

Jaime began to package his phallic works as love letters to the neighbor,
a woman the townspeople often gossiped about at the pileta, calling
her a prostituta. My mother never cared how the neighbor made her
money—only that she stood up to her brother.

The neighbor returned his notes and chastised his unwanted behavior.
"Ella no se dejaba," my mother said. Jaime responded by drawing on the
wall of the communal outhouse sketches of acts so obscene the block
became constipated, as people avoided the shitter. Everyone ran in fear
of Jaime. But not this neighbor. My mother drew strength from her example and began demanding Jaime pay her to do the laundry, give her
enough money to buy food and permission to go to Carnaval that year.
She was fifteen now, after all.

Though she never drank, my mother was a born party girl. The drive
my first drink ignited in me she naturally possessed, no preservatives
added. It was an energy ingrained from a childhood spent on the streets,
what the locals called una callejera. She made meals from the fruit of
trees, friends with whoever happened to be kicking a ball outside, a
dance hall from music pulsing through open windows, car doors, and
storefronts. A party wherever she went.

Isolated in that rural town in New Jersey, I knew my mother didn't
belong in Mendham. She was a descendant of one of the largest, most
raucous, and most famous parties in Latin America, La Ceiba Carnaval.
The annual two-week-long celebration straddles May 15, a day of tribute
to San Isidro Labrador, a Spanish farmworker made Catholic patron
saint of labor and peasants, anointed for his service to the poor and

love of animals. The tradition originated as a pilgrimage to drink holy water from the meadow of Isidro's hermitage in Madrid. Colonization transplanted not only the practice of Catholicism but a twin city of San Isidro to the Caribbean coastline of Honduras. The people of the isthmus transformed it. Partygoers across the country, the hemisphere, and even the world gather for the festivities now known as the Honduran Mardi Gras, tripling the region's population, with guests estimated at more than five hundred thousand each year. Though the party literally went down in my mother's backyard, she never counted as one of the celebrants until that day in the photo.

My mother remembers very few things about her childhood fondly, which makes this day's story historic. She tells me over and over again how she and her friends "bailaron punta, compraron pan de coco a las vecinas garifunas y toneladas de baleadas." They judged the beauty queens (verdict: they'd seen better on the corner), followed the parade all the way down San Isidro Avenue until it culminated on the beach, and stayed out through the night. Early on, Jaime had zoomed past on his motorbike, ordering her to go home. When she refused, he said he'd be waiting for her when she got home.

While my mother danced and laughed and ate and swam, my uncle envisioned her touched, licked, and kissed by men. The images conjured by his incestuous jealousy told my uncle she must be punished. He tore the leather band from the sewing machine my grandmother had left behind and boiled water. Triggered by rage, he placed the strap inside the scalding water and set the two in a bucket outside to broil—the cocktail intensifying with each hour she was gone.

Fearing retaliation for her disobedience, my mother did not return until the next day. As she approached the house with her friend Cristelia, she watched her brother rise from the porch and reach into the bucket. "¡Pero no hice nada!" she begged as he pummeled her. The blasts from each lashing rang out through the crowd like the firecrackers from the festivities the night before.

"¡La vas a matar!" Cristelia cried, begging for help from frozen on-lookers. She decided to run to get her family when the neighbor appeared with a machete over her shoulder. "¡Deja a esa niña o te corto en pedazos!" she told my uncle, breaking his bloodthirst. He dropped my mother's body, inches from death, and walked away.

It took weeks for the neighbor to nurse my mother back to health. When she could walk, she had to leave. Desperate to be nurtured, my mother tried to stall, but the neighbor could no longer slow her enterprise, and my mother, at fifteen, would be at risk among the men who came to the house looking for sex.

———

When my mother was twelve, my grandmother Beatriz had decided she was old enough to fend for herself. All my mother knew was that Beatriz wasn't coming back. The official word came by way of her grandmother Chong, who pilfered the money, gifts, and letters Beatriz sent to my mother from the United States. Chong told her that Beatriz's tourist visa had expired, but she found a Puerto Rican to marry for the papers so she could stay. They had met at a plastics factory, the same that would employ my father.

Beatriz was part of a wave. In 1965, Lyndon B. Johnson signed into law the Immigration and Nationality Act, lifting the immigration ban and ushering in an influx of people from the global south to the United States. My grandmother went to the local consulate, which granted her a tourist visa, initiating my maternal family's migration to the United States and leaving three sons and a daughter behind in Honduras. Her daughter, my mother, was born on February 9, 1958, in La Ceiba. She named her Celia, though the birth certificate records the day in January and misspelled my mother's name with an *i* instead of an *e*—C I L I A.

We know this was a typo since Beatriz had named my mother Celia de Jesús in honor of Beatriz's childhood friend who took her own life after her parents forbade her marriage to her first love—mal de amores, they romanticized. No one ever corrected the spelling of my mother's first name, but when she married my father, she dropped the middle, replacing her belonging to Jesus Christ with belonging to my father. At their divorce proceedings decades later, he asked for his name back. She and the judge refused.

Moving back to New Jersey from Texas meant I had access to one of my living grandparents. Many kids at school loved their grandparents and saw them as allies against their parents' discipline. But my grandmother wasn't the type. Throughout my parents' twenty-year marriage, my grandmother often told my mother to leave him—and us. She made a performance out of the threat. "Tu papá es un viejo," she jeered at my sister and me, telling us my dad was an old man near death—way too old for a hot young woman like my mom. Her canned vulgarity made my sister scream, but I always cried, which disturbed my grandmother more than my sister's violent outbursts. My mother would tell us to go play in the next room while they cooked, as Beatriz belly laughed, relishing our distress.

———

My sister and I were desperate to go home after our visit to the prison. We told our mother we missed our father and warned her he must be waiting for us. But Beatriz insisted my mother come back to her house and help her with a plan to get Jaime out. My mother, hesitant, demanded to know why Beatriz believed so adamantly in her son's word over his victim's testimony. "¿Qué gana ella?" my mother asked. What could she possibly stand to gain?

My grandmother lived with my two other uncles, Javier and Hugo, in the same dark apartment my mother had fled before Karla and I existed, across the street from Morristown Memorial Hospital, where she worked, and we visited her every week. She shared a room with Hugo and slept with the married neighbor on their bed whenever Hugo was out. My uncle Javier occupied the next room with his wife, Patricia, to whom we would have felt inferior if it weren't obvious something was off. "¡Esa retardada mental!" I could hear Beatriz call Patricia as she and my mother cooked the white woman's dinner.

Few things were precious to my grandmother: her sons, her sewing machine, and her couch. The commodious centerpiece was beached like a whale in the center of the cramped living room—a gift from her lover, José. While poor, Beatriz felt she was far too sophisticated to cover her fabulously fuchsia furniture in plastic. "¿Cómo jíbara?" she'd say. "¡Qué va!"

I agreed she should not wrap her furnishings in a condom like my aunts, whom she called hicks, did, but she'd forgotten to remove the plastic wrappers atop the gold detail running down the arms and legs. When my sister and I noticed the vulnerable display of preservation, we took turns peeling off the long strands of plastic. It was so satisfying a game; we made a contest of who could extract the longest peel without tearing. My sister won, but I was caught with the evidence in hand—strewn about the carpet as if a snake had just shed its skin at my sides.

"¡Deja de tocar, traviesa!" Beatriz shouted, slapping my hands before running to the kitchen to tell my mother we were damaging her property. No one wanted her to have nice things, she claimed as we tried to explain that we were helping—that you were meant to peel this layer and now the couch would shine more brightly.

She might have believed us had we been little boys. According to my grandmother, every trait the women in our family exhibited had a pathology, a behavior that must be corrected aggressively. At the same time, men's actions were ignored or justified by ours. Jaime, her eldest and favorite son, was a prime example of the damage ser traviesa could wreak in the life of an innocent man.

Used loosely, *traviesa* means naughty, but my understanding of the term was more specific. *Traviesa* meant I liked to touch everything. And it's true. I'm very tactile, a liability for my young mother. I dropped glass figurines at the Hallmark store, excitedly groped silk dresses at Macy's with my sticky fingers, spilled innumerable cups of coffee, soda, and juice at McDonald's—I liked to help pour the milk and sugar into my mother's drink. "Look with your eyes, not your hands," my mother would say in an effort to mediate my childish curiosity and the store clerk's suspicion. "You're gonna have to pay for that."

My grandmother's apartment had a lot of interesting things to touch. I liked the feel of the warm cloth she used to wrap homemade tortillas, the cold steel of her sewing machine. I spun around on her stool—the sharp edges where the leather had split from use pricked my bottom. I picked at the orange sponge that spilled from the crack and begged her to teach me how to sew.

One day, she finally gave in, placed me on her lap, grabbed a piece of scrap fabric, and stepped on the pedal below the machinery. She told me to keep the fabric straight and be mindful not to get my fingers too close to the needle. I nodded, eager to comply, afraid she'd stop if I bothered her with questions. She placed her long fingers on mine, her petal-pink manicure digging into my knuckles, and pushed. At first, she guided my hands gently through the movement. I smiled, proud of my work, as she smirked, raised her eyebrows, and nodded. She pressed the pedal harder, and the needle jumped rapidly, looping thread into a fastened hem faster than I could control. I resisted her pressure, but she applied more, forcing my tiny hands toward the needle like a dare. I ripped my hands from under hers before I could be stabbed and turned to watch her erupt into laughter.

"Para que aprendas," she said as she tossed me from her lap. My grandmother didn't believe in establishing the home as a safe harbor like my parents; it was a training ground. The United States was a rapid, demanding, and shrewd place where lessons were learned the hard way. She'd been here longer than us, and she knew better. Even with me and my sisters being born in the country, she was the one who'd learned how to play the game. If anything, being born here was making us soft.

"La comida ya 'sta," my mother interrupted, ignoring her tirade. Beatriz ordered me to fetch my uncle and his wife to come eat. Upset, I turned the corner quickly and entered their room without knocking. I stood confused and undetected for a moment before my uncle screamed, "¡Chucha su madre!" tossing the covers over a mushroom cloud of smoke. When I ran back to the kitchen, my mother and grandmother laughed. I pretended not to understand why they laughed, and I never told anyone what I saw. I knew enough to know they weren't fucking. But I didn't yet understand that what they were doing was getting high.

When I walked into my uncle's room that day, he and his wife were sitting, clothed, cross-legged on the bed facing each other. They held something that appeared precious between them. Gingerly, he lowered a flame to the glass and inhaled deeply. Sparks flew.

Although it is not my secret alone, I'll confess that my grandmother was right about one thing: we did destroy her couch. Not at first, but slowly. We sought our revenge by scraping the gold veneer from her prize—bit by bit.

8

D(rug) A(buse) R(esistance) E(ducation)

Before televisions were hung flat on the wall like works of art, I would sit on the floor propped on my elbows, craning my neck far back to look up at a small, curved screen inside a black plastic box set a few feet off the ground. I liked being up front so I could always be the one to switch the dial once the nightly news was over and my father let me change the channel.

The evening's regularly scheduled programming was interrupted one night for a special address from the new president. The first nationally televised speech by George Herbert Walker Bush, on September 5, 1989, was billed as a "heart-to-heart" between the president and the American people. We were being called to a mission against the "gravest domestic threat" facing the nation: drogas.

I was six years old and had just started first grade. I was into Cabbage Patch Kids and a new show called *Saved by the Bell*. Drugs were pretty meaningless to me at the time, outside of Nancy Reagan's "Just Say No" campaign, which seemed simple enough. Drugs were animated in my world by people—the ones who used them, the ones who sold them, the ones who got hurt by those in the first two groups, and the ones who never touched the stuff, like my parents.

I don't remember much of what Bush said that night, nor did I grasp the implications of pouring billions into the so-called war on drugs despite its effect on our family. What I recall is that ridiculous bag of crack cocaine. The way the president extracted what appeared to be a chalky block of soap from his desk drawer and presented it to the camera with a trembling hand of condemnation—the sound of my parent's gasps and murmurs. "Qué barbaridad," they sighed.

My mother and father, regularly at odds, could be easily divided on political issues, but they presented a firm and united front against drugs. They said they'd witnessed the devastating effect of drug use in their own families and communities, which was one of the reasons they moved us away from it: to protect us. My mother began to talk loudly over the TV as Bush casually shared a conversation with Jim Burke, the chairman of Johnson & Johnson and head of the Partnership for a Drug-Free America, who supposedly spent many a restless night haunted by the thought of teenage girls all over America who, rather than being in school, were giving birth to children addicted to cocaine. It's funny how he read my mother's mind; she practically screamed for my teenage sister Karina to come hear the harsh reality, hoping that, despite the fact she had never used drugs, it would scare her straight.

Who could forget the salty illustration of one's brain on drugs as an egg fried on a cast-iron pan? The infamous commercial that asked American kids if they had *any questions*?

Indeed, I had questions. None would be answered. The story was what I internalized, fearing I knew someone who reflected back this cautionary tale—a member of our own family who affirmed this terror was true. Pressure beat down on my shoulders as I sat up from my elbows and turned to search my parents' faces. I wondered if they were thinking about my uncle Javier, too.

Propaganda was nothing new to my parents. They'd arrived in the United States during Nixon's age of "law and order" to the declaration of the war on drugs as the second civil war, one the government was prepared to spend billions to win. What they didn't understand were the reports of escalation in the news. Why did Bush need more money than his predecessors, more than the last four presidents combined? Why, after so many years of zero-tolerance policies, was the problem only getting worse?

Because of people like you, Bush told us that night, recycling the good ol' dog whistle propaganda from the Nixon and Reagan eras that intentionally cast drugs as a foreign agent determined to destroy innocent citizens. "Americans have a right to safety in and around their homes," he said, which meant we had to double our financial assistance to police so they could *clean up our streets.* Safety was compromised by criminals, and criminals were people who used drugs.

That night, as a little girl desperate to fit in, I feared the implication of what I had heard and how that reflected what I was experiencing at school. Kids already treated me differently. They laughed when I got tongue-tied and a Spanish word would slip out, teased when my mom came to pick me up from school, pulling up in her beat-up Mazda beside the BMWs and Mercedes. Though I was born here, my parents weren't. I had to be an agent for these suspicious interlopers, obviously in the wrong place, my face a dead giveaway.

Of what? I had no idea.

But when the president called drugs the greatest threat to our national security and said they were being smuggled from the same places my family came from—sold, profited, and used by people who looked like us here, stateside—I knew that meant we were the threat.

Cocaine, like us, wasn't from here, not originally. It came from "beyond our borders" in Latin America. The "Andean nations" was Bush's term for the place, specifically Colombia, from which cocaine and crack were brought onto American streets, where they proliferated in the so-called ghettos, spread by the crooked poor and leaked into pristine suburbs by people like us. We weren't Colombian, but no one cared or understood that. As immigrants from the Global South, we were all alike—guilty, accused of invading the town, the factories, the school, the sandbox. Now drugs threatened to invade small towns because we were the kind of people who carried them like fleas.

———

In my uncle I saw the USian caricature of drug users brought to life. When the president spoke of spooky zombies and hardened criminals, I felt I couldn't deny his claim. I knew one. And every time one showed up on television, they looked like my uncle, never my uncle's wife.

I wish I could erase the image of that memory from my mind. The one that made a bogeyman out of a person I wanted to know and love. I wish I could spend pages telling you about who he was, but I don't know him all that well. My mother kept us at a remove. She didn't believe in redemption or change, nor did she trust the promise of a magic pill, like my uncle did. The only way to avoid pain was to outsmart it and stay clear of it. What mattered to my mother were his actions—the predictability of his recidivism and what that meant for her and her children. So, she moved us away and kept us away.

On the drive to Beatriz's house for our weekly visits, I'd search for him on the corner where he'd become a fixture. I feared his temper but admired his rebellious spirit—though it had made him a consistent ward of local police. Javier's behavioral issues, which would likely be diagnosed today as neurodivergence, got him kicked out of school just shy of fourth grade, and he never returned. Written off at such a young age, Javier resonated with the counterculture of the '60s, passing a joint outside all day with men twice his age as his peers and his sister walked to school and back, performing manhood as he witnessed it. The violence he displayed was an expression of his anger; the deeper meaning behind that anger was irrelevant. No one interrogated the environment or questioned the adults—parents, teachers, schools. They didn't even blame the drugs. It was no one's fault but Javier's.

He arrived in the United States months after my mother, dependent on drugs, and settled into a way of coping that never evolved beyond the maturity or abilities of a child. He didn't pursue his diploma, though he had the opportunity—a revealing and persistent outcome for an immigrant from Latin America. Statistics show that of the more than a million immigrants who come to the United States each year, most are more likely than US-born citizens to attain a bachelor's or advanced degree—save those from Mexico, the Caribbean, and Central America, who are less likely than USians even to graduate from high school.

Illiterate and unable to articulate his feelings without fits, Javier chose to forget, escape, and smoke—reappearing to pillage the kitchen, eat in one sitting a week's worth of the food my mother's benefits fetched for the whole family, destroy my mother's school projects, and lock her and my sister, then a baby, out of the house. Violence shielded him from accountability. Everyone treated my uncle like a land mine—once detonated, completely disposable. Shreds of his indiscretions were scattered everywhere.

What I sensed then and what I know now is that he and I shared the same sensitivity to the world's unkindness, la desgracia, as he would say. He mirrored its brutality to establish a fortress around himself, a scare tactic he was sure could prevent more pain from rushing in, and he used drugs to tend to what had already penetrated. His misguided attempt to cope became a red herring, distracting us from the truth. The only thing people talked about, the only thing that seemed to matter about Javier, was that he used drugs. In America, that's the whole story.

In the spring of Y2K, my uncle was picked up for possession of fifty grams of marijuana and five grams of hashish. A few months later, on August 14, he was charged again with possession (of fifty grams of marijuana) with intent to distribute on or near school property. His post-up spot was blocks from the local high school. Just as Bush had warned all those years ago, my uncle appeared to be "a dealer or an addict hanging around a school playground," waiting to ensnare. Likely, he was walking home with a fresh stash, but the cops got him on a technicality, and he was charged.

During that time, Bush's oldest son, George W. Bush, was running for president amid accusations of illicit drug use. "Families must set the first example of a drug-free life," Bush senior had admonished Americans that night in 1989. That's precisely what my grandmother had done for her children and what my parents had done for me. It's strange how that didn't work out for the Bushes or us, and how drastically different the consequences were.

While still a Texas governor, young W. pooh-poohed his illegal activity as youthful "mistakes," vowed he had been "drug-free for twenty-five years," and went on to become president.

The day my uncle was released from jail, he walked into the apartment to kiss my grandmother goodbye. He didn't say what was happening or where he was going. My grandmother says the police placed handcuffs around his wrists and surrendered him to Immigration and Naturalization Service, the bureau known after 9/11 as ICE (Immigrations and Customs Enforcement). According to the Drug Policy Alliance, ICE arrested more than sixty-seven thousand people in 2019 on drug charges—that's one every eight minutes. The government has been able to expel approximately forty thousand people each year since 2008, all justified by drug law violations. Simple (pot) possession escalated in 2013 to become the fourth-leading justification across all infractions and the number one cause, among drug violations, for deportation, with the power to bar a legal permanent resident from ever leaving or returning to the United States.

I remember my uncle Javier as the most handsome of my mother's four brothers. I like to think we have the same wide, wild smile, though he didn't smile much, ashamed to expose the teeth he'd lost, which aged him far beyond his actual years. I remember driving past the corner, his corner, eyes quickly scanning the spot where I could always catch a glimpse of him—seeking that sense of relief.

One day, my uncle was outside on the corner at the intersection of Speedwell Avenue in Morristown, like always. The next, he was gone.

9

The Rhythm Is Gonna Getcha

The night Jaime got out of Northern State, we celebrated. We danced with him. My sister and I wore high pigtails fastened with giant scrunchies and identical pink dresses. The bustles of our skirts puffed wide as hula hoops as we twirled our bodies around in circles. My uncle placed his hands beneath the fabric wave, bolstering the undulations faster and faster as he shimmied his shoulders to the drumbeat. "Ohwe Yahowa Ohwe Yahowa . . . " we sang from our lowest registers in a chorus and leaned our mouths toward an imaginary microphone he held between us. At first, his breath was sweet from rum, then it was bitter with beer.

We trailed behind him like ducklings. We mimicked his conga in a line and belted out "the rhythm is gonna getcha!" It was the '80s. Gloria Estefan was on the radio, and my uncle was what would soon be classified as a registered sex offender. When he couldn't stop molesting children, he threw himself in front of a train.

On August 2, 1989, Beatriz held an open-casket wake at Doyle Funeral Home on Maple Avenue in Morristown, New Jersey. Services were also held in La Ceiba, Atlántida, Honduras. New Jersey Transit paid. My uncle died less than a year after being paroled, nine years after arriving in the United States from Honduras. Some said it was a vendetta killing ordered by the survivor's mother; others said it was an unpaid debt owed to drug dealers, finally collected.

"They put him back together like Humpty Dumpty," gossips whispered. "¡Dios mío!"

Beatriz approached the casket after a short sermon and stood before the audience, the trembling mother of a pedophile, and blamed the train conductor for killing her son.

"Mi hijo," Beatriz wailed, falling to her knees. "Parece un monstruo."

"¡Tu hijo es un monstruo!" my mother screamed, demanding she acknowledge what my uncle had done, grabbing Beatriz by the shoulders, sacudiéndola, just as Jaime had done to her.

That was my first funeral.

I always had a morbid fascination with Jaime's death. When I got sober, I started investigating his story, looking for clues, trying to dispel more mysteries, blow the dust off old secrets.

At first, it was a rugged trail to chase. Before the police could convert to digital, the precinct that held my uncle's record caught fire. The paper trail was gone; anything before the '90s was now dust. My partner, Freddy, searched vintage editions of the local paper online and found a curious report on his death but nothing on his misdeeds, save a speeding ticket. It felt odd to find his name and address listed in a small paragraph announcing all municipal court infractions, among five others, all charged a sixty-dollar penalty. Soon after, the same paper would report his mysterious death. In a column called "The Week in Review," *The Daily Record* described his death as a "deadly shortcut":

MORRISTOWN—A Morristown man was struck and killed by a NJ Transit Commuter train as he strolled onto a stretch of the railroad he was using as a shortcut through town. Investigators said rush-hour traffic on nearby

Route 287, coupled with the low noise level of the electrically powered train, probably prevented 34-year-old Jaime Alfredo Bustillo from hearing the train until it was too late.

As Freddy read the cryptic clip out loud to me, decades after my uncle's death, I realized the story of his suicide had never been corroborated. Did I make it up? According to my grandmother, when he left the apartment that day, he kissed her goodbye and told her he was going to a job interview. He walked to save money and crossed the tracks to save time. His death was likely an accident. In my grandmother's memory, her sons never leave without kissing her goodbye.

The woman fielding calls at the police station told me to try the courthouse. If he was locked up, that had to pass through the Morris County Courthouse, and they would have those records. After several calls, hours on hold, and a mansplaining clerk, I received an attachment from NJCourts eFiling three months later. The type was too faint to read on the computer monitor. Knowing the file dated back to the mid-'80s, I'd purchased an HP laser printer in anticipation of this issue. I printed the fifteen-page dossier and read the evidence for the first time. Jaime had been charged with three counts of aggravated sexual assault of a minor, a girl just five years old. He was evaluated by the Adult Diagnostic and Treatment Center in Avenel, New Jersey, which revealed documented evidence of a clear, repetitive pattern of sex-related offenses. After this, he moved to lessen the charges to sexual assault by changing his plea from not guilty to guilty. The state removed the term "aggravated" from the charge and initiated a bill for $25,000 to be paid to the state of New Jersey—nothing to the victim or her family.

Before Beatriz came to the United States, she had shared a bed with my mother. Jaime would come into their room in the middle of the night, and my grandmother would pretend she didn't feel it. She'd claim she saw a ghost. "¡Un fantasma!" she'd scream when my mother demanded she open her eyes. But she wouldn't; she called my mother a liar and said she'd imagined the groping when she knew well it was her eldest son forcing himself upon her only daughter.

When Jaime died in 1989, my father, my sisters, and I prayed my mother would be able to sleep. That she'd put down the knife she'd grab in a stupor, that she'd be able to tell the difference between my father and her brother in the middle of the night. But she remained haunted. Her nightmares never stopped. She still swaddles her body at night— tightly wound in a blanket, curled into the fetal position, because it's harder to unravel and touch her that way. She covers her face from a hovering ghost—the man who stood over her bed as a child.

I wasn't the first or the only person to believe my uncle chose his fate that day. Rumor was he'd done it again and would rather die than return to prison. My uncle's lust for power drove him to prey on the most vulnerable. He denied his own vulnerability until it killed him.

At his funeral, whispers of relief circulated as they lowered his body into the ground; death could be processed when assigned a meaning. "Todo en la vida se paga," they said. My uncles were bad actors, sprung from a bad seed contaminating the American garden, and they had to be plucked out, uprooted, and discarded. As we strived to distinguish ourselves from them, deny our humanity and the harm perpetuated by our secrets, it was as if no one realized my uncles were the most assimilated of us all.

America wasn't a dream. It was a race. And the only way my family could run it was as a relay, with me as the anchor. Stories became my only escape. By telling a story, I could transform my home into a monument, my uncle into a sacrificial lamb, and my mother into a happy housewife. But the dream's comedown was harsh. Soon, I'd need something stronger.

———

Because my parents refused to admit to their romance, I've mythologized love all my life. I've seen only one remotely amorous photograph of them: a glossy square image, outlined by a neat white border, creased and curled at the edges. My mother, eighteen years old, wore a shimmery peach dress fastened to her shoulders by thin straps tied in loopy bows. She sipped a glass bottle of Coca-Cola, her favorite, through a red-and-white straw, and looked up at the camera doe-eyed, lips pursed. My father, thirty-two years old, his shy smile barely visible between the enormous sideburns that carpeted his cheeks like shaggy pork chops. The only thing that eclipses the 'burns for your attention is the size of his shirt collar and the glow of their youthful beauty.

That night, my father had picked her up in a Volkswagen bug that was yellow as an egg yolk, my mother said. She loved that car, so he let her drive it whenever she wanted. It was 1975, a time when a steady factory job made you a real papichulo para una recién llegada.

"Of course we loved each other!" My mother says decades later, almost chastising me as if she doesn't remember screaming "I never loved your father!" the day she left him during my junior year of high school. I guess she doesn't realize her declaration's impact on me or that it confirmed so many things I'd observed. Since I was a little girl, I'd known that her leaving my father would be for her own liberation.

At six years old, I was still sleeping in my parents' bed. I wouldn't start in bed with them, but I'd sneak in on my mother's side once I thought everyone had fallen asleep, before my parents' yelling broke us all out of our slumber. My mother would nestle me between her and my father to protect herself from my father's unwanted touch. He knew this, and as he lay in the foot-to-pillow position that indicated his frustration, he'd taunt my mother until somehow—whether he believed I was awake or not—he got her down on the floor beside the bed. My mother complained the entire time. I pretended to be asleep.

"¡Calláte, cochino!" she said, slapping my father's back. "Con la niña aquí. ¡Dios mío!" It was over quickly, and my mother walked across the room to her dresser. I heard a drawer creak open—the whisper of gauzy cotton down my mother's legs and up again, the snap of the elastic waistband against her belly. The sound of a fresh pair of underwear.

"Se dice cállate, bruta," my father finally replied, correcting her Spanish under his breath as he returned the pillows from the floor to the bed and resumed his backward position, reluctant to provoke her temper after the transaction that had temporarily given her the upper hand.

10

My Mother's Daughter

When I was sixteen, I worked as a waitress at Guiseppe's, a local pizzeria, slopping up disintegrated paper plates full of bite-size squares of plain pizza sliced special by the Mexican chef and drowned in whole milk by the kids who came in with their nannies after school. I'd collect the loose change left behind as my tip, slip the coins into the pocket of my red apron, press my hidden hands into the dough of my belly, and wait near the door for the next customer as I squeezed welts into the fingers of newfound fat I counted since I started working there. I'd swear I wouldn't have pizza or pasta for dinner after my shift, but it was impossible to pass up a free meal. I usually had enough to take home to my father, too. He loved the garlic bread.

It got busy on the weekends and turned into a proper restaurant or, as the owner called it, a trattoria. We offered a full menu, and I was a good server—fast, flirtatious, and eager to please. I never forgot a special or one line of an order, and I knew how to sweet-talk the cooks in Spanish, puro Latinos. They looked out for me. The uniform was black and white. Any combo of your choice, my manager said, so I got creative. Sometimes, I wore a button-down, à la Carolina Herrera, and a pair of trousers, or a black miniskirt with a V-neck tee.

I mostly wore low-waist bootcut pants in that paper-thin jersey fabric from Joyce Leslie, the kind that usually had words stamped across the ass. Of course, I went with plain for work. I thought I looked cute, but my manager didn't like getting the chefs too riled up. I was reprimanded often. "Too sexy," she complained, and blamed me at sixteen for the lack of restraint of grown men. But I made good money for a kid and gave my mother cash each month for my used hunter-green Jeep Grand Cherokee. My escape.

Things at home were falling apart. When Karla went away to college, Karina moved out, too. The nearly empty nest emboldened my mother to finally stake her independence, and soon, she stopped coming home. I took over the upstairs bedroom, and my father retreated to the dingy basement to sleep in the empty twin bed. He used the former marital bedroom to keep his things clean and dress for work but refused to sleep in their bed, as if the mildew he inhaled as he slept could be exhaled into my mother's lungs—a sign she must come home.

It was up to me to take care of my father—cook him dinner, do the laundry, entertain his grievances. Each night, he unburdened himself to me as if I were his mistress. I was old enough, he said, to know the truth about my mother.

While other mothers maintained the facade of a happy marriage, my mother refused to pretend. My father looked feeble and forlorn when they separated, while my mother grew feral and fearless. She held out her palm as my father placed cash in her hands before slamming the door, white foam collecting in the corners of her mouth as she left us both behind.

My father began following her and suspected she was fucking her boss, a chain-smoking Jersey boy who drove a white van and owned a cleaning service. When I expressed the slightest doubt in his theory, he told me to watch my mouth. "¡No me hables así!" he said, reminding me that he was the father, and I was the child, still living under his roof.

The home we shared was a single-story ranch tucked far back from the main road on a misshapen lot among four other small houses. The derelict property sloped down, causing frequent flooding, mold, and decay in the basement where my father had tried to build two extra bedrooms to accommodate our five-person family in a two-bedroom home. Before Karina moved out, I often slept on the couch.

I wasn't sure where my mother was. I'd stopped asking. My father said she had a boyfriend down the shore and that he'd seen a picture of her on his boat. It seemed a little cold still to be at the beach, but it was possible.

Mother's Day had just passed, and she hadn't come home. My mother spooked easily, like a cat, so I never put pressure on her. But for Mother's Day, I wanted her with me. It was my one request. I bought her flowers and a card. I even sprang for a pink balloon in the shape of a rose, inscribed with gold letters that announced "I love you, Mom," and I left the offering on her bed pillow. When she returned, the flowers were wilted as if at a graveside.

My father passed by the doorway as often as I did to stare at the death of the woman we once knew. He mumbled under his breath, then came to my door. He asked rhetorically, "¿Tu mamá nunca llegó?" He didn't want my mother to hurt me, but he was glad she had failed the test. Now I understood. "Mira como es tu mamá." He was right about her.

11

Sick as Our Secrets

I was raped the year my mother left my father. My mother was raped after my grandmother left their home. My grandmother told me she stabbed the man who attempted to rape her. We all left the place where it happened as soon as we could.

The story of my mother's rape is not my story to tell, and yet I've told it before. It is a story I've heard since I can remember, and perhaps I felt that it entitled me to share it, or maybe it's because of my resentment that since it happened to her, it could not, *should not* happen to me. This was the kind of fantasy the American Dream professed to make possible. While many equate it with prosperity, in my mother's interpretation, America was safe; her dream was safety. For her and for us.

I'll tell you what happened to me because I want you to know there is no safe place. Gender-based violence is not endemic; it is epidemic. At sixteen my mother was drugged and raped in La Ceiba, Honduras. And at sixteen, I was drugged and raped in Mendham, New Jersey.

Over three generations, none of us escaped violence.

—

I was going to the prom with my friend Ant—a faux-platonic invite, the kind of teenage pact made by all misfits, a rescue. I was devastated that the boy I had a crush on had reunited with his girlfriend. I'd be forced to watch the perfect prom king and queen canoodle lustfully on the dance floor as I slowly danced an arm's length away from my friend's body, or so I imagined.

I went to the mall to buy my dress. The year before, we had all gone together to find my sister's prom dress—me, Karina, Karla, and Mom. It was an event. Many hours, across several stores and dozens of dresses. Finally, a unanimous vote: a white sequin tube top paired with a ballerina-pink tulle ball gown skirt. It was rare for Karla to choose something so girly, and my mother could not get enough photos to commemorate the occasion. Karla pretended to be annoyed, but I knew she wanted my mother's approval as much as the rest of us.

In a crowded corner on a sale rack at Macy's, I found a two-piece like my sister's. A corset top with a matching ball gown skirt in a soft shade of opaque green they called seafoam. Jeweled embellishment subtly accented the neckline, the spaghetti straps showed off my prominent clavicle, and the plastic ribs of the corset snatched my waist. It was perfect. It made me feel beautiful. I was pretty, but not the kind of pretty that meant anything in our town. You had to have a certain taste, a palate for the exotic, to call me hot. Not many boys did.

Macy's didn't have a cloth garment bag for me like the one they gave Karla, but they wrapped it in a long plastic bag and let me have the hanger. I draped it carefully over my arm, cradling it like a child, and walked to grab a Frosty at the food court. It hurt to do it alone. I don't know why people always say the youngest child is the most spoiled. When my turn came around, everyone had lost interest.

—

When my mother reads this, she'll say, "Everybody is going to think it was my fault." It's not.

It is true that if my mother had been home, I would not have gone to the party a few weeks before prom. She would never have given me permission. My mother was strict; her rules humiliated us. If a boy called the house, she'd say, "Jessica who? She doesn't live here," or "Karla can't talk to any boy! Don't ever call here again." We tried our best to sneak away from her and help each other. She once dragged my sister out of a party by her hair because she was sitting on a boy's lap. Witnesses say she slapped the boy, too. I remember his parents called our house and threatened to press charges. The boys stopped calling.

If my mother had been home when I didn't make it back that night, she would have been like an animal in the streets, hunting me down, and those boys would be dead. (Incidentally, two of them are.)

It's also true that my father was home. He believed in deferring to my mother as a primary form of parenting. "Pregúntale a tu mamá," he'd always say when my mother denied our requests in his name. My mother was the enforcer, my father the whisperer.

When I got home that next morning, I was sick, disheveled, raped. My father knew nothing of what had happened, where I'd been, or why I hadn't called or come home. But he was disappointed in me, so he gave me the silent treatment. I braced as I heard his slippers scrape the cement of the basement stairs, shuffle past the peeled edges of the kitchen's cracked linoleum floor and across the few paces of the carpeted floor to my doorway. He stood there, smacked his lips, turned, and left. Silence. A punishment more painful than any childhood spanking. I was another woman who didn't come home to him, who didn't sleep in her own bed.

—

I couldn't remember much. That's why it was easy to lie to me for so long. So I want to be as clear on the facts as I can because they will call me a liar. A whole town. Save the other victims and the eyewitnesses who have contacted me or whom I've interviewed. So many people were complicit. And I hope this haunts them as it has haunted me.

I didn't tell anyone because I believed the lie they told about me. It isolated me, silenced me. It was the lie that took my family from me. With large gaps in my memory erased by Rohypnol, they knew I could never credibly refute what they said I'd done. Although it seemed impossible in the state in which, they say, I'd gotten drunk.

Rohypnol is a benzodiazepine commonly referred to as a *roofie*, similar to Valium but ten times stronger. Its effects magnify when mixed with alcohol and begin within thirty minutes of ingesting, peak after about two hours, and last up to twelve. The most common symptoms are incapacitation, loss of muscle and motor control, drowsiness, slurred speech, and amnesia. It is a potent tranquilizer—victims and users become paralyzed. Some are able to observe events, even keep their eyes open as their bodies metabolize the drug, but all experience partial or total loss of memory— ideal components for a premeditated attack at a house party.

———

Here's what I remember about the party: It was a small town, but these people had acreage; they weren't homeowners, they were property owners. It was dark when I drove from the edge of Chester Township into the foothills of Mendham, where the biggest mansions lined the winding streets on the way to Bedminster. Gray stones crunched beneath my tires as I pulled into the pebbled driveway. Ahead was a small garage. It looked like a barn. Maybe it was a barn? To the left, a house—a giant house, a mansion—and a large field. I can't recall if there was a bonfire that night, a staple of Ben's parties. I only remember being inside the house.

I went in and followed the sound of music and conversation up the stairs and into a room I assumed was Ben's bedroom, where people were gathered. All upperclassmen. I scanned the room for a friendly face, but no one made eye contact. I was driving, so I didn't want to drink. If I ever got caught, my parents would kill me. But when Ben came over from across the room with a red Solo cup, I couldn't refuse.

I went that night because I thought a boy I liked would be there and because Ben called me to invite me personally. "Don't spread the word," he said. "It's just gonna be a small thing, a few friends, and I really want you to be there." I truly believed I'd made it into the inner circle just in time for prom. I didn't see any of my friends there, and I wondered who had given him my number as I sipped my cup and awkwardly stood outside a group, hoping the boy would stop by, but he never showed. As Ben draped his arm across my shoulders, I felt as if he had broken an egg over my head, the icy yolk dripping down my chin. Then it all went blurry.

I remember the stained mattress on the ground. No sheets. My whole body felt numb as I lay on my back and stared at the pitched ceiling above. The room was very dark; it appeared to be the attic. A small light emanated from the door. It was cracked open, and a few guys stood in the doorway— Ben, Dillon, Chris, and Mike. Maybe a few others behind them? They huddled like a sports team calling a play, came to an agreement, and one entered the room. It was Mike. He stood over me, grabbed my arm to lift my body, and suddenly let go. Like when you boil pasta and throw a noodle against the wall to see if it'll stick, so you know it's ready.

I dissolved, no control, no resistance. He sat beside me on the edge of the mattress, and the others closed the door.

I will never know what happened to me that night, all night, on that filthy mattress, for hours. But that's where I woke up: the syrup of raspberry Smirnoff sticky on my chest, the sour stench of beer from the tapped keg and sawdust—wood had been freshly cut. It smelled sweet and cedar, almost wholesome. My father always smelled like sawdust.

I'd never gotten drunk before, so I didn't understand what I felt. I assumed it was a hangover and prayed I hadn't done anything too embarrassing. My head pounded, and I struggled to get up from the floor, limbs still partially numb. When I finally stood, I noticed my fly was down, the top button of my jeans undone. I zipped myself up, grabbed my purse, and ran down the stairs. My legs gave out on me, and I fell, hitting the gravel driveway.

The stones were sharp. It hurt so bad, but the shock helped wake up my legs. My foot trembled as I pressed the gas pedal in reverse and tore out of there. I had to take the back roads: long, windy, snakelike—deadly in my condition. In some parts, they're flanked by high banks and hedges. As I nodded out, I slid off the road, came to, and quickly regained control of the car. I had to pull over a couple of times.

I didn't want my father to see me disheveled and assume the worst, so I ran to the house, right into the shower, and collapsed into bed. My new prom dress hung in the crick of the accordion door on the outside of my closet. When I brought it home, I had decided not to smoosh it alongside all the other, lesser clothing items. This was special—a piece. And I didn't want it to get wrinkled. But most of all, it made me happy to see it. As I stared at that dress, something told me to put it on. And something told me to get a knife from the kitchen. I put on the gown, slipped the knife under my pillow, and lay in bed like a zombie bride.

That was the day my mother finally came home.

I heard the weight of her overnight bag, no doubt full of laundry, slam down on the piano bench. She walked slowly to my room and found me, overdressed, in bed. "You look like Sleeping Beauty," she said as she took my picture. It was what she always did when she thought I looked pretty.

———

By summer, my sister came home from her first year of college. My mother was around more. My father spent less time in the basement and started sleeping on the couch. I had a boyfriend and was barely home—I spent all my time at his place. When his parents caught us having sex,

I was forbidden to be in his house. We began having sex on my white wrought-iron daybed. The unsteady IKEA hand-me-down shrieked at the slightest touch, which only seemed to make my boyfriend thrust harder. I begged him to be mindful of my father, who was often down in the basement, but I never told him to stop.

My father told Karla that while searching for a pruning tool in the basement where he'd made himself a workshop, he'd heard us above on the iron daybed. He ran out of the house through the basement door and waited until my boyfriend's car was no longer parked in front of our mailbox.

The story he told me was about how he tied a noose in the basement. For many weeks after my mother's desertion, he would go down to the basement to tie knots, set the stage, and go over his plan. He said the sound of my footsteps stopped him on the day he was going to make an attempt. It happened that winter, the season I kept bringing my pinche gringo boyfriend to the house all the time, my father told me. That day, my boyfriend helped me drag an enormous Christmas tree into my carpeted bedroom as a big fuck-you to my mother, who disapproved of the holiday. It was then that my father decided to live. For me, he said.

12

Thirst Trap

In Spanish, we don't say "I'm thirsty." We say "I thirst" or, more specifically, "I have thirst." "Tengo sed."

I had only ever seen designer goods in fashion magazines, when I spotted a Louis Vuitton monogram pochette perched on the shoulder of an underclassman during my senior year of high school. I didn't know the girl well enough to approach, but she was in my PE class. I made note of where her gym locker was and took my time changing for class. At first, I only wanted an up-close look at the bag, but when I opened it, I found tons of cash. I took forty bucks, shoved it in my bra, and ran out to the gymnasium trembling but exhilarated. When nothing happened, I did it again. I hit a different locker each time. I could not believe how much money these fifteen-, sixteen-year-olds were carrying, and I figured I needed it more than they did.

Rumors about theft started circulating, linking the window of opportunity to phys ed. For a long stretch of my senior year, I was the last person out of the gym locker room, yet no one ever accused me, not to my face. I have no idea why. After the rape, they accused me of everything else.

I coveted other people's things, other people's lives. My mother cleaned houses and took care of rich kids to try to cover our needs. I would always go with her on jobs, de metiche. I liked to pretend I lived in these big, beautiful mansions—be super nosy and go through all their fancy things. I'd promise my mother I'd be busy in the bathroom and sneak into the daughter's room, find her closet, and grope expensive garments hanging on pillowy silk hangers—never worn, Nordstrom tags still attached. I stood on my tippy toes to audit their wardrobes for hours, considering each piece, shifting the hangers one by one with a single pointer finger, the way I would one day flip through Diane Von Fürstenberg's new spring line from the third floor of her showroom, staring across the Hudson at New Jersey and thinking how far I'd come, barely surviving but connected enough to get high for free, and fantasizing that one day I'd have it all the way I fantasized about it as a girl.

Some say addicts are born. As far as I'm able to recall, I was always a little klepto, though I never stole from my mother's clients. I didn't want to get her in trouble, for her to be ashamed like the day at the supermarket. But the desire to take what I wanted bloomed from trying to replace what I already felt had been stolen from me. My hands reached out from the hole inside me left by that original theft, a thirst I could not slake.

The first time my mother caught me stealing, it was candy from the grocery store. I was four years old. Grocery shopping was the one chore that also tested my mother's impulses. Though, even when my mother hit her heaviest weight, you'd hardly see her eat a full meal. Before I'd gulped down a cup full of fountain soda and felt full, my mother would beg me to have a bite of the single hamburger from my McDonald's Happy Meal. She'd eat the rest before tossing the cardboard box in the trash, careful not to discard the plastic toy, what I wanted most. At dinnertime, she would serve the whole family and scrape the leftovers off our plates at the sink, her back shielding her movements, her shifting shoulders a dead giveaway that she was licking them clean. She waited up at night until we'd all fallen asleep to slip into the kitchen.

My mother deeply resented her addiction to food. Unlike her mother, led only by her own desires, she battled them until she was starved. In the middle of the night, when no one could see her give in, she'd devour entire boxes of cookies, whole bags of chips, every leftover in sight—and hate herself.

Of all the treats in the store, my mother told me I could have only one. I had to choose, so I picked cookies. But then I saw the Duncan Hines chocolate cake mix, gummy bears, and marshmallows. I was distraught by the idea of choosing just one. She put her foot down. "Mucho dulce, mija," she said to me. I pouted as my mother moved on, filling our cart with essentials. At the checkout, I faced another wall of temptation. I begged for a bag of Skittles, cherry Life Savers, watermelon Bubblicious gum, but my mom remained firm. As she paid, I slipped the Life Savers into my purse, a hot-pink patent leather Barbie tote bag with plenty of room for one doll, a *Berenstain Bears* book, and as much candy as I could reach.

When we got to the car, my mother noticed my round, red mouth full of hard candy and quickly discovered my stash. Immediately, she drove back to the store, forced me to apologize, and returned it all to the manager. My mother thought the shame would scare me straight. But all I learned was to hide my thirst, like her.

13

Lightweight

I'm supposed to be talking to you about how I was the first in my family to do something extraordinary, so this is where I should tell you that I defeated what had tossed me off the beam as a kid. That I triumphed over rape, slander, homelessness. Escaped a broken home and beat the odds by overcoming my family's prison records. Despite it all, I became editor of the school paper, got a full-ride scholarship, and wound up at Harvard. Right? That I didn't let my trauma pull me under. Would this make the book worth reading? Would it make my story worth listening to?

It's only fair to tell you that I didn't. I was an adequate student, below average by graduation. From the academic institution my parents sacrificed for me to attend, I achieved little more than survival and labor. I didn't raise the level in my parents' water glasses, though I left Jersey determined.

While packing to leave for our respective colleges, my boyfriend found, under my bed, my old yearbook from sixth grade, my last year at Mendham Township Middle School, the year we lost the house. As he paged through, laughing at the young photos of his now-much-older friends, reading messages from classmates to glean who might have liked me or who I liked back then, he found the picture of me with the school newspaper staff. "What the fuck, you were on the school paper?!" he asked rhetorically, incredulously, even as he held the evidence in his hand. I smiled as I looked down at the photo, barely able to remember myself. "What happened to you?" he said, eyes squinting as if I had somehow become unrecognizable. Disappointed, he shook his head.

In true Hoppe fashion, I packed very little when I left to register at Northeastern University, but I brought that yearbook, willing to do whatever it took to redeem that little girl. I chose the School of Criminology and Criminal Justice because it offered the major closest to pre-law. I had no real sense of my academic interests, nor did I think I could trust my own judgment, so I went for my father's. He always wanted to be a lawyer.

Around eight years old, my father was taken out of school and made to work in the mercados. He hauled crates and barrels of goods off ships, dragged bales of grain, lentils, cardamom, and cumin across hectic dirt roads to set up and sell at the open-air market. He haggled prices with the local baker or the housekeepers who managed the large estates. He worked for love, desperate to be acknowledged for his negotiation skills and savvy from a young age. "Tenía inteligencia," he recalls, pointing to his temple and giggling like a boy, as if it were something he had and lost. He believed his life in the labor force didn't reflect his intelligence. When he tried to make a case against mistreatment at the Shade Tree Commission, he was disparaged in the paper, called sensitive and opportunistic. They tossed him a small settlement to keep him (and his family) quiet and forced him to retire, which hurt him most. He had no idea what to do with himself if he wasn't working.

Unaware of the generational baggage strapped to my back, I kept my faith in the storybook trope of new beginnings. I wanted to start fresh—forget the past, turn the page. Finally free from the confines of a small town and the small-minded attitudes that had held me back, I had hope, a modicum of power to think Boston would be a do-over.

Reuniting with my sister Karla in a new city made me feel safe again. Growing up, I had always felt she was my protector, shielding me from bullies at school. She had established herself there over the previous two years, built a solid friend group, and lived with them in their own apartment off campus. I soon moved in with her. Five girls in a one-bedroom, one-bath was a mess that is fun only in college. The guys we hung out with lived upstairs. Both our doors were always open, all walking in and out freely, many dating or at least sleeping with each other and partying almost every night. It felt like a spin-off of *Friends*.

I worried I was an imposition on my older sister and her friends, so I made myself helpful—cooking, cleaning, and pouring cocktails. A sort of at-home bottle service that began hours before we even left the house, the "pre-game" was the best time of the night. The only part I'd ever remember.

Back then, my drinking looked like everyone else's. But I recall always creating an excuse to run back in the house: I had forgotten keys or my cell phone or to put on my necklace, or I was wearing the wrong shoes. I'd sneak to the kitchen and pour myself an extra shot or two from the frosted bottle of cheap vodka in the freezer. Warmth for my bare legs, I justified—a layer to help me endure the bitter New England cold.

At school, I found myself in familiar waters. Each semester was the same. I'd start out in the front row, super-prepared for class, and raise my hand enthusiastically. I'd drill my pen onto the page, focused on making sure my notes were perfect. But when I couldn't keep up, I'd tear the page from my notebook, crumple it into a ball, and flip to the next. It gave me a thrill to give up on myself, quietly, privately. Though it killed me to have to pretend—to lie when I felt disoriented, nod *yes* when I meant *no*, agree when I knew something was wrong, say *I'm good* when I needed help.

Despite my best efforts, I couldn't seem to skip from stone to stone, each step building upon the last, like the other students. Instead, I found myself in a loop. But when I felt like a failure, I knew I could always work my ass off. I was exhausted, but I needed things to be different. I couldn't afford to stop or rest.

I crammed my classes into three days to accommodate a four-day work schedule at a restaurant to cover living expenses, and I took out loans to pay tuition. Northeastern University is known for its work-study program, which means you spend equal time in the workforce as you do in the classroom. The idea was that you would graduate with a job in your chosen concentration.

Karla attended Northeastern, too, and as a finance major scored a job with Merrill Lynch. So I felt confident I'd be landing my dream job next. On a whim, I applied for and got a competitive internship at Ralph Lauren the summer before my senior year. When I learned it was full time and unpaid, I used my student loan money to take time off waitressing and give myself a shot at a creative profession. I had hoped my free labor would position me as a shoo-in for a spot at the corporate office in the merchandising department come fall. But I didn't get the job. Two white kids from Harvard did.

Devastated, I resigned myself to get back on track and redoubled my efforts toward my studies. It was absurd to believe I could make it in fashion, I thought. Prior to the internship, I'd aced my midterm in organized crime. The class was fascinating, and I loved my professor, who in turn favored me. But when I started partying every night, I stopped showing up for class, and my already tenuous grades completely slipped through my fingers. The day she handed me my final, she slapped the graded test facedown on my desk and waited for me to look up and meet her eyes. "What happened to you?" she said. I flipped the corner to peek at the result and saw a capital *F* circled in red pen. My first.

I managed to make it to graduation, though on the day of the ceremony I woke in bed with my friend, wondering if we'd finally slept together. Still drunk and already late, I ran to the bathroom to brush my teeth, splash water on my face, and scrape the smeared mascara from under my eyes. With no time to change my outfit, I threw my gown over the sequined minidress I had worn to the club and bolted to the stadium in last night's strappy sandals. Despite the pouring rain, I arrived without busting my ass as they began to seal the doors. I could barely hold my head up through the ceremony, my cap falling off my head repeatedly as I nodded out. Luckily, the enormous stadium made me appear as a speck to my family in the stands, my disgraceful behavior indiscernible. My parents, in the midst of their divorce proceedings, had no idea what condition I was in and barely noticed that my gown had not one sash, award, or adornment. I told them I was a success, and they believed me.

I've never read my official transcript. If I did back then, I don't remember. But my adviser told me law school was a long shot, even if I scored high on the LSAT, and would put me at least another $100,000 in debt. My academic career ended unexceptionally, and I turned my focus to making a *career* career out of the story of my internship and typed up my resume as follows:

Education: Northeastern University, Boston, MA, 2001–2005,
Bachelor of Science, Received in April 2005, GPA 3.8

I thought it was a modest embellishment.

14

Dependent

I'm a Jersey girl. I'm from shorelines and turnpikes, bridges and tunnels. I'm from a place where they write songs about being born again and running away but staying proud. Concentrated, a punch in a small package, like Jon Bon, Bruce, or Snooki. (Did you know she's Chilean? Did you know she quit drinking after she found alcohol in her breast milk? She's a cycle breaker like me.) Growing up, I had little appreciation for my first real home. I thought of New York City as the promised land my parents imagined the United States would be when they were growing up in La Ceiba, Honduras, and Guayaquil, Ecuador. As they had, I believed that the unlucky place where we found ourselves at the start was temporary; our true home was somewhere else. For me, it was across the Hudson River, a mile-and-a-half drive through the Holland Tunnel.

Once I got my license, I began sneaking across alone, mostly to take dance classes at Astor Place or audition for a commercial; once, to date an NYU professor whom I had convinced on a flight back from Miami (seated separately from my mother) that I was a student there. On our first date, we played Frisbee with his dog in Washington Square Park and ordered takeout at his place. I told him the truth that night, assuming it would end things, but he said he was still interested in dating me. I was a junior in high school. It scared me that he still wanted to hook up, and I never saw him again. Soon, a letter from the city threatening a warrant for my arrest due to unpaid parking tickets arrived at our home and was intercepted by my father. My secret solo trips to the city were over.

When I finally moved there after college, I learned it is customary for landlords in New York City to require an income that is forty times the cost of rent to grant the privilege of applying for an apartment. Just to put your name down. Cold-call interest in a place will garner a terse response demanding your most intimate financial details. You oblige, maneuver, lie even. Under these criteria, it seemed impossible that I would ever qualify for a lease on my own. I would need a roommate, partner, cosigner. I would always be dependent.

I wanted my arrival in New York City to feel like a homecoming, but I had no place to live. My sister found a spot in Battery Park with her friends, and my boyfriend's family got him an apartment on the corner of Mott Street and Houston. I lied to my sister and told her I lived with him, that I was welcome there. I lied to my boyfriend and told him I lived with my sister and friends down by Wall Street. Technically, I had no home. As usual, everyone was making it but me.

My boyfriend in LA told me to sit tight and find another job before I left. My boyfriend in London told me to quit and come be with him in Europe. "I'll take care of you," he said. "We'll travel." I didn't think twice.

When the crash hit in 2008, I lived with my sister in a one-bedroom split in SoHo. Our 400-square-foot railroad-style apartment was on the first floor of a walk-up on Thompson between Watts and Grand and featured windows that looked out onto a brick wall. I slept on a springy futon couch from IKEA. My share of the rent cost nearly my entire salary. I was an assistant buyer at Intermix, a high-end boutique with a then-innovative shop-your-closet assortment. White shopping bags emblazoned with the signature hot-pink logo littered the city from NYU to the North Fork. With barely an item under $100 or a size above a US 8, Intermix cast a rigid type—landing the job said something about me. I'd made it. I was *in*.

What making it actually looked like was mindlessly redistributing unsold units of our bestselling "going-out tops" from Bal Harbour to Fifth Avenue, from the narrow bowels of a misshapen loft where I worked atop a piece of plywood that served as a desk for nine women. Separated by mere inches and tufted hot-pink partitions, I sat directly beside my boss, who, despite her cartoonishly dead-inside tone, could shut down the room with a hair flip.

The fact that my dream job turned out to be dreadfully unglamorous and deeply unfulfilling was not a reality I was prepared to process. I'd literally gone into debt to get it and was actively accruing debt to keep it. To escape, I invented the life I felt I should have, uploading vague and blurry photos of my awkward jaunts into New York City nightlife onto Tumblr each night. My catalog was always askew after this rando I met at a rooftop party reached over my shoulder and tilted the lens of my chrome-red Nikon as I clicked a pic of friends. He said all you had to do to make a photograph interesting was change the perspective. Force it off-kilter.

I was making $37,000 a year when executives corralled the entire staff into the stockroom for a meeting. Dozens of employees filed in to listen to the cofounder announce our salaries would be cut by 30 percent. I tried to quantify this percentage into a meaningful sum— dollars, subway rides, meals—when I heard my name. I hadn't realized tears were streaming down my face.

At my annual review, I was told by my boss that I "wear my heart on my sleeve." This was bad for business. After two years, they determined I had no potential as a buyer, and I would not be promoted from assistant to associate. If I chose to leave, they'd sign off on my unemployment insurance.

I told my LA boyfriend I had accepted their proposal and was going on a long-term trip with my mother to Costa Rica. Not sure when I'll be back, I said. He never asked me to come to LA. My London boyfriend booked me a flight to Heathrow with no return. Construction began on our block in New York to build the James Hotel, triggering a bedbug infestation throughout the neighborhood. But I was long gone, leaving my sister to clean up our mess alone.

I arrived in London for the first time at the start of the following year, as winter warmed into spring, wearing faux-leather leggings, knee-high boots, and an Elizabeth and James blazer. The day of my departure from New York, brunch with friends had escalated into an unofficial going-away party. I nearly missed my flight. Nauseated, I could not remain seated at liftoff, nearly tackling the flight attendant who tried to intercept my run to the bathroom. The painful purge cleared my head enough to question what I was running away from and whom I was running to—I hardly knew my boyfriend. I asked the flight attendant for a glass of wine.

I had met my boyfriend Luca, who would become my ex-husband, high on cocaine. The first time I'd ever tried it. My friend had invited me into the bathroom at an underground lounge in the West Village, the kind of place that was a restaurant to everyone upstairs and a club to close friends and A-list models downstairs. He pulled a small baggie from his pocket and held a key of powder under my nose. I remembered my father's warning. He said drugs turned people into zombies—once you started, you couldn't stop. Siguen hasta la muerte. The only thing on the other side was death. I told my friend I was good with my tequila, confessing the echo of my father's admonition. My friend laughed heartily and inhaled the bump. "Nothing bad is going to happen," he whispered in my ear. "I promise." I loved it when men made promises to me.

I was twenty-four years old, and this was my first time seeing coke in person. I tried to play it cool but was scared to try it, though tons of the girls I worked with in fashion used coke, and most of the dealers were corny white boys who sold out of a JanSport backpack and could get any prescription they wanted from their parents. It wouldn't be the same, though, if I did. In many cultures, drug use is viewed and utilized as protest, part of the fight against oppression. It functioned as a release valve for overworked laborers or a fuck-you to the Man for counterculture creators. None of this occurred to me at the time. But I did want to defy the repressive rhetoric I'd internalized. I didn't want to be afraid of anything anymore. I wanted to let loose—just like everybody else.

Only when I tried it myself did I decide that all that propaganda was bullshit. I loved cocaine from the moment I tasted it. Coke straightened out my sloppy slurring, cut my appetite and drinking in half. Most seductive was how it satisfied a hole the size of a god I carried inside. At least for ten-minute intervals. It contained the chasm that split open in my soul, the gnaw of its spread, heat no longer quelled by booze but inflamed. The wrath that alcohol unchained in me by the end of the night (every single night, without fail) was lassoed by a relentless devotion to instantaneous pleasure. For once, I allowed myself to be seen desiring what others had; it was less humiliating than fits of rage. I retired my reputation as Tequila Boom Boom and turned my rent-stabilized East Village apartment into a place my friends and I called la factoría, sharing lines of cheap eight balls off my vanity mirror and stumbling downstairs to head out for the night no earlier than the official start of morning.

During civilian hours, I wound up behind a receptionist desk at a finance firm while my white cohorts ascended the ladders at *Harper's Bazaar* and Ralph Lauren, their lifestyles still subsidized despite the economic crash. I started to wonder if my late-night activity was keeping me from the success I so desperately wanted.

15

Red Flags, Green Light

My sister got married in Playa Hermosa, Mexico, in 2013. That year it was rated one of the world's most beautiful beaches: a worthy backdrop for the first wedding in our family—we could only afford civil ceremonies before. The event was a sandy, intimate celebration we'd planned over boozy brunches. After I changed my profile pic to a portrait of us from Karla's ethereal wedding, a guy from my past randomly used the opportunity to say hello. I was single for the first time since high school and determined to remain so for a while, to recover from a series of bad breakups. Still, alone on my couch in the East Village, I chatted with this guy for hours. And when he asked me out, I couldn't say no.

From the inception of our romance, even that very first date, it was clear the guy was struggling—red flags more conspicuous than Times Square. Yet we dated for nearly three years. I needed love, and he needed money.

While we were together, I worked as an executive assistant and hustled on the weekends to resuscitate my fashion career, growth hacking to build a following on Instagram. He took all my photographs. I was enamored of his vision of me, and soon he was booking clients, making a living through the lens of my camera at my suggestion. I came home to a new couch, state-of-the-art EgglestonWorks speakers, a full Cary Audio system. All swag, no cash.

He was always short, and I always covered it. I bridged the gaps. I hid on the roof and cried for hours. I drank. Alone. One bottle a night quickly turned to at least two. I berated him. I berated myself. It didn't make me feel powerful to be responsible for a grown man the way I hoped it would. The way it had always emboldened my exes.

I couldn't walk up the stairway to our front door without stopping at a bar first. I tried to leave many times. His parents would call, show up outside my office, sit me down at a coffee shop outside Grand Central, and convince me to stay. "He'll never cheat on you," his father said; for a girl like me, that's all it took. I was found collapsed in the hedges outside our home, screaming at EMTs in the back of an ambulance, making out with an ex on Montague Street blocks from our door. I have no memory of any of these nights, only torn clothing and broken heels, scraped knees and bruised shoulders, lost phones and missing credit cards. Ashamed and tormented by the unknown, I asked him to forgive me.

He helped me retrace my steps, suggested we use the iPad to track my phone, and kept the locator active without my knowledge. Through each cry for help, he monitored my whereabouts from the couch, as desperate to control me as I was to control myself. I aimed my efforts at my drinking. I punished myself with weeklong cleanses.

I set rules.

No drinking during the week. No hard alcohol. No beer: too many calories. No wine: too much sugar.

I broke every one. In the end, it was vodka straight.

———

Jared wasn't the kind of boyfriend who took the heavy off your hands. We once got in a heated fight about why he wouldn't offer his seat on the subway to a pregnant person; he claimed his was the feminist argument. This debate occurred at the start of our relationship, and by the time we ventured on our first let's-fix-it trips, the shock of his selfishness had worn off.

All Jared needed for four nights and five days in Mexico was a standard carry-on. I envied him as I dragged behind, hauling my overstuffed luggage. My duffle definitely breached TSA regulations, and I felt anxious about breaking the rules. As I struggled through JFK at 5 a.m., I could hear Jared whistling, though I couldn't decipher the tune. Burdened by my indecision and bleary from lack of sleep, I envied how casually Jared strolled and wished he'd turn to see me.

I had stayed up late the night before to pack. My goal was to get my belongings past security in one carry-on and one "personal item" by stacking bags within bags and transporting wide-brim hats by layering them on my head. Jared tossed a couple of T-shirts and shorts in a leather bag his parents had given him, a piece from the surplus Wilson's Leather they sold, and went to bed. He forgot to charge the camera, even though I'd asked him to. I plugged it in myself and tried to get a few hours of sleep.

My luggage was disorganized and heavy. I noticed that a seam of my black nylon Tumi bag had torn as a result of my insistence to fit just one more pair of shoes, but I managed to get it all on board and into the overhead without being asked to check my bag. A triumph in my book.

Jared slept practically all five hours of the flight to Mexico, save one long trip to the bathroom. And when we landed, he handed me his bag and offered to carry mine. "Here, babe, this is much lighter," he said, and I smiled, appreciative of the chivalrous gesture; he did notice me, I thought.

During the nineteenth century, references to pot in the United States were made using the plant's formal name, cannabis. No matter where it was discussed—medical journal, trade publication, or local paper—cannabis was always what it was called. But after the political upheaval in Mexico caused more Mexican migrants to come into the southwest territory seized by the United States, it was called something different. Suddenly, it was *marijuana*. The "marijuana menace." It was called this to target and punish people who looked like me. Cannabis was white, but marijuana was brown.

———

We breezed through immigration, pausing as a couple to answer questions about our trip, which was *for pleasure, four nights five days, nope, nothing to claim.* Stamped and sailing through, I was on the lookout for our driver when we were stopped again at a customs checkpoint with a device they call "red light green light." I was told to place my bag on a scale and press a giant red button overhead, which will, at random, trigger either a green light (you are free to proceed) or a red light (you must take your bag to an agent who will perform further inspection).

Jared was cleared as a twinge of fear shot through my body. Then my light blinked red. Confident I had nothing to hide, I sauntered over to the desk, placed Jared's bag on the steel table, and greeted the agent in Spanish. "Open the bag," he responded in English, covering his hands with rubber gloves.

———

Cannabis was banned in Mexico in 1920, seventeen years before it was in the United States. Mexicans would cross the border into the United States to purchase it from pharmacies. Mexican oligarchs who controlled the media often pushed fearmongering headlines, racializing drug users and correlating recreational use with violence. Sound familiar? The States likely stole this strategy from Mexico. Most immigrants did not smoke pot, but US officials dressed up drug use as a foreign threat. Drugs and otherness were fused and forever instilled into the US consciousness as a *them problem*, codifying racism into law.

———

I couldn't find Jared anywhere. "It's my boyfriend's bag," I told the agent as I scanned the room.

"Hey, pay attention," the agent snapped. "This is your bag."

"Take this out," he said, pointing inside at Jared's stuff. "I have to search it more underneath."

"Go for it," I clapped back, offended by the feeling that I was being profiled by the white agent. I turned again to look for Jared, who stood at the far exit, poised beside the automatic doors. The hue of his cheeks blanched from pale to translucent as he looked on from afar, feigning busyness by fidgeting and scrolling through his phone. I began to lose patience with the inspection, releasing an audible sigh, and the agent finally returned the bag.

———

During congressional hearings in 1937, the US Narcotics Commissioner Harry J. Anslinger presented so-called evidence to support federal restrictions on marijuana, with the help of testimony from the editor of the *Alamosa Daily Courier*, Floyd Baskette. According to the official court transcript, the letter stated, "I wish I could show you what a small marihuana cigaret can do to one of our degenerate Spanish-speaking residents. That's why our problem is so great; the greatest percentage of our population is composed of Spanish-speaking persons, most of who [*sic*! Such an enthusiastic *sic*!] are low mentally, because of social and racial conditions."

———

"What the fuck was that?" I complained as I rejoined Jared. We stepped out of the airport, struck by a wave of humidity and the wickedness of his laughter. "Thank God!" he cried.

Jared's humor was sanguine, prideful, as he explained how we'd managed to smuggle his weed into Mexico. At home, he'd torn the seam of his pants and stuffed as much pot between the denim and the lining as he could. In flight, he'd fished it out of his crotch from the bathroom and hidden it in his carry-on. He'd then handed that carry-on to me.

Jared never outgrew his habit of trespassing—dumb shit like breaking onto a roof or a backyard, a closed-off street, or a park. It was as if all signs read "Welcome" to Jared. Boundaries were meant to be crossed. A broken rule for Jared was a broken law for me, though he thought of himself as my passport. When the only person who ever took us anywhere was me.

———

A full moon is the result of exposure. Positioned at a direct angle to the sun, the moon is fully illuminated, not by emitting her own light but by reflecting the sun's light off her surface. Though we only see one side of her from Earth, we perceive the moon to be on full display.

Is this a sign of the moon's grace, allowing herself to be seen? Or is it the greed of the sun, forcing the moon to reveal what is safer in the shadows?

What is hidden feels wrong, deceptive, deceitful. I was called a liar when I said I could not remember what happened when I drank—that I was lost, my body obscuring itself from myself. People felt deceived, and I understood. So did I. I asked my doctor for hypnotherapy.

I wanted the truth, I said, sure it was the solution. She refused, listing the potentially dangerous effects of summoning the suppressed. She said to trust that my body knew best, that suppression was an act of preservation. (Later on, people in the rooms said memories can be recovered over time—if you stay sober.)

The moon is rumored to have a dark side. This is a misconception. All parts of the moon are exposed to the sun in equal measure, though as she spins on her axis, she twirls around us on Earth, fixing our perspective on one view.

The moon, guarded as she may be, is known for her gravitational pull—the energy that rules the ocean's tides—purging all that lies beneath the surface not with light, but by force.

I wouldn't take a picture for years without a drink or Jared. His eye was the only one I trusted. I liked the way he captured me, how he exposed me. I often took a bottle of rosé with me to loosen up into poses he suggested. In some photos, I'm visibly, shamefully drunk—red, eye drooping, slurred speech in videos: Jared loved to record me drunk. I needed the drink to show up for me, to help me present an image, but the liquor was corrosive. I was deteriorating, edges blurry, like a snapshot left in the rain.

Astrological lore is inspired by nature. On August 18, 2016, the full sturgeon moon, named for the fish known as "stirrers," peaked on the East Coast at 5:27 a.m. Like the sturgeon that whip up the mud at the bottom of the Great Lakes in search of food, this late summer moon energy is said to roil the murky waters of denial.

During the summer of 2016, I gave zero thought to the lunar calendar. I had no plans to manifest, perform rituals, or harness the ripe energy of the moon. After waking up on Friday night, naked from the waist down, alone in our bed, all I knew was there was an eviction in my name—the money I'd made and Jared were both gone. I thought he'd been paying our landlord all that time, but we owed $11,000 in back rent.

Luca was away in Italy for the next two weeks. Before he left, he gave me the keys to his apartment and told me to go there if I was in trouble. Too ashamed to face my family, I went to his empty loft and scoured the kitchen for booze. He didn't drink and kept none in the house. Unable to relax, I looked at my phone, at the deluge of notifications.

The echo of traffic at the entrance of the Holland Tunnel was deafening, and I contemplated sleeping in the crawl space used for storage where he kept a mattress. But I knew when he returned that we couldn't share a bed—we were past that—so I stayed and tried to sleep in the bedroom as long as I could.

The next morning, I called out sick from work and contacted the property manager. I was informed that there was no way to stop the eviction process. Jared's father had somehow procured a lawyer, most likely a favor from a friend, who negotiated a deal. If we paid two months' rent right away, no paperwork would be filed in court. The rest of the back rent would be split and allocated across the remaining months through the end of the lease in October. All would be off the books, our records kept clean.

"So, you want me to pay it," I told Jared.

"If you do," he said, "I'll pay you back every penny."

I cleared my belongings from the apartment and cut a check to management from my savings.

16

Unreliable Narrator

I held my phone with two hands, cradling it like a grenade. Seated in the narrow waiting area of my therapist's office in Greenwich Village, I rehearsed my speech. The fact that I felt the need for preparation proved I no longer trusted myself to tell the truth. Last night, a stranger had pulled the pin, and I knew my confession would detonate.

After a decade of care, my therapist, Rebecca, had become like a mother to me. Her office was where I came to talk shit and garner sympathy before going back to my job, my boyfriend, and my family, better prepared to gather their needs like a sponge, only to wring it out again at Rebecca's feet the next week. But how had she missed *this*? My drinking had become a problem. How had she allowed me to obfuscate for so long?

The door opened, and I heard Rebecca's voice. With a whisper and a gentle touch on the back, she reassured another client as she left, then turned to signal me inside with a smile. Rarely face-to-face with Rebecca's clientele, I stood quickly to get a closer look—to observe their body language and interpret their level of intimacy so I could judge it against ours later.

The woman was young and thin. She wore a simple suit, tasseled loafers, and a charm bracelet, pearl florets cast in gold fastened to her minuscule wrist, unmistakably Van Cleef & Arpels. She stroked the leather strap of her Longchamp bag, a repetitive gesture that betrayed her neurotic thoughts, and nodded in agreement to Rebecca's parting words. Emerald eyes rimmed red from crying: she was the one I constantly compared myself to. I even compared crises. *What is her dilemma today?* I wondered. Daddy issues, eating disorder, breakup? Something actually worthy of pity, unlike mine. Who felt sorry for common drunks?

———

Once a week over many years, talk therapy has made me a storytelling expert. The goal of narrative therapy, as explained to me, was to isolate the issue from the self, identify a solution, and map a path toward it—with me as the victor as opposed to the victim.

"You are not the problem," Rebecca told me countless times.

When I used blaming language that exposed my contempt for myself, she gently redirected me. Tenderness triggered an immediate response; *What are the tears?* Rebecca would ask, then guide me through memory to find an idea, image, or imprint that informed my response in the present day. I was still hurting from past pains because I could not locate myself within my current reality.

This time, I held reality in my hands. It was physical, material—the irrefutable testimony of an impartial stranger. The only obstacle circumventing this truth from accountability was me—confirmation that, like all the perpetrators in my life, I was a threat to my own safety.

Stepping across the threshold into Rebecca's office, I felt like a needle pressed into a pincushion—I just needed a little push to know I was held. My steps that had echoed on the hardwood floor in the hallway now fell on a shag rug that padded and blunted all sound, signaling a change in territory.

I had become familiar with the thoughtful curation of safe space here. The asymmetrical shape of the room seemed to welcome imperfection, and although natural light was obscured by the alley nearby, Rebecca avoided harsh overhead lighting. Medium and low light warmed the room with amber tones, no doubt a soothing suggestion.

As I thought was customary for therapists, Rebecca sat in the corner, in a leather chair opposite me. I took my place in the center of the couch, reached for one of the embellished accent pillows, and tucked it into my lap for support as I counted the books on Rebecca's shelf in pairs. To calm my hyperactive and anxious mind, I'd played this secret mental game since I could remember. I counted traffic signs on the highway, paintings on a wall, houses on a block, but always by two, until I lost track or interest. Odd numbers threw me off.

Rebecca lowered herself into her chair, and I paused my count. I already knew the number was twenty-nine—it pained me that it wasn't thirty, but I let it go. She flipped her hair and casually leaned her weight to the right—the sign that she was ready to listen. Without alcohol in my bloodstream, I felt the full force of my nervous system and the drive to please her. But I'd made my decision.

I explained I would not be speaking for myself today. I'd received new information and needed her to level with me. Arms extended as if to distance myself from the stark reality of this stranger's messages, I read them to Rebecca verbatim. The web of cracked glass scraped my thumb as I scrolled the iPhone screen. I gave no commentary, excuse, or supplication. When I finished, I asked, "Is this true? Is this what's happening to me?" I braced myself for impact. "Am I an alcoholic?"

She nodded. *Yes.* The rule in alcoholism, she explained, is to determine whether your life has become unmanageable. Admitting this is the first of the twelve steps of Alcoholics Anonymous. A program she wanted me to try.

"Near-death sounds unmanageable to me," she said.

———

Delirium is described as an acutely disturbed state of mind, most commonly brought on by intoxication, fever, or psychosis. In the days that follow an episode of heavy drinking, the body may experience withdrawal resulting in delirium tremens, or DTs. It was rare for me to get the shakes, but it had been a few days since my last drink—the cops had confiscated my magnum of Belvedere, so there wasn't a drop around the house to scrounge. The shakes were something that happened to grimy old men, though. I was quivering in shock, I told myself.

I never thought of my impulse to drink as corporeal. I didn't know my body well enough to be able to pinpoint the origin of what enslaved me. I knew alcohol took effect in and took a toll on my body—I lived with the destructive consequences—but the habit was cultural. It was social. I considered drinking as part of the story, cliché as it may have been. I was *blowing off steam, cutting loose, letting my hair down, taking the edge off.* Clichés become cliché by their ubiquity, and if drinking is everywhere, it's normal, and if it's normal, it's okay. Right?

"Why are the rules always different for me?" I asked Rebecca.

She seemed to consider my question but instead asked, "Do you remember when you came to me? The incident with your hospitalization?" She was referring to the night of my 51/50 hold—when I was put in the psych ward in order to determine whether I posed a danger to myself or others. Did I want to die or kill someone? Or both? I managed to convince them it was neither. "I hoped that was just a stupid mistake, but can you see the pattern now?"

———

The 51/50 hold had happened ten years before. I woke up in a public bathroom, mouth sour, jaw throbbing from temple to molar. Eyesight fogged by gunked mascara, I focused on the plastic band around my wrist. I felt it before I could see it: the sharp edges of plastic fastened through doughnut holes, blue bruises blotched underneath. I wondered if it was the pass for entrance to the club I had gone to the night before. But it had my name on it—my full legal name, the one no one knows, an accessory more common to a hospital ward than the VIP section.

My stomach spasmed, and I threw up again. It must have been again because my abdominals were tired and sore. I still wore my wedged platforms—high-heeled shoes the color of buttermilk, although they'd been sold to me as nude, and beneath a hospital gown, my slip dress, a flirtatious A-line silhouette that billowed off my curves from the pleated breast line to mid-thigh in the shape of a fluid triangle. The dress was cobalt blue, my ex-boyfriend's favorite color. Before I pushed him off me that night, I had hoped he'd like it.

———

Please find the police report issued to our institution by the NYPD attached:

Resident at the corner of Mott and Houston called regarding a domestic disturbance approximately 10 minutes after midnight on Tuesday evening June the 13th. Officer Fitzgerald and Officer Ortiz arrived and found his girlfriend hiding in the bathroom. She cooperated with authorities when asked to come out. Appeared to be heavily intoxicated but no visible signs of harm, when asked she denied any physical injury. She was offered an escort home which she refused. We issued a warning to not return to the premises, which would then constitute trespassing and result in arrest. No keys were found on her person or belongings. A second call was made shortly thereafter requesting emergency assistance as the person in question had returned to the building. Unable to re-enter the apartment she had migrated to the roof and was attempting suicide as a result of his infidelity. We found Ms. Hoppe outside the 5th-floor window after a neighbor reported hearing the woman scream for help. We apprehended her safely and escorted her to Bellevue shortly after 1 a.m. The greatest threat she posed was to herself. Against our recommendation, the boyfriend/resident insisted on pressing charges, requesting a restraining order be filed and Ms. Hoppe detained again upon her release from the hospital. No further arrests have been made as of this morning.

From the back of the ambulance that night, the cops had allowed me one phone call. With my hands cuffed behind my back, they held a phone to my shoulder as I gave them Karina's number. I was too afraid to call Karla, blocks away, who might have murdered my ex-boyfriend. Karina was totally discreet. She only asked a few questions, and when I left the hospital, she offered me emergency mental health services provided by her company, Novartis. This program connected me to Rebecca, who had worked with me consistently over these tumultuous years to maintain my access to affordable therapy. Without my sister's gentle intervention and the advocacy of my therapist, I would have had zero protection against a rapidly accelerating disorder.

———

When I was in Bellevue, I disappeared for a day without access to my phone, and Karla feared the worst. I took a cab from the hospital to her place and passed out in her bed, covered in contusions I couldn't explain. I opened my eyes again as the sun set on the Hudson River and watched it sink behind the Statue of Liberty. My back ached as I reached around to finger the sores along my spine and suddenly recalled the impact of the police officer's tackle from the windowsill and the tearing of my flesh against the carpeted hall of the apartment building. *That's when my dress ripped. That's why one of the spaghetti straps now hung off its seam.* The reality of what happened the night before began to leak into my consciousness. I got up and went to the bathroom.

I stared into the mirror, avoiding all signs of my battered body, and there it was again. I promised myself I wasn't going to touch it. The *it* was a microscopic blemish halfway between the bottom of my nose and the top of my upper lip. This sensitive middle passage, made of skin like chewing gum, is called the philtrum. It's the dent that marks the formation of your face, a pinch where the three sections of the puzzle merge. We all have it.

At first, the tiny bump appeared as just a bit of raised skin; squeezing it would only worsen things. I'd been down this road a million times and knew how easily I scarred, how a three-day ordeal would become two weeks if I couldn't control myself. *Don't fucking touch it,* I sneered to myself. I could never resist the urge to rip it off.

In twenty-four hours, a bulb of pus formed at the top, and it was all the permission I needed. At first, I pressed with the flesh of my fingertips, careful not to break the skin. I pulled the skin away from the shadow of my nose and inspected it more closely. The whitehead was still there. My eyes watered as I pushed, now using my nails, which were thin and sharp as razors after I'd peeled off my gel manicure at the hospital.

I regretted it the moment I drew blood. I knew how my skin would respond. I rolled my eyes at the horrid little bitch who lived inside my head and covered my mess with an ointment to soothe and a powder to dry and prayed for a miracle by morning.

———

As Rebecca and I talked about what had happened to me a decade before, we began to circle back to the present—the reason I clutched my phone so tightly, the message that told me I had almost died in a black-out. Rock bottom. I had to be done. Rebecca understood alcohol had become as precious to me as any friend, and I would miss it. She advised me to grieve the loss as I would a death. I had witnessed the attachments my niece and nephew formed to their blankets and dolls and the powerful influence they projected onto these objects for comfort, soothing, and safety. This was like the bond I felt with booze, she explained. *How pathetic*, I thought.

Without it, I would have to start from scratch, like an infant, and learn what I hadn't been taught in my childhood about self-love, self-care, and self-soothing. I tried to offer myself the same compassion I felt toward our little ones, but alcohol was not a cuddly stuffed animal—it was a carcinogen—and I was not newly born.

17

Rock Bottom

I went to my first AA meeting on Thursday, August 25, 2016. It was in Tribeca. Down the stairs of an upscale treatment center, I followed the sound of voices to a small room at the end of the hallway. I was late as usual, and there were no more seats left in the small circle, so someone told me to have a seat on the floor. My ass itched after a while of sitting on the stiff carpet the color of mist, not gray and not blue—intentionally neutral. Sterile even, no snacks or the classically advertised coffee. Maybe they only did that in the morning? It felt awkward to see a celebrity there: *What the fuck is his problem, ya know?* But I focused on the story I heard that night. A painter now in her sixties was prone to self-harm as a coping mechanism for untreated childhood trauma. I was astonished by how much I could relate, and how desperately I needed to admit that out loud. To speak. To identify myself in this room, because I was finally in the right place. So I raised my hand.

Hi, my name is Jessica, and ummm . . . this is my first time here. I've never been to one of these meetings before. I kinda had no idea they existed.

Seems I missed the whole cultural memo on the AA thing. I guess I never felt I deserved help or that people like us did. Anyway, I'm here because a woman, a total stranger, contacted me on the internet. She says she saved my life. It happened about a week ago, and I don't remember anything.

According to her, not that she has any reason to lie, she was hanging out with her friend on the steps of the Whitney when she saw a cab stop and a woman and all her messy shit spill out onto the road. Screaming, stumbling across a major multiple-lane highway in New York City like a psycho: the fucking West Side Highway. That was me.

I got to the divider thingy, you know, like the huge cinder block kind, and in these big-ass heels, I climbed up onto it like a balance beam. I blacked out and couldn't figure out how to get through or around it. I fell and rolled over it! The light changed, and the cab took off, so I'm now trying to cross the other side as the uptown traffic is headed my way. She started freaking out, thinking she was gonna watch me die, but I got to the other side and ran into another divider with the fence on top. I got up on the rail-thin divider again, and she ran. She said I was too "intoxicated," her words, to realize there was no sidewalk and I would be hit. She screamed at me to get down, reached over the fence, grabbed my arm, guided me along the fence to a break and walked me to the Whitney steps. She and her friend changed my shoes—I had sneakers in my gym bag—and called me an Uber from my phone. Before I left, she got my name; that's how she found my Instagram. She kept Googling me, afraid something happened to me and I was dead. About forty minutes later, the same Uber driver came back and said I was being such an asshole in the car—putting my feet on the ceiling and yelling. He dropped me downtown at Bowling Green. He said he watched me go to a bench where a few people saw me and stepped in to help. Who knows what happened after that? I woke up in my bed, fully dressed from the waist up. I had all my belongings except my phone.

This story is crazy—like I can't fucking believe I did that, and I know in my bones that it is 100 percent me. The thing that got me, though, was the question she asked. She said, "Do you know what's happening to you?"

(Breaks down) *"Do you know what's happening to you?" No one has ever asked me that. Like it's not my fault.*

After a big night, it's always like: Do you even remember what you said last night? How'd you get home? I can't believe you did that; you were so wasted . . . *It's humiliating. And I deserve it, you know. But this woman said she just wanted to make sure I was okay and maybe give me a better understanding of what happens to me when I drink. Her mom has been sober for thirty-some-odd years, and I could ask her anything. I just kept thanking her. Shaking, I couldn't control my body. I was shaking violently, and I felt so cold. It's August.*

The days after this happened, I couldn't leave my room. I holed up at my ex's place with a magnum of vodka like that's ok. I could feel something was wrong, that something happened, but I didn't know what. But this . . . this is insane! How do I not remember that? But lately, I can't remember shit. I passed out in a taxi and woke up in the back of an ambulance. My boyfriend heard me screaming at the EMTs from our third-floor window and rushed down to get my ass. I woke up the other day, and my Acne jacket was shredded down the left side like I had toppled over. Scrapes and bruises all over my back, arms, legs. But I woke up in my bed.

I'm just so afraid to go home. My boyfriend won't get help. Turns out I need the fucking help. I went out to dinner with an old ex (I know, a lot of exes, I'm a messy bitch) and texted my boyfriend to come get me. He combed all over Brooklyn Heights and found me making out with my ex around the corner from our house. When I woke up alone in bed, I ran to the living room, where he was asleep on the couch. His face was so swollen from crying, his eyes beet red. He told me I cheated, and I believe him, but I don't remember. He said I kissed my ex but I didn't get in the cab with him. When he tried to get me to go back to his hotel, I ran in the opposite direction. My boyfriend watched from behind a bush and just sat there and observed, sick fuck. If I was too drunk like he said why didn't he step in?! Why didn't he help me? But it was my fault. I own that. I needed an excuse to break up, but he forgave me. I felt like a monster; I couldn't leave him.

My sister even told me I can't be around her kid if I drink. How could I do that? I love my niece more than anything. How could I jeopardize being able to see her? Like hello, *how did I not know? How do I not know what's happening to me? Why did I never understand this as a disease, disorder, or whatever—something deserving of help and not shame, criticism, and chaos? But I didn't. I swear I didn't understand this, not the way y'all described it, as a . . . what was it? A spiritual malady, a physical allergy, and a mental obsession? I have that. That's me to a* T.

I hate myself for not knowing enough . . . about this, about myself. That's what I told Claire—the woman who saved me—that I hate myself. And I do. But that night when she told me, my whole body went cold, freezing in the middle of summer; something entered that room, a very strong presence, and I caught my reflection in the mirror, and I just said, "No," like the word came up from the bottom of my feet through my whole body. NO, *I said out loud. Because I heard, clear as day, someone or something ask me,* Do you want to die?

I wasn't drunk, but I dunno; maybe I'm crazy?

It's clear my body is shutting down on me. I just don't know how to do this. Be sober? What the fuck does that even mean? What would I do with myself?

Anyway, I'm here because my therapist told me to come and see how I feel. And I feel like you told my story. I identify with everything the speaker said, and we're nothing alike. I want what you guys say you have, the miracle or whatever, but I'm terrified. I'm scared. I have never been able to face myself.

18

Intemperance

Addiction isn't the kind of diagnosis where people send thoughts and prayers. They set expectations. The first step is to admit you have a problem. You diagnose yourself, claim it, and dive inward, sleeves rolled up. You won't be alone (if you don't want to be, and trust me, you won't want to be), but the onus is on you.

As unrealistic as it may sound, I had no idea I was an alcoholic. What was clear to me was that I had problems that drove me to drink. I couldn't afford the things I needed. I couldn't get my partner to respect me. And something was deeply wrong with me, my insides radioactive.

If I could finally get my shit together, solve the material issues, and find a man who knew my worth because I'd finally be worth something, then I wouldn't need to drink so much. It never occurred to me that this cycle must be resolved in reverse order. Unless I removed the drug, I could never access the self who actually believed I deserved the things I claimed to want. My dreams weren't a lie—I wanted them. But I couldn't imagine my life without alcohol. At the same time, I couldn't see myself as an alcoholic.

On August 27, 2016, I took my last drink. It was a nip of generic vodka I'd snuck into the bathroom off my sister's bedroom. After I felt no immediate rush, I got into the bathtub, lay down, and waited for the alcohol I'd poured into my bloodstream to wash over me, to take effect as it had faithfully done in the past. I stared at the spot outside the tub, where I kneeled to bathe my baby niece every Sunday, determined to prove that a real childhood was something this family could provide. It was from her perspective that I realized alcohol had stopped working for me. And I was the one preventing the cycle from being broken.

I knew I was on the hook once I shared what Claire had told me. I knew my family was the only anchor strong enough to hold me, so I divulged my secret to my sister, brother-in-law, and mom. My mother was inconsolable. "You didn't learn it from me," she said, oblivious to our family history, failing to consider her own father's addiction. I tried to assuage their fears by sharing my therapist's recommendation to go to AA, where I could begin my program with ninety days of abstention. "I'm gonna do it and see how I feel," I pledged.

"Do what you need to do," Karla said. "I can't lose you."

I understood what she meant. We'd always been more sensitive to each other's pain than our own.

———

The only person I miss drinking with is my sister. Our parents never drank. Alcohol was a habit we acquired in college.

One night, while out to dinner with our father in New Jersey during Christmas break, my sister and I ordered a bottle of red wine. We were fast becoming winos, though we thought of ourselves as sommeliers. An understanding of wine, having a signature drink—drinking, period—was a mark of sophistication we proudly brought back home along with our degrees and jobs as profesionales, as my father said.

I'm not sure how much we had to drink that night before suddenly my father reached across the dinner table. "Nonono," he said, sliding the glass across the slippery polyester tablecloth away from me by the stem: "Ya no más." Karla and I met eyes across the table and laughed, assuring our father we were good.

"Una mujer borracha es lo más asqueroso," he said. "Uno tiene que saber controlarse."

"AsqueROsoooo," I repeated, with emphasis bolstered by liquid courage. "Guess we're nasty women, Ku," I joked to my sister, using the nickname I invented as a baby when I couldn't roll an r yet. "Honestly, control yourself, Jess," she joked back. We laughed heartily.

After Karla lost her first child, she began to fear we would all die. Suddenly and without warning from one day to the next, we'd be gone. She'd grown her baby inside her so carefully for weeks and weeks, until the doctor said the baby had started to grow hair. Karla, blessed with long, thick hair like the tail of a horse, imagined she'd passed down the trait of beauty she admired most about herself, the one we all coveted, too. She pictured combing the baby's hair with her fingers at first and later a brush, but the baby started to die the next day. And she never got to touch her hair.

She was having a girl and had named her Paloma. At five and a half months, my sister's placenta ruptured, and the baby began to lose oxygen. On March 19, 2014, at Jersey City Medical Center, Paloma was born still, as they say, but they mean dead.

The night my sister returned home from the hospital, we drank shots of tepid vodka alone in her kitchen. Karla was concave from grief, catatonic with shock. A fearless girl all our lives, she was now a woman consumed by paranoid fear, who wrapped her hair around her neck and pulled until she gasped for air. She told me about her visions: how, within seconds of an unanswered text, she saw my body pushed onto the subway tracks, bludgeoned, discarded in an alley, hit by a bike messenger, and comatose—she could never sign the papers to take me off life support, she said. "Please be careful," she begged.

I brought the alcohol because I wanted to perform an exorcism, and booze was the only ritual I knew, though it was growing unreliable as of late. I recognized the possession in Karla—the same radioactive cavity that haunted me had calcified the womb that once nurtured my niece and set out to devour my sister. She needed to get it out—plunge it like a fucking toilet.

Alcohol was the only substance I'd encountered that was toxic enough to snuff out my suffering, smoke rising. At the hospital, when the room was full of a family expecting a child alive, unable to speak or breathe after her sudden death, I offered to buy us pizza down the street. I called in the order from the hospital room, requesting the various toppings each of us preferred. It was perfectly legitimate.

But I also knew the restaurant was next door to another one, the place that became ours after my sister moved to Jersey City with her man. It was across the street from the PATH train station and blocks from her home. I'd text Karla when I was close, and she'd have a drink waiting for me after my commute as if it were a reward. At least, that's what that first drink felt like: a reward. We spent hours sipping and swiveling on those stools, planning her bridal shower, her wedding, and her baby shower until my sister was tipsy enough not to notice I'd switched to tequila straight, and I'd confess to our new bartender friend how I got the nickname Tequila Boom Boom. When Karla got pregnant, the bartender started serving her water and quesadillas.

Before grabbing the pizza, I walked into our spot alone and slipped into the one empty corner at the bar. The bartender was there. She tracked me from the entrance and met me where I stood to order. Without a word, she placed a rocks glass in front of me and filled it with tequila. I drank and nodded for another. She gave me three, returned the bottle to the well, and came back with a bill for one.

I set off back to the hospital, pizza in hand. Orange grease bled through the bottom of the pizza boxes onto my forearms as I walked along Grand Street. I watched the sun set behind the austere blocks of the hospital building, the watercolor sky streaked with the same orange that dripped down my arms. I was halfway there when I collapsed onto my knees and screamed so loudly cars shrieked to a halt. I stayed on the ground until the purge had been satisfied and then returned to face my family, grateful for alcohol and desperate for more.

This was the release I wanted for my sister.

I brought the elixir and acted as her healer. I felt nothing as we went shot for shot. I told her to scream. Her eyes, vacant wells of blackness, began to dart as the alcohol traveled beneath what was stuck, and her mouth opened like a snake catching its prey. I heard a scream so primal the memory still fills the drums of my ears until I am dizzy. Longing for the sister before the amputation, the one who laughed and slurred and dreamed aloud with me, wondering if the drink was the magic that unburdened us for a while. The one we'd been looking for since we were kids.

19

The Baptist

Two years later, my sister gave birth to a daughter who lived. When my niece Bella was born, I was passed out drunk in the waiting room, a half-empty bottle of Grey Goose in my purse. I was never unprepared again after Paloma died.

When we were starting to plan for Bella's first birthday party, I'd been a few months sober. I remember we were at my sister's house when we received the news from Honduras that my grandfather had died. My mother cried like my sister had the night she lost her daughter. An old wound cut open—the last hope for the love of a father lost forever. The love my sister was desperate to give, the love my mother was desperate to receive. "I love that man. Don't ask me why," she said, angry she never got a chance to say her goodbyes. She'd tried.

—

I was immersed in recovery when my grandfather died—I was doing cognitive behavioral therapy, meditating, eating a clean diet, engaging in frequent exercise, avoiding sex and relationships for a year, and going to daily group therapy in AA. I had a sponsor and was halfway through the twelve steps. I was alive. Sobriety empowered me.

I read books on neuroplasticity and learned it was possible to redirect a toxic behavior imprinted over years. I could pause, interrupt the emotion enveloping me, and examine the evidence behind my train of thought. Not to immediately transfer my feelings from negative to positive but to accept them—much like riding a wave by floating on your back. Without fighting the current of life's challenges, I could attune to the reality of my present circumstances. With that presence of mind, I could accept life on life's terms without turning to a mood- or mind-altering substance to cope.

A dead grandfather I never knew wouldn't trigger an old pattern, but my mother's feelings never lost their charge. "How does it feel to have had an alcoholic father and now an alcoholic daughter?" I asked her.

"¿Qué? What do you mean, Jessy? I don't see you that way. And my father drank, but he always worked y siempre andaba bien vestido, well dressed, like you."

The idea of attaching that label to me jarred my mother. She blamed herself: "Where did I go wrong?" She blamed me: "This is not how I raised you." We knew so little about alcoholism, yet assumed so much about the alcoholic.

"Don't say that about yourself," she said. I knew identifying in this way placed me on the other side of an invisible, impenetrable line my mother had created in her mind about her family—good and bad. Those who suffered from addiction, her father Jaime, and her brother Jaime, were her greatest tormentors. What would it mean to place us shoulder to shoulder? Would it change how she saw them or me? Would it lead to a greater understanding of the disease? Would it make it easier to see what had happened to our family?

I rejected the shame, the correlation between addiction and otherness, addiction and badness, addiction and criminality, and said, "But I am, mami. I'm an alcoholic."

She cried for me, for him, for her. I pressed my chest to hers, drawing forth the tears of generations from our eyes—she, in mourning; I, here, baptized.

———

I don't feel entitled to claim injury at the hands of my grandfather. How can I really know how deeply his abandonment affected my mother? How has that injury impacted me, as her daughter, throughout my life? Other than that, I did have to take up quite a bit of the parenting on his behalf to dress the wounds he inflicted. I could file the hours I listened to the same despicable stories, wiped the sweat off her brow or the tears from her cheeks as softly as I would an infant, and lied to her like I was the parent and she was my child because what could I say but *I know he loved you*. What kind of monster wouldn't?

When I learned he was an alcoholic that day; it made me feel less alone in this family. I wasn't a random deviant; the sensitivity runs in my blood. I didn't blame him for my fate, but now it feels strange to romanticize it, to imagine that alcoholism is the legacy bestowed upon me, a secret handshake between us, a mission he failed to confront so that I could. I don't want to give him that power over my life, nor do I have that space in my heart for him. I didn't know him.

But I do harbor a feeling, a worry, that because I never knew him, I would never know me. Sober, I decided I wanted to find out.

20

Inheritance

My grandfather was born Marco Aurelio Bustillo on May 19, 1930. When he was a boy, his mother changed his name for an unknown reason to Jaime Acosta Bustillo. He passed this name down to his first son, my uncle Jaime—and then disappeared. The senior, a fatherless boy himself, may have thought of abandonment as tradition and emulated his father in this way.

His birth certificate, a handwritten civil registry recorded in a journal that had begun in the mid-nineteenth century (1841–1968), *Registro Civil de Honduras*, describes his mother, María de Jesús Bustillo, as soltera. It also unnecessarily divulges an intimate detail. Although the account is brief, the transcription makes a point to include that the twenty-five-year-old mother was also a grandmother to a child who died shortly after birth.

I shared the document with my family, and the previously unknown information upset my mother. "Why did they have to *said* that?" she replied via text, confused in her tenses as usual, a quirk in her bilingualism that I have always loved. All her English language verbs occur in past tense, all the action has been committed: her conjugation style is like future tripping. "Who cares if she was a grandmother or what? Wtf," she ranted furiously, as if she could argue with the Christofascist institution that likely persecuted the unmarried woman for giving birth without the testimony of a man.

———

The two crumbs of information that I was fed routinely as a child regarding my Honduran ancestry were 1) que Honduras era el culo del mundo, that Honduras was the shithole of the world, and 2) that Honduras, more than any of the Central American countries, was the biggest USian bootlicker.

Around the turn of the twentieth century, the American writer William Sydney Porter, known as O. Henry, arrived in Honduras and holed up in a hotel in Trujillo for six months, a stint that ended in January 1897. He scribbled his observations of the exotic country, musings that would eventually be fashioned into a book of short stories entitled *Cabbages and Kings* and published in 1904. The novel in stories takes place in a fictional land (based on Honduras) that he named the Republic of Anchuria, which he called a banana republic.

Economists, journalists, and political pundits latched on to the term *banana republic*, which reduced the value of a nation and its people to an export. It winked at the culpability of despotic US entrepreneurs and their collusion with the US government, CIA, and military as they worked together to control the isthmus in order to ruthlessly extract the world's most valuable resources from it. The term *banana republic* tells the story of US dominance and casts as fools the formerly enslaved people and Indigenous and mixed-race peasants who courageously and cunningly fought against the legacy of Spanish colonialism. This glorification of US imperialism erases the vital and true account of one of history's most consequential and radical labor movements.

Turns out O. Henry was actually in Honduras because he was on the run from the US government for embezzlement. Upon his return to the United States, he was sentenced to five years in prison for stealing $854.08, the equivalent of approximately $30,000 today. He published fourteen stories under pseudonyms during his three-year incarceration and moved to New York City after his release. O. Henry, an ex-con, published a story a week for a year in the *New York World Sunday Magazine*. Many books followed.

O. Henry died at forty-seven due to complications related to alcohol use disorder, which included cirrhosis of the liver, diabetes, and an enlarged heart. My grandfather suffered the same health complications, which required open-heart surgery and the implantation of a pacemaker. The second and last time I ever saw him was in the hospital. In need of an interpreter, he summoned my mother.

———

An intensely political era known as the "decades of Dictators" served as the backdrop of my grandfather's coming of age. In 1933, when my grandfather was a toddler, Tiburcio Carías Andino took official control of Honduras and installed a puritanical and violently repressive dictatorship that lasted sixteen years. My grandfather grew up in Coyoles along the banks of the Río Aguán. He was a country boy, un jíbaro se decía, until he was sent north to study in La Ceiba with his father's side of the family.

The northern coast of Honduras was known as the land of opportunity due to the development of large banana plantations and the construction of the Tela Railroad Company. Recruiters, mostly gringos, aggressively solicited potential workers from the youth in the central and southern regions. To seduce my family, they murmured the first iteration of the American Dream—the reason to send their boy away. When he graduated from trade school as an electrician, he figured with his education he could avoid field work harvesting and pruning the fruit. The engineering departments of plantations oversaw the railways, machinery, and factory lines.

"He never said 'no' to a job," my tío Ernesto told me via FaceTime. "You know the line? At the factory? The conveyor belts that boxed bananas," he said. "If that ever broke, they called him." I stared into the small screen of my phone as he mined his childhood memories, decades back, for the few details he could recall with confidence. Su rostro, my uncle's face, his countenance, his mug, sparked my memory of meeting my grandfather. He looked nearly identical to the man I met as a child, with the same purple lips, deep as the skin of a plum, the same color that outlines my lips like a pencil before my father's pink blots through like the etch of a kiss at the center.

——

I was six years old when I met my grandfather. One day, for no particular occasion, we drove from the suburbs of New Jersey to the Bronx, where he had a place near Tremont Avenue. My parents, two sisters, and I all filed into the hallway of his railroad-style apartment, and we stood awkwardly in an assembly line before him—my mother up front and father behind us, each parent securing the perimeter. It was my first visit to New York City.

"Estás gorda, Chili," my grandfather said in place of *hello*, unable to make eye contact with my mother, who seemed warmed by the sound of his nickname for her, though needled by his insult. Like him, she'd always struggled with her weight and resented being called fat.

My father extended his hand to my grandfather above our heads, presumably to ease the tension of the moment and soften the disappointment of my mother, who had expected a heartfelt reunion. "¿Estás son sus hijas?" my grandfather asked my parents as he reached for my cheek with scorched, jittery hands that appeared to be covered in moss. I was terrified, but I knew what this meant to my mother, so I stayed still and let him touch me.

The apartment was dark and cramped. Brine wafted off a half-eaten pot of white rice, mixing with the peppery zest of cilantro. The sharpness of sliced onions lingered. They had just eaten before we arrived and had nothing to offer us—a gesture my mother would make note of as proof she was unwanted.

My grandfather stood to accommodate us, his back hunched, belly swollen, and insisted my father sit in his La-Z-Boy. My grandfather's wife, Rosalba, emerged from her bedroom, even less eager than my grandfather to meet us. The story was she hated my mother because she was jealous of my grandmother, my grandfather's first love. Though he had many mistresses and at least ten children, Rosalba was by far his longest relationship. *She won*, my mother thought, and imagined Rosalba as the wedge between them.

It was the summer, and his place had no AC. My grandfather's face was red and sweaty, and how much it resembled my mother's amazed me. I whispered this into her ear, and when she repeated it to him, he offered to buy us ice cream. We followed him to a bodega, where he strolled knowingly to the far cooler and instructed us to pick a Popsicle from the display under the register. "Quédense ahí. No me sigan," he said, commanding us not to follow him. He and the cashier greeted each other like brothers, and the cashier wrapped my grandfather's glass bottle in a brown paper bag, rolled the top down into a collar, and handed it over as the imprint of condensation revealed a gleaming gold label underneath. He was met by more friends just outside the shop and stood on the corner with them all afternoon, even though we went back to his apartment. He never returned while we were there, and we left without saying goodbye.

———

It was hard to believe a daughter could forget the day she lost her father. But my mother wasn't the only one who couldn't say for sure. I asked my entire family—no one could confirm the date of my grandfather's death. This fact told the story much more than the details I was desperate to find. His death was a version of *away* he'd accustomed us to.

How could we know the difference or suffer the loss? He'd been gone all our lives.

Who really knew anything about their absent father? Where did they go . . . ? What took them away? What could have been more important than being a parent? Do they want you to care if they're dead or alive? Should I believe their actions tell the story of who they are? How they feel? How long can a heart sustain hope from the withheld?

These questions haunted my mother, though she believed her father could answer them, if only she could find him. Estranged for her entire life, her memories of him are few. Violent alcohol-fueled fights between him and her mother; weeks, then months, of abandonment, his absence resolved by scouring the local bars. The barmen and regulars knew my mother well. Some tried to help her out.

My mother would rent a bike with a quarter and traverse the entire city in search of him. "¿Está mi papá 'quí, está mi papá 'cá?" she whimpered at five, six, seven years old. She wandered into brothels and discotecas en el Barrio Inglés, where she met a barkeep who owned a place full of mirrored balls, flashing lights, and the most beautiful patrons. "Abro la puerta y veo las lucecitas de colores y digo 'oye, qué bonito.' Pero yo que puta sabía, solo que era un bar donde había hombres vestidos de mujer."

The owner tried to shoo my mother away until she noticed my mother was the same age as her daughter, and they became playmates. My mother found a home among drag queens and stopped looking for her father after a while.

One day, my mother got word that her father was in town and raced over to Chong's. He'd gone to visit her grandmother. It was a mystery what kept my grandfather loyal to her. She wasn't his mother, but he gave her money and paid his respects regularly. It was more than he did for his children.

Innocently, she ran to him and chased him down the street like he was a heartthrob. She was his fandom. My grandfather was dressed neatly, wearing slacks, loafers, and a short-sleeve button-down shirt with one breast pocket. Inside, he had placed a pocket protector with several pens clipped in a row. "¡Qué bonito!" she squealed as she reached toward his neck, nearly running to keep up with him. "Dame uno," she begged, desperate for something that was his. He hastened his pace and refused. He told her the pens were imported—from Europe, the United States, some fancy far-off place. "Esta pluma es muy fino." It was far too expensive to spare.

My mother was a quick study. Often bored at school, she challenged the ill-equipped and militant nuns who taught a tired curriculum. They'd send her home for the slightest infraction, a stain on her white knee socks, unkempt hair, no pencil, no textbook. By eighth grade, she'd been expelled from three schools for fighting. Her mother wanted her to attend a local trade school for secretarial work. But she was too bright for that and didn't want a career taking notes for men, a life of being dictated to.

A few days after she ran into her father, her older brother, Ernesto, sat at the kitchen table scribbling in a notebook with their father's pen. My mother tore it from his hands and insisted it was hers, "*Ayyy, esa pluma es mío! Yo se lo pedí a mi papá y no me lo dio.*" They fought, and he took it back. Their father had chosen to give it to his son, not his daughter.

"It was his attitude that hurt me," my mother said as she sat in my kitchen and rifled through her purse. "Ahora tengo miles de plumas. ¡A mí qué me importa un pluma!" She broke down as she held a handful of pens, the love she'd tried to collect. I watched as she seemed to become aware. As if, at that moment, she understood the meaning of her obsession with pens.

"All I wanted was love. I wanted him to hold me and say 'I love you.' He was so mean to me."

I embraced her—held her tightly as her body heaved with sobs—whispering sorries into her ear.

There are secret doors that separate my mother and grandfather that will never be unlocked—harm I could never understand, wounds I cannot heal. I've spent my life trying because I wanted more of her. I wanted all of her. Without the love of her father, something was missing.

"He chose his friends over me; he'd rather drink with them," she cried as we drove back home after our visit to the Bronx. "Pero cuando me necesita, ahí sí me reconoce." When he needs me, he'll call, she predicted, and he did. He got sick. He called.

I cannot change my mother's memory of that afternoon. But my understanding has shifted. I know my grandfather never chose alcohol over her. I imagine the moment he saw her, he believed he needed a drink. I know this is the kind of self-medication we learn, and some of us are more susceptible than others. I know we carry generations of pain, and because we don't tend to this sorrow—because we don't know how to—we continue to hurt others. But there is no one my grandfather harmed more than himself.

Alcohol didn't rob my mother of her father's love, and being an alcoholic was not what made him unlovable. But it did keep them apart. What she misunderstood about his addiction and what he kept hidden for fear his daughter would not be able to understand, what he may not have understood himself—this lack of awareness was the unbridgeable chasm between them, and I could not let that come between us.

I understood my mother's confusion because as much as I had hidden my drinking, I also hid what it took to stay sober. I worried more about not making others feel uncomfortable or concerned—appearing transcendent, rather than being honest. She had absorbed an image of the addict—we all have—but seeing me fully would require her to interrogate that. Which would inevitably push her to have compassion for her father.

Dysfunction persists through silence, and silence is facilitated by shame. The isolating symptoms of addiction inevitably lead to a cycle of demoralizing behavior—a perpetual state of humiliation. The moment I told my mother I was an alcoholic was reclamation. I couldn't lose my family. There was a legacy to protect.

21

Concepción

How do you make sense of someone you never knew? How do you retrieve an entire history from scattered breadcrumbs?

I started reading. One book in particular caught me: *Roots of Resistance: A Story of Gender, Race, and Labor on the North Coast of Honduras*, by Suyapa G. Portillo Villeda, a Honduran academic and historian who shares the same name as one of my cousins. The book is the true story of Honduras. Nothing like the things I was told. Or that's not quite right—maybe it's that it contextualizes the clues, the hints in what I was told. You know how adults never really explain anything to you when you're a kid or make you feel like something is too complex or mature for a child's ear? (This must be how they delude themselves into thinking you don't pick up on all their dirty jokes.)

I was reading that book around the time my tío Ernesto called. I was excited to hear from him at first. My mother had been my chief research assistant on my Abuelo Project (as I dubbed the quest for information regarding my grandfather's life). And although hers was the only narrative that mattered to me, I knew I needed more to get the whole story.

My uncle told me what he knew about my grandfather. It wasn't much, but it was a new perspective.

"He was a gentle soul for sure," my uncle said as he described my grandfather as a man who avoided confrontation at all costs. "It was only when he drank that he lost his temper. And you know he had his bad habits . . . he loved women."

My mother was told my grandfather chose Beatriz as his first wife because she was a virgin. This bullshit story was debunked by the birth of my uncle Jaime six months after their wedding day, on April 18, 1953. My grandmother claims she was twenty and my grandfather was twenty-three. I can't know for sure because I cannot find the marriage certificate or her birth certificate. All I know is that the story of immigration is one of constant revision: At the start of my research, my grandmother gave her date of birth as November 4, 1938. After I asked about her marriage to my grandfather, the year became 1933.

Their wedding portrait is tattered now. A curious white crease is permanently etched into the gloss of the photographic paper and forms a shape across my grandfather's brow and under his nose like the mask of Zorro. I imagine my grandmother crumpling it dozens of times after each betrayal, abandonment, or brawl, then, regretful after a reconciliation, taping it, bending it, and unfurling it again, though it could never be restored to its original form. The photograph is framed and displayed prominently in her apartment to this day. She promised to give it to me when she dies.

I took a picture of it with my phone. I stare at it sometimes. My grandfather's expression is curious. Below his tidy mustache, there isn't a smile or a frown. It's his eyes that signal distress: his turbid stare and the slight forward tilt of his head, the bend of surrender in his neck. The colorless photo surrounds him in a deep sepia and my grandmother in a halo of white. Beatriz's expression appears as bright as a lightbulb, her cheeks so prominent they graze the lace edge of her veil as the heart-shaped neckline of her gown flirts with the secret she shields with a bouquet. I can't tell what kind of flowers are in it. She's stunning. We all take after her.

But there is someone who looks even more thrilled—over my grandmother's shoulder beams my great-grandmother Chong, short for Concepción: a Catholic name that might indicate that she was the creator of the virginity tale, one that gave her the leverage to broker the marriage between her daughter and an up-and-coming young professional.

Even after my grandparents' separation, Jaime maintained a steady cash stream to Chong, who pooled the revenue for her own household rather than redistribute it to her daughter, his estranged wife. It's unknown how many lives my grandfather was responsible for on an unstable income. He'd been groomed from childhood to believe in the opportunity the agricultural industry offered. Though his experience therein was tumultuous, what else was there to believe in?

My grandparents had three sons within the first three years of their marriage, while crops were ravaged by a pestilence known as "Panama Disease." I learned more about this in my reading. Decades of monocropping exhausted the once-fertile soil and decimated jobs, as relentless USian owners manipulated the Honduran government for more land concessions and moved to stomp out the formidable uprisings of the labor movement with the help of the US government and CIA.

Unlike in neighboring countries, Honduran workers like my grandfather operated without the shield of any labor code. Perhaps in an act of protest, my grandfather became as unfaithful to the fincas as he was to my grandmother and worked for competing plantations.

Two US-based and -backed companies dominated the northern coast region; the first was Cuyamel Fruit Company, which in my grandfather's time became known as United Fruit Company and eventually Chiquita Brands. The second, Standard Fruit and Steamship Company, was acquired in the 1960s by Castle & Cooke, which branded banana and pineapple exports under the Dole name. I learned through my research that bosses at these companies used drugs to extract faster labor from workers, then offered other drugs—mostly depressants—to numb their pain and drudgery, to overcome increasingly long laboring days. Then the cycle continued: the bosses would offer stimulants to counteract the effects of the depressants, to sober up the workers and make them more efficient. That's just what happened with my grandfather.

In the spring, on the year of my grandparents' first wedding anniversary, the newlyweds and first-time parents struggled to negotiate their future against the tide of upheaval. Unfettered exploitation fomented dissent among workers against company control. Though the plantation paid a pittance, Beatriz was pregnant again, and they needed the money. She quickly realized the game at play and resented that my grandfather fell for it. The game was this: the company offset low-paying jobs by offering cheap provisions, treating basic necessities like food and home as perks to avoid paying workers a living wage. *Comida, casa y caramelo,* my grandmother called it, *pero poco sueldo*—an expression repeated by an ex-wife still trying to make sense of her own abandonment.

Caramelo, or candy, is a euphemism my grandmother used for booze. While on the job, it was common for an overseer to encourage workers with a swig of something, though they forbade drinking and the purchase of alcohol off the property. Overworked and underpaid, alcohol dulled the pang of workers' oppression. Many viewed partaking publicly, purchasing from illicit vendors, or fermenting their own brews as acts of rebellion and indulgence. A rare pleasure.

The finca made sure to get my grandfather drunk, pliable, and dependent—first on the job, then on the drugs. They sent him home to his wife if he got out of pocket at the commissary. Women reported that drunkenness often led to serious violence. Though brutal, the consequences of the revelry did not, for the most part, interfere with their work and were largely treated as commonplace. Inebriation became a workable defense against the company police and in court. And it was often a way of expressing masculinity, the kind of machismo labor that propped up banana harvesting empires. Violence and inebriation were permissible because both allowed the state to function; Toxic masculinity was one of the pillars upholding the banana republic.

Three years passed after the birth of my mother's older brothers—a period of separation that didn't last once Beatriz got pregnant with my mother. "Así a la fuerza," Beatriz answered when my mother asked why she continued to have children with such a mujeriego, "Borracho . . . ¿Cómo se dice? Drunk, drunk," she repeated in English.

My mother was five when Beatriz left my grandfather for good. She was twelve when Beatriz left her. My grandparents were legally married for fifteen years. Beatriz was his first call when he got off the boat in Sacramento, California.

22

Abandono

My curiosity about my grandfather led me down a research rabbit hole. I wanted to understand more about how he might have started drinking, what working conditions might have propelled him to turn to alcohol, to cope with disillusionment. Did he realize how his alcoholism fit within larger systems of oppression? Or did he just internalize it as yet another failure? The myth of exceptionalism was as sickening as the drink: a lesson of the American Dream I must unlearn to get well.

What I found was the story of an oppressed people who wouldn't go quietly. On April 26, 1954, workers and organizers within the labor movement executed a coordinated strategy across plantations that would destabilize the country's economy, halting an entire nation. The sixty-nine-day action began at the United Fruit Company, quickly spread to the Standard Fruit Company (whose workers joined for eleven days), and then went nationwide in a show of solidarity. The only games in town were on strike.

Just before this, as the Carías dictatorship ended, a document known as the Rolston Letter was exhumed. Originally from 1920, it was finally published in the *Vanguardia Revolucionaria* on October 20, 1949. It revealed much about how the colonizers and elites felt about the workers—their malleability, character, and purpose. H. V. Rolston of the Cortes Development Company wrote to company lawyer Luis Melara, "Estos pueblos envilecidos por el alcohol son asimilables para lo que se necesite y destine." These people debased by alcohol are assimilable for whatever is needed and intended. In other words, let's soak them in booze and make them do our bidding.

Rolston's plan in 1920 was to take control of the northern coast and build an empire. Alcohol would play a key role in the operation. His plan was well in hand by the time this letter was published. His blatant disrespect for workers' humanity and his description of the intentional manipulation of workers through alcohol validated their grievances. It proved without a doubt that their employer was an abuser, something they had felt for so long but had been denied incontrovertible proof until the letter made the rounds. Here's what Rolston wrote:

> It is indispensable to capture the imagination of these subjugated peoples and attract them to the idea of our agrandisement [*sic*], and in a general way to those politicians and bosses that we must use. Observation and careful study have assured us that a people degraded by drink can be assimilated to the demands of necessity and destiny; it is in our interest to make it our concern that the privileged class, whom we will need for our exclusive benefit, bend itself to our will; in general, none of them has any conviction or character, far less patriotism; they seek only position and rank, and on being granted them, we will make them hungry for even more. These men must not act on their own initiative, but rather according to determining factors and under our immediate control.

The letter's legitimacy has since come under scrutiny, but regardless of its veracity, it reflected the lived reality of so many laborers. It ignited a reaction that lit the fuse on a strike, becoming a lightning rod for the labor movement that would be cited in leftist circles for generations.

———

I wonder what my grandfather thought of the movement. Which side was he on? There is nothing I can find in my research that can tell me for certain. No one in my family knows. In my fantasy, he was a handsome operative with the rebellion who carried a dog-eared copy of *Prisión verde* in a canvas bag over his shoulder wherever he went, espoused radical leftist ideals, and wrote manifestos under a pseudonym in the *Vanguardia Revolucionaria*.

But the facts? The facts tell me he was a fatherless boy forced to make his own way far too soon in a turbulent and violent world, without the love and guidance that would have smoothed his way. He was no match against greedy imperial forces. This is a common story, and one that is still alive and well today.

The only definitive evidence of his feelings is that he got the fuck out of there. And as much as I would love to believe I'd be on the front line, locked in arms with my compatriots, I know I'm a runner. I get that from him. I'm my grandfather's granddaughter.

———

Hurricane Fifi dealt the final blow to my grandfather's career as an electrician. The storm hit the northern coast of Honduras on September 18, 1974, drowning infrastructure in rainfall for miles—mudslides swallowing villages whole. Thousands died and 95 percent of the banana crop was decimated. The moorings were the quickest to repair, and my grandfather decided to jump on cargo ships that delivered food around the world, predominantly to Asia, and began a consistent route from Sacramento to Vietnam, until one day he got off in California.

He decided to stay. Unsure of how to acquire legal status on his own, he called my grandmother. Beatriz convinced my mother to petition for his naturalization.

Once on the East Coast, my grandfather worked in the kitchen of a Midtown Holiday Inn as a dishwasher and later a cook. On his days off, he rode a train upstate to pitch in at a hotel called the Pinnacle. When my tío Ernesto, nearly a dentist in Honduras, arrived in the United States in 1984, my grandfather got him a job at the Holiday Inn. At night, the entire kitchen had to be cleaned and broken down. The guys showed him what to do. "You have to socialize," tío Ernesto told me when I was in my rabbit hole. "But, you know men, we don't have much to say." They instructed him to grab their biggest steel stockpot and fill it with equal parts ice and beer, a dash of water. My uncle relapsed after having been sober for five years in Honduras. But he saved up money and called my mother. Eventually, he wound up at our place in Mendham and later became a dental prosthetist. He was my grandfather's favorite of his four sons.

———

Bananas breathe oxygen just like the rest of us. They're alive. And as they absorb air they swallow pathogens—viruses, bacteria, parasites, trauma. No matter how protective their outer layer appears, the inner tissue is made of mush—soft and vulnerable to bruises. When harmful agents penetrate, bananas instinctively attack and metabolize them by producing ethylene. The more gas the fruit must produce to combat its environs, the more quickly it ripens. Fighting causes rot. The process of ripening is called senescence. Isn't that a beautiful way to describe death?

Humans react similarly to their environments. The effects can be measured in our cells and passed down in our genes through generations. The study of this is called epigenetics.

It isn't an exaggeration to say my mother survived on bananas. When she had nothing to eat, she'd pick them off trees. Mangoes, too. When she recalls these stories, I wonder what it was like to live in a food production hub, from which sustenance was shipped around the world, and starve for days. On some level, I know the answer to my own question: it lives inside my body, a famine coded into my DNA.

But my knowing isn't a part of my consciousness the way it is for my mother. My discoveries about our family and her childhood trigger regressive fits, bouts of anger, and mostly tears. "I can't help but cried," she writes in our group text. As I push my mother to her edge, I feel guilty but persist. I need this.

"Mom's reverting back to her childlike behavior," Karla texted me directly, off the group chat, an intervention. She lives with my mother—my mother helps take care of her kids, my niece and nephew—and is sensitive to my mother's moods. "I'm sorry," I reply. "I was worried that might trigger her."

"She's actually OK. She cried. Let it out," Karla wrote. "She's mostly hurt, I think." I'm relieved to read this, though I know my sister wants me to back off. My sister, the middle child, does not appreciate any tilt toward imbalance. She understands why I dig, but she resents the lack of control it lays bare in her home. Hers is a home full of children, with little room for inner children.

———

"I'm opening my heart to you because you won't judge me. Otherwise I just keep my mouth shut, I don't like to lie. I have to be myself, so most times I stay quiet. And my father was the same way. When you've been abandoned, you expect people to abandon you," tío Ernesto told me on a FaceTime call over the summer.

It was hard to hear my uncle's recollection, hard to hear him justify my grandfather's behavior by saying it was the expectations of a daughter that caused the injury, not the actions of a father. These were convenient rationalizations for my uncle. But a man can be many things to many people. My grandfather was a small benefactor to my uncle, a kind and generous old man to my cousin, a callous abuser to my mother, and a violent batterer to my grandmother while, still, the only man she says she ever loved.

My therapist once explained why it is crucial for one parent to never speak ill of the other to their child. Because no matter whose side the child thinks they're on, they are still a part of that parent, and the parent is still a part of them. A child can't help but internalize the insult when one disparages the other.

I think that's why I hang on to the story of my uncle Javier—the same reason I cling to what I've learned about alcohol and my grandfather. The addicts, the ones we knew of in our family, were so vilified—but we all deserve the dignity of our journeys.

23

You Never *Have* to Drink Again

No one tells you that healing turns stones—that our minds don't Ctrl-Alt-Del what we've decided is behind us now. We don't automatically find inner peace. Instead, the mind unfurls: not like a flower, but with the bite of a split onion. It's messy. Life's challenges are even more palpable. You feel like a target—it's as if your mind says, *You're ready now.* But who gave this bitch my consent? Who said I could handle this in my condition?

Unable to contain my curiosity, I felt driven to face everything I'd avoided all at once, everything I buried beneath the rocks. I lifted each to find the slithering worms of repressed memory. But meanwhile, I could barely tolerate the simple chores of daily life. I avoided every mirror in the house. I never checked the mail; I couldn't even bring myself to unlock the box. Typing the password to my online banking app made me lightheaded. I'd sit on my bed for stability, but the room would still spin and spin. Substance use disorder fucked with my chemistry until I felt nothing without a simultaneous impulse for escape. I had found relief in the usual places: alcohol, drugs, a scroll on social media, shopping, or sex. I had sought to maximize the feeling in any direction, up or down; it didn't matter.

My sponsor suggested I write down what came up in the moment. A trick for detangling neural pathways is to get it all out of your head and onto the page. You separate the feeling from the craving. The sentient takes shape, is brought into focus, so you can trace your steps to the trigger. Whatever the next step, I wanted to take it as myself. And I had to find out who that was.

The pages started out ugly, words scribbled illegibly in black pen, hot-pink highlighter, whatever I could find. My scrawl gave voice to my fears, which miraculously made the fears less terrifying. Tucked into the cover of the black Moleskine is a note from my sponsor written in her signature style, "Something to help build your creativity." (Heart, CNH.) Inside, on yellowed, warped pages watermarked by tears, I'd written so many exclamation points, lists, and styling—literally writing down what I planned to wear in a week. I wrote it all, quickly, messily. The disgusting thoughts, the irrational fears, the hopes, the crushes, the dreams, the disappointments. Writing things I thought I'd never admit to anyone helped me decide my life was worth saving. I unleashed a stream of consciousness every day, a new habit, like brushing my teeth every night before bed. The process of recovery followed the process of narration. It was the biggest writing assignment of my life.

I chose my sponsor because of something I'd heard her say in a meeting. I was told to listen for what resonated when picking a sponsor, for someone who has what you want. "I have no secrets today," my sponsor said, and my spine straightened like a marionette pulled on a string. I'd never wanted anything more in my life.

When she finished her qualification, I raised my hand to tell her and the entire room, *I want what you have.* I then told the story of what people in AA call "my first drunk," how I'd been roofied, raped, and then blamed. I realized the very idea of keeping that night a secret meant I blamed myself, too.

The basement in Alphabet City felt reminiscent of the underground world we'd all been a part of once upon a time. *Are we creatures of habit—or is it nostalgia?* I wondered as the meeting closed. The crowd dispersed, the space surrounding me growing wider as people formed groups and left to grab coffee or brunch. I felt faint and remorseful, an effect referred to as *share shame*, when a woman came up to me, as fellows often do with newcomers. Finally, a rescue, I thought.

"You're gonna find your part in it," she told me. "I'm sorry?" I replied, new to the lingo. "Just keep coming back and do the steps, and you'll see. We all have stories like that, honey. Best to take it to a women's meeting or your sponsor."

My soon-to-be sponsor was still at the front of the room, surrounded by people who approached to offer thanks and praise her message. I stood in the corner, crossed my arms over my white tee to cover the embroidered red roses where the designer imagined nipples would be, about five inches above mine, and tugged at the hem of my denim mini-skirt. I had done as I was told and in turn been completely undressed by a woman with decades of sobriety. I had found the courage to be vulnerable, and I wasn't believed. How was this place different? How was this safe? My therapist always told me, "Your instincts exist for a reason." But now I was an addict. "You can't trust your feelings" was the message in the last meeting. "Feelings aren't facts." A slogan that made sense at the time was now used to deny what I knew, as if I had never left high school.

I told my sponsor what happened, and she assured me nothing could be further from the truth. "Fuck her," she said, and took me for a green juice to discuss. "You did absolutely nothing wrong. Not then, not now." We were both survivors of sexual assault; she was putting her life back together not by moving on from or getting over what hurt her but by absorbing the truth of her experiences and integrating them into her daily practice and recovery. As she explained this to me, I felt from my new friend that sense of security I'd always projected onto romantic relationships with men. I listened to her when she suggested I begin with morning pages, just me and this notebook and my truth. It would be a practice free from agenda.

Pen to paper was the first gesture of trust I offered myself.

Eventually, I learned the voices in my head—the shrieks and the murmurs—were a part of me, echoes of the harms I'd endured, projections of prejudice and fears. I would have to get used to interrupting them, challenging and speaking over them. In the shower one night, I put my hands on my stomach. My muscles relaxed, warmed by the temperature of the water. My shoulders settled their blades into repose as a groan erupted like thunder from some unknown source. I sucked in a gut so tense I could hardly squeeze it. Taut, bloated, bracing.

I wanted to soften in the places that had gone hard. That sounded like freedom to me.

24

Sinvergüenza

As I approached one year sober, I was thirty-four. I had no job, no savings, and a couple of months left on my unemployment insurance benefits. But I was full of hope. This was the longest, most honest commitment I'd ever made to myself, and I was determined to celebrate it.

The day I was fired from my job as an executive assistant after I reported abusive treatment by a coworker to HR, I went directly to an AA meeting. I shared openly about the shame of being let go, my frustration with unjust office politics, and my fears for the future. After the meeting, the group consensus was that this was the program in action; some called it God's plan for me. One woman shared she'd had an identical experience during her first year and shortly after was offered her dream job.

"Everything happens for a reason," she said, patting my hands like a mother, though I was nearly her age.

Six months later, I was still waiting for God, the universe, or whatever, to notice the 347 days of good behavior I'd accumulated and reward me accordingly. In the meantime, I conjured a plan to reward myself.

That I had been working as a secretary tells you how well my freelance writing career was going, though you'd never know it from scrolling through my online avatar, @Nuevayorka. She was mucha muchacha, and like the song by Juan García Esquivel made famous to gringos after being featured in *The Big Lebowski*, everything was mucho—mucho fabulous, mucho exotica, and recently mucho spiritual (read: spiritual not sober; sober wasn't cute, yet). With social media presence becoming valuable capital, my growing Instagram following was my most substantial currency—enough to negotiate a barter for a free vacation. After a quick Google search and a couple of copy-and-paste emails, I got a bite from a yoga retreat in Costa Rica.

I'd traveled alone only once before. The previous Christmas, I'd left my family in Buenos Aires to fly to the southernmost tip of South America, where the Tierra del Fuego archipelago becomes the gateway to Antarctica. They call it El fin del mundo. It was the farthest I'd been from home. I needed that much distance from the dangerously circular path of my past. I hoped the detour led the way to my escape.

By my second trip, the pride of rigorous solo travel had not worn off. After thirteen hours, three planes, and a shuttle down Calle Pura Vida, I arrived in a small town along the coast of the Nicoya Peninsula called Montezuma. The proprietor of the retreat spent hurricane season in Switzerland but had made all the arrangements for me ahead of time. I was welcomed warmly and checked in slowly. As I climbed the slight slope up the mango tree grove to my private bungalow, I breathed in the sweetness of independence. I was neither companion nor stowaway. This time I paid my own way.

I pulled the string of the ceiling fan, the only AC available besides the canopy of the trees, and collapsed onto the king-size bed. Exhausted after half a day's travel, I stared at the sloped ceiling. Beads of sweat sprouted across my entire body as I lay there, completely still, uncertain of what to do next. Pride didn't make the solitude any easier.

Much of the village was visible from my balcony. I figured I could traverse the entire place in thirty minutes if I upheld New York City walking standards, but I didn't want to behave like a tourist, so I slowed all the way down, braided my swollen curls, and stripped off half my clothing.

Losing my job meant losing my health insurance, which meant losing my birth control. I'd have to pay nearly $100 a month out of pocket, so with no one in my life, I stopped taking the pill for the first time since I was eighteen. The five pounds I'd wanted to shed since that age melted off my petite frame within weeks. My breasts fit securely into my bikini top, with no unsightly spill, my tummy was flat, and there was a keyhole gap between my thighs. This state felt temporary, which made me desperate to be seen.

"¡Hola!" I said to passersby as I walked to the town center, hoping my satisfactory Spanish would help me pass, if not for a local, at least una Tica. But Central American or not, the town is small enough that any new face is a foreign face, and if you're coming from the United States, eres gringa, no matter what.

I flew over my mother's country to arrive near the place I've always longed to go. In the neighboring country, the people's credo is a version of it's all good—it's all life—a far cry from my mother's tales about these countries. In my mother's memory, it was all bad. No life to be had. That's the way it goes with mothers and daughters—whatever they teach you to fear, you charge toward faster.

As I reflected on this, a man pulled to the side of the road and offered me a ride on his motorbike. My family has a history with men on motorbikes, so I declined. "Pura vida!" he shouted as the back tire kicked sand onto my plastic flip-flops.

———

There are no apparent borders in Montezuma. To the west, the land simply comes to an end on a craggy cliff, where a tree the size of my building back home offered me a place to contemplate the fact of my being very much alive without a clue how to live.

I decided to start with an adventure. In order to reach the hiking trail that leads to the famous falls of Montezuma, I had to cross a river. Because I was alone, I couldn't do anything or go anywhere without my headphones—even in paradise, I couldn't be fully present. The squeal of monkeys, the song of tropical birds, and the roar of the current whipped up by last night's storm were all drowned out by the sound of SZA. Unable to hear the imminent danger I faced, I stood in the water ankle-deep and watched a father and son skip a few well-placed stones. I tried to casually follow their lead, but I slipped and was swept downstream for meters before catching on to a rock large enough to wrap my arms around, grounded deep beneath the river. As I caught my breath, I felt more alone than I ever had before. I began to imagine how far the charging current could drag me, wondered how long it would take for my body to be found, when the song switched to Princess Nokia and I hoisted myself up. Channeling strength from the rapper's lyrics, my playlist intuiting my needs, I crossed the river and trekked the challenging path. Convinced of my invincibility, I climbed down a steep hill and saw two boys in the distance. When I arrived at the bottom, I registered friendly faces. The redhead spoke to me in tragically broken Spanglish. I laughed and said, "I speak English." He smiled. "Oh, well, that's easier," he said, blushing. "I'm John."

The gringos hopped into the deep water but were quickly outshone by the local boys who swan-dived and backflipped from high cliffs that hung over us. They also sold handmade jewelry made of crystals from the foot of this magical waterfall, where I, too, took a huge leap and in doing so overcame my fear of heights. I bought a necklace from them and wore it every day until the gold plating rusted, leaving an imprint on my skin green as a Spanish olive.

John and I crossed paths again that night, seemingly by chance, although he later confessed he had been looking for me. As we walked around the small town, I learned he was twenty-seven and entering his final year in medical school. We both lived in New York City. I noticed he struggled slightly, one foot dragging behind the other. I asked if he wanted to slow down or rest. "I'm good." He shrugged, then guided me toward the dark shore and told me about bioluminescence. "It's like underwater fireflies," he explained. "Through this chemical reaction, totally natural, the sea life—fish, plankton, jellyfish—all light up. You have to see it."

It stormed every night in Montezuma. Blasts of lightning illuminated every corner of the pitch-black jungle like spotlights—shocking bursts bright as day, then suddenly dark, night again. We'd have to get in the water to see it, create a current to reveal the famous electric blue. I knew this was a play for romance, but I worried we'd be electrocuted.

As we waded into the warm surf, he reached for my hand. I buckled as I felt the stab of a rock beneath my foot, and as he tried to catch me, his glasses fell into the water. We splashed around searching for them, and the moment evaporated. I wiggled my hand away from his, sat on the beach, and wondered why I was forcing this uncomfortable evening with a random stranger. I felt relief when he finally found his glasses, and we headed back toward town. As we passed my hotel, he told me it was his last night—*Fuck it*, I thought, and invited him up to my treehouse.

I had a promise in mind, a wish that after a year of celibacy and sobriety, I would be rewarded with the perfect partner. John could be it. What are the chances of meeting at this far-flung locale on my first anniversary? I told myself it was fate, but our lack of sexual chemistry quickly dispelled my fantasy.

When it was over, I expected him to leave, never to be seen or heard from again. My downward spiral could commence in private. But he stayed and asked me questions. When the power went out from the lightning storm, he suggested we try the hammock. He had a bus to catch soon and wanted to spend his final few hours in paradise with me. We lay naked, legs intertwined, and watched the storm from my private porch, sneaking peeks at each other's bodies in the seconds of light. I had never allowed myself to be on such display before. I felt bold and confident. I was coming into myself.

I continued seeing him back in New York. Though he was often unavailable, there was no one else, and I figured he was harmless. The sex never improved, and I never spoke up. Even when it became painful, I moaned encouragingly to make him cum faster, and I'm sure he thought I liked it. I chastised myself for not asking him to stop or slow down or tell him what I wanted. After all I'd been through and all I'd learned, I still had no respect for my body. I still protected some dick's feelings over my own. I have no idea why he didn't use condoms or why I didn't insist. I figured I was too old for a slipup. Doctors had told me for years that pregnancy would be difficult because of polycystic ovary syndrome. When I shared this with John, a medical student, he agreed and carried on without protection.

Three months of noncommittal dating passed, and it was obvious the relationship had no future. Things had nearly faded completely when I missed my period over Thanksgiving.

There had been scares in high school. My boyfriend said his parents sat him down and told him we must come to them right away if anything happened. They knew a doctor. As if my only chance in life was to trap their son with a teenage pregnancy. As if I'd want to keep it.

The first time I settled in Italy with Luca, 1 didn't get my period for two months and started to panic. He took me to the doctor and paced in the tiny exam room while I lay on the examination table, my legs spread in stirrups. They never took my blood or urine. The doctor just thought he'd eyeball it from my cervix and press down on my abdomen as my boyfriend screamed, "Lei è incinta? È incinta?" He gesticulated obnoxiously with his hands, catching a nest of wires attached to a beeping silver box. The nurse immediately appeared to untangle him and roll the equipment away to safety. No one told him to calm down. The doctor, undisturbed, took a seat behind a wide mahogany desk and determined that I was built like a man in my upper body. "Wide shoulders," he said in a hard Italian accent, tapped his own, then lowered his forearm to make a muscle with his biceps in a faux bodybuilder pose, and he and my boyfriend laughed. Once the doctor had concluded his jokes at my body's expense, he told me I was not pregnant—that my body was most likely adjusting to a new time zone, country, food. My period came the next day.

Then there was the time I got hate-fucked by an angry New Englander while away for a weekend. He sent me a $700 check after I texted him my period was late. After it came, I kept the money; I used it to pay rent.

Unlike many of my cousins and family friends, my sisters and I managed to avoid teen pregnancy. This was a great point of pride for my parents. But as we all sailed, childless, past the age of thirty, they became superstitious, calling for God's will but insinuating we'd waited too long.

By the time I got pregnant with John's baby, I'd completely lost faith in the program, but I had nothing else, nowhere else to go. I had spent a year in the twelve steps, following every rule, completing every step, picking up service commitments, developing a spiritual practice, abstaining from sex and relationships—all in an effort to come out the other side cured, perfect, worthy of love. Addiction was the obstacle to the things I desired, the person I wanted to be. I had found that out, removed it, and was poised with my hands cupped toward the universe, ready for my rewards to fall from the sky. If I couldn't get my act together sober, I was irredeemable. An unplanned pregnancy—an unforced error—a fuckup so catastrophic in my mind, it triggered a psychotic break. I am petrified to reveal where my thinking wandered from the day I tested positive in my bathroom to the day I performed a medical abortion alone in my studio. Petrified that I will be accused of substantiating the claims of those who call themselves pro-life. That I will be disowned by feminists—called a hypocrite.

But the truth is, I did not want to have an abortion as much as I did not want to have a baby. The choice was not easy, and the process was not painless. And I don't think I have to say they are for you to know I believe what I did was right.

The abortion health care I received was a privilege. I went to a Planned Parenthood clinic near my home in New York. I was cared for by trained, thoughtful, conscientious women who never made me feel like my symptoms were wrong. I was supported in every way and applauded for my actions. But state and federal regulations require that doctors who perform this care follow certain rules, many of which are intended to provoke the pregnant person into reconsidering. My breakdown was by design.

I don't know if the sound was meant to be on, but the rhythmic whirs filled the dark, windowless sonogram room, and I heard the sound of a heartbeat just like I'd heard my niece's as I held my sister's hand. I was eight weeks pregnant, the technician said. Two months pregnant. I texted John; we were both shocked at how far along I was.

Profound, lifelong cultural programming based on colonial violence had penetrated my family, my school, and my world, forming a mythology around goodness, womanhood, and motherhood—one I consciously rejected but unknowingly internalized. These were never my ideas. Understanding how my psychological state spiraled, I went back to the source to finally unravel the wires of self-sabotage.

25

Land of the Free

Rumi wrote, "Sit with your friends. Don't go back to sleep. Night travelers are full of light, and you are, too. Don't leave this companionship."

My mother has been my companion in darkness my whole life. We have traveled through the night hand in hand, always, and, I believe, over many lifetimes. But this is where we split. In this loss, we parted ways. Motherhood is where our companionship has changed. I wonder if she will ever be able to understand me. Will she forgive me for what I've done? Will she ever be able to understand why I had to?

Abortion has been legal in the United States all my life. At thirty-nine years old, I watched the decision that protected it as a national right be overturned. One of my first thoughts was, *Thank God I already had mine*.

Honduras is one of six countries in Latin America and the Caribbean that ban abortion without exception. Though my mother says she never took the law into consideration, she was aware of the penalty. Women suspected of having abortions appeared on the cover of the local newspaper—gossip fodder for the so-called God-fearing masses. My mother witnessed the horror of a clandestine procedure firsthand. It was a harrowing experience that resulted in her cousin's disownment—a story I'd never heard until after I had my own abortion, when I was assigned a feature about Honduran reproductive rights. I told my mother about the assignment, and she told me what she had seen in Honduras fifty years before.

After my mother survived the beating from her brother that nearly took her life, she had nowhere to go. Chong was the head of a large family home, where many children and grandchildren cycled through, coming to their matriarch in their times of need. My mother inherited her mother's reputation as the family's black sheep; therefore, the open-door policy didn't apply to her. Her stay was always conditional, dependent on housework and childcare.

At the time, my mother's cousin Luisa was staying at Chong's with her two daughters. Chong referred to the girls as *micas*—when my mother recounted this detail, I recognized it instantly; it was the exact term my grandmother used for my sisters and me. Unlike *mija* or *mijita*, terms of endearment, *mica* was used to disparage girls, to call them brats. My mother despised the word and felt protective of the little ones but did not want to be tied down by Luisa's responsibilities. She wanted her freedom but needed a place to stay, she said.

Luisa took off around noon one day, leaving my mother with the kids. My mother ran to catch up with her, to tell her she couldn't watch the girls, and saw Luisa get in the passenger seat of a car and drive off with a man. No one knew who he was. When Luisa came back after a few hours, my mother was desperate to go outside, ride a bike, see her friends, grab a Coca-Cola.

She walked to Luisa's room to tell her she was returning the children to her care. But when she opened the door, she saw Luisa crouched in the corner of the room, hands gripping her knees, hemorrhaging. Pale, damp with sweat, and half-conscious, she kept pushing as Chong placed towels and a bucket beneath her stained skirt.

Water seemed to fill my ears as my mother described the scene to me while we sipped coffee on my couch in Brooklyn. My palms pricked, numbness spreading through my fingertips. "Y salía ese chorro de sangre y una cosa negra," she said, recounting a propulsive jet of blood so crimson it was practically black. I set my mug on the ground before it could spill, drew my legs into myself, wrapped my arms around my knees and listened.

My mother had felt sure Luisa would die. "She had no blood or color in her face, like a ghost. Chong was in and out of the room, bringing her hot water, towels, broth, and things to clean her. It was frantic." Chong made sure to keep the door closed and everyone out—privacy was her priority. Keeping Luisa's abortion a secret was as critical as the fight for her life.

Once Luisa recovered, Chong put her out. Luisa left, took her girls, and went to San Pedro. She went on to have many more children, eight total. Twenty-five years later, Luisa and my mother reunited in New Jersey. My mother told me her face of stone never softened.

"It scared the hell out of me, me pegó un susto horrible," my mother said of the whole ordeal with a shudder. "Esa mujer se estaba muriendo. So, when I got pregnant, I remembered what happened to her, and I did not want to do that."

When my mother learned she was pregnant with her first child, the US Supreme Court had just enshrined in law citizens' right to choose. One month after my piece went live, just shy of its semicentennial, *Roe v. Wade* was overturned.

The World Health Organization qualifies legal abortion as one of the safest treatments in the world—as safe as a penicillin shot. Clandestine procedures can be lethal.

It is the rhetoric, the shaming, that kills us.

26

Nine Days with Unborn

On the forty-third day of my cycle, two weeks late, I went to my usual Pilates class. Our waifish Spanish dream of an instructor began her scripted intro, asking who was new. "Anyone here for the first time? Any hangovers, babies on board, anyone? Any mommies? Not sure yet?" she joked. I'd heard this spiel a thousand times, but for some reason, that day, I began to calculate the dates and numbers in my head, reaching for an out, and for the first time in my thirty-five years, I answered: *yes*.

Instead of panic, I floated into momentary bliss. I allowed myself to fantasize about what it would be like while it was all still hypothetical. My bladder had become abnormally weak, and I had to get up in the middle of class to run to the ladies'. *I can't make it through one hour of Pilates without peeing?* When I got home, I dug through my stash of toiletries for a First Response left over from my last scare in September. I pissed hurriedly on the stick just for good measure, as I was already late to meet my family for Thanksgiving. As one line lit up, I exhaled. I was almost embarrassed at my internal hysteria. It was so silly to think I could be pregnant, so dramatic of me. And then came the second. Two. Fucking. Lines.

On the forty-sixth day of my cycle, I saw John. I had to drag him out of a house party in StuyTown to tell him he'd knocked me up. He had planned to break things off with me that night but stopped dead in the street, rosy cheeks suddenly sallow. He tried to hold me as I cried. I squirmed away, uncomfortable in the arms of the man whose child I was carrying. He said, "Let's get a cab." We were silent the entire ride. He didn't want the taxi driver to overhear our conversation. It made me feel like he was ashamed of me, of my condition.

John, like me, had never been in this position before. He was young and a year away from graduating from medical school. I was seven years older, had $1,000 in savings, and had been sober one year. He was squeaky clean, nerdy even, known during his residency for having a strong constitution and the temperament of a puppy. He was the good guy who somehow managed to get an apology every time he let you down.

"It's your body," he said. "I can't tell you what to do. Do you know yet? Have you . . . ?"

"I can't keep this baby, John," I admitted for the first time out loud.

He exhaled deeply, a gleeful *phew!* "Okay, good, because I don't want the baby either."

Either? I thought. A term so callous it landed like a slap across the face. John had no idea what I wanted. Nor did it matter to him.

I stayed silent. John walked toward me, and I bowed my head. It rested on his chest, a barrier between our bodies. I didn't want to be touched. I didn't want to say it was okay. But I was too exhausted for honesty. All I could do was pretend.

On the forty-eighth day, Unborn and I went to Planned Parenthood. I didn't name him Unborn; the financial adviser at Planned Parenthood did. And I can't say how I began to imagine it was a boy. But I started to think of it as him that day.

After my pregnancy test, I was told my options. I already knew what they were. I'd done my research. I chose the pills, believing it would be less *invasive*. The earliest appointment they had was Friday, and it was Monday. The nurse handed me tissues and an appointment card and sent me to the third floor. Maribel, the financial counselor, was sweet and pretty. She was Puerto Rican and reminded me of my cousin. As we discussed my lack of health insurance, she advised that I, as a pregnant woman (the first time I'd ever been referred to as a pregnant woman), and Unborn would be taken care of. I had barely been listening to her, but the term was the bullhorn I needed to regain consciousness.

"What?" I interrupted. "Unborn?"

"I know, it's horrible," she replied. "It's just in case anything happens and you change your mind." My mind split like a branch. I could almost hear an audible snap. Like when you're walking through the woods in winter—crack, crack, crack.

I left and walked to the coffee shop on Broadway and Eleventh Street. Unborn wanted bagels every morning, and I was determined to give him anything he wanted while I had him. I sat and ate the multi-grain bagel with butter. It wasn't toasted enough, but it was delicious. I sipped my coffee and walked to an 11 a.m. AA meeting. I rolled my eyes as I entered begrudgingly. *Promises, my ass*, I thought as I searched for the darkest corner of the room. I resented every word uttered by every person who spoke and was fully tuned out when the man speaking finished, looked around the room, surely to find the most miserable-looking person, and said, "Would you like to share? The woman way in the back corner there."

"Fuck," I replied audibly, prompting a small laugh around the room. I shared vaguely yet honestly. I couldn't lie in AA. But I also wasn't prepared to admit that at 457 days, my disease found me stealing a sonogram of the baby I was planning to abort at the end of the week from a nurse at Planned Parenthood as she turned to grab paperwork from the printer.

"Pass," I muttered through sobs.

At my sister's house, I woke up twice in the middle of the night to pee. After the second trip, I decided to sleep on the couch. I remained awake all night, conscious but drifting, utterly untethered to anything earthly. When morning came, I blinked my eyes open and began to breathe deeply, willing myself to get up, to find strength. I heard my inhale, but then a short, tiny, alien gasp I hadn't exhaled. My heart began to race; surely, I was starting to lose my mind now, hearing things. I sank my head under the covers and took another deep breath when I heard the *hhhhssss* again. I began to panic, but I wanted more, further confirmation. I held my breath to be sure, waiting for the first sounds I'd ever heard Unborn make. I heard it again.

Another branch. Another snap.

I believed this was Unborn breathing. Was he letting me know he was there? Was he speaking to me? What did he want to tell me? I wanted to burrow into myself and connect to the cells growing in my body, but I feared I would never emerge. I was disappearing. I was losing the feeble grip on my sanity I'd been fighting to maintain over the past five days.

On the forty-ninth day of my cycle, I woke up with John. We'd had sex the night before. We used a condom for the first time. The wrapper was on the floor, half-hidden under my closet door. He slept in, missing his first class, and got up around 8 a.m. As he dressed, he sheepishly explained he'd have a long day and would most likely want to sleep in his own bed. I assured him I was okay. We usually saw each other once a week. "Nothing is going down until Friday," I shrugged. "We can return to our regularly scheduled programming." He said he'd be back Wednesday and left.

Restless, I took Unborn for a walk through Washington Square Park, blasting the saddest music I could find. I wasn't sure if I wanted to indulge the suicidal thoughts or drown them out. I had been crying publicly for days and gotten pretty addicted to it. Plus, I felt like anything less was sort of disrespectful to Unborn.

I thought of my mother, who had almost died giving birth to my sister at age seventeen—an unplanned pregnancy after being raped. She risked her life several times for the sake of her womb. Although our lives would be troubled and painful, we were loved and often happy. She taught me that the seed of life is sovereign and the physical call to motherhood is never to be disobeyed, for I am not my body at conception. I am, instead, the product of my body.

I began to rub my belly. My stomach felt bloated—bubbling uncontrollably. I craned my back and held it openly as I walked, wanting people to acknowledge that I was with child. Flaunting it—craving the morbid experience of acting the loving mother, while counting the days until the abortion. Many smiled warmly, I'm sure confused by my performance as I barely showed. I heard another snap.

On the fifty-second day of my cycle, John came over for dinner. I made tacos. He told me he wanted to go away for residency next year. "San Diego, I would do," he said, his life sailing along undisturbed. *Go fuck yourself*, I thought. We ate in silence.

When we got into bed, he asked what I was thinking. I didn't want to tell him anything Unborn and I had shared during these days together. My world with Unborn was private. I didn't answer and fell asleep with my back to him.

That night, I woke up several times to pee. In the morning, hours away from my appointment, I got up and took a long shower. John was awake when I got out, and we discussed what to do. I told him I wanted to go alone. I wanted to spend my last hours with Unborn. He loved bagels, and I wanted to be sure we could sit and enjoy our last one together.

I arrived at PP and waited in line—nervous but relieved to begin. The receptionist couldn't find my name. I wasn't in for today. My appointment was yesterday, they said. I begged, I sobbed, I said I'd wait all day. A young man walked over and gently escorted me to his office. They couldn't do it today, he explained, practically whispering the words in the sweetest southern accent I'd ever heard, though I barely registered a thing he said. He was very sorry but the earliest was Monday. I held myself upright by focusing on his hair. The style surprised me—a bleached-blond mohawk a rulers-length tall, jet-black roots. I wondered how long it took to do his hair every morning. I admired his commitment to self-expression.

I texted John, two girlfriends, and my sister. Their support began to annoy me. Too many voices in my head. I was plagued by the idea that I'd fucked this up on purpose. That it was a sign from the universe— *don't do it*. All I knew for sure was *I couldn't be my mother*. I had to break the cycle.

On December 4, 2017, I returned to Planned Parenthood and checked in. At the office, the doctor gave me one pill that she said would stop the pregnancy from growing. At home the next day, four pills dissolved into my cheeks, contracting my uterus with labor pains, a feeling I'd never conceived could hurt this much. I tried lying down, stacking pillows a dozen ways, but I couldn't breathe on my back. The pressure forced me to my feet; I had to stand, though I felt weak. I began to pace the studio, but my knees buckled through each contraction, a grip that seemed so malicious I assumed it had to be punishment. The doctor had prescribed a mild painkiller, but all I had was my sobriety, and I worried I'd misuse the meds and lose everything. I crawled to the bathroom when I was sure whatever was coming would explode out of my asshole. I draped my abdomen over the tub basin, grinding my teeth and writhing until my body gave way to exhaustion. I dragged myself into bed until hours later, when the force of a flood catapulted me to the toilet around midnight. I howled and wept for hours until I passed out again, arms wrapped around the basin, unable to let go. I woke up the next day on the cold tile. Eventually, I used the twelve pack of jumbo-roll toilet paper John bought me for the at-home procedure as a pillow. I'd asked him to leave once the medication took effect, and I never saw him again.

———

On day four of my new cycle, I slept at Karla's house. My period was heavy, and I'd bled through my pajamas but thankfully not on the bed. I lay back down, and my mother joined me and caressed my arm. "Qué flaca, mija," she observed my frame, thinner than usual, and asked if I'd slept well. I couldn't tell her what I'd done, but her instincts were never off. "Cuídate, bebe," she said, cradling me in her arms, "I love you." The rush of those words and my mother's touch almost made me believe I deserved them.

All I could think of was my dreaded follow-up appointment at Planned Parenthood. And when I would open my eyes in the morning and not have them immediately fill with tears. When I would stop putting my hands to my belly trying to feel for the squiggling. I wanted to know when this would start to get easier.

———

I couldn't change my clothes for days. A full-body long-sleeve jumpsuit was probably the most impractical choice, but it was the only thing I could bring myself to wear. The fabric was worn and soft, a shade of indigo dark enough to mask the bloodstains. A super-vintage Liz Claiborne style that buttoned all the way to the top. I was covered from head to toe. I was untouchable. Swaddled. And despite the rush my body experienced each time I stood in the tiny room where I'd flushed my guts down the toilet, I'd have to slow down and unhook each button until the garment wilted. I'd stand tall, upright, my bare chest pointed heavenward. Broken, hollow in every possible way, I'd lower my body to the toilet. I did this countless times. Like a meditation, over and over again. Until I was able to flush it all away faster. Until I didn't feel the morbid need to kneel at the basin and stare, hallucinating that I had dug up the first seed I'd ever planted.

———

Everyone has a place where they stash their secrets—some token, some physical evidence of the things we want to bury but won't let ourselves forget. Old rusty instruments of self-harm, literal or figurative. I keep my sister's and mine together in a cabinet above the refrigerator. I have to stand on a chair to reach the shelf where I store past-due bills, a box of family photos, file folders of old tax returns, half-written journals, and one children's book titled *I'd Know You Anywhere, My Love* by Nancy Tillman. We bought the book when my sister learned she was pregnant for the first time, with the baby she lost.

Inside the sleeve of the book, I hid the last sonogram taken of that baby. Three years later, I placed the sonogram of the baby I aborted eight weeks and one day into my first and only pregnancy there, too.

In Spanish, *dar luz* means *to give birth*. The literal translation is *to give light*. Not give life, but give light. I could not see the light night travelers possessed, the one that Rumi saw, until I got sober. Still, I had no light to give away. There was nothing to spare from the glint of hope I'd recovered in a year, and the warmth I'd always found from my mother's shadow was gone. I refused to cast a shadow of my own.

In my family, every woman I knew got pregnant. There was no such thing as family planning. As a result, so many women suffered, and so many children were mistreated. No one chose until my sisters and now me, though our choices led us on divergent paths, theirs toward birth, elevated, mine toward abortion, hidden.

The day my mother told me about Luisa, I told her what I'd done. My throat ached as I admitted that I'd chosen like her cousin, not like her. That it was hard, but it was the right decision; I'm glad now that I did it. She reached for my face, "¿Por qué no me dijiste?" she said, grabbing my chin tightly, the way she did when she brushed my hair when I was a little girl. She tilted my chin up, but I kept my eyes closed, tears wetting her fingertips. She asked why I did it alone, wondering how I managed and saying she understood the pain I described. At that moment, I was just her child.

Despite believing that her pregnancies, although unplanned, had saved her life, she did not believe this was the case for every woman. "Those were different times. I'm not in your body. I don't know what's right for you. And that guy wasn't going to stick around," she said. "I would have been there for you."

All this time, I'd been wrong. I believed that keeping my abortion hidden from my mother saved me from ruin, but hiding it was the only thing left that allowed me to believe I could be ruined. I never imagined that I could be set free instead. It took me thirty-six years and the awakening of my decision to learn that my life had value.

My first year of sobriety didn't end with the start of a great love story. I didn't get the guy. It ended much like the nights I spent using—on my knees, on the toilet, dripping in snot and sweat and vomit, half-naked and disoriented. That was the same, and it made me angry, but for once not with myself. Against the most powerful tide I'd ever faced, I'd made it to shore. I refused to drift into an identity I didn't choose. To sacrifice myself. For once, I chose me. Over everybody else, I picked me.

27

Family Disease

"You people eat too much," my mother said, still in her pajamas, laughing the words, talking to herself out loud. I buttered a bagel on the counter, a rare indulgence. She smacked my butt, shuffled past me, and lifted the lid of one of the doughnut boxes from yesterday's trip to the bakery to inspect the frosted leftovers. The rich aroma wafted through the room. I bit my lip and considered swapping the bagel for a doughnut, now sure I craved the taste of sugar not salt. She giggled shyly, glanced at me from her peripheral, and turned her attention to her grandchildren, who wanted her to get dressed to go to the beach. She said she would clean up and join us shortly—filing everyone out of the rented beach house. She needed time alone.

There's no world I can imagine where my mother, starved from infancy, eats too much. Or could ever come close to enough. Like me, she was born allergic to milk. And like her, my grandmother was unable to breastfeed. Pregnant and out of options, my grandmother would boil oats in water and spoon-feed the filmy residue to my mother as a baby until she could process whole food. After nearly a year of malnourishment, my mother crossed none of the milestones essential to healthy development. Unlike the boys, four sturdy sons my grandmother boasted she'd given birth to, my mother grew bird boned with a belly distended like a balloon and a big mouth. She learned to cry like hell.

My mother was in her sixties, deep into diagnoses for decades by that point, when my grandmother told her the story. Beatriz had made a joke of what she called my mother's weaknesses all her life. She was the last to walk, taking her first steps far behind her brothers, though she is not the youngest child.

Who could take baby steps under such deprivation? Who could survive it and stop worrying about scarcity around the corner? Who could believe they could ever be sated? Who is neutral about survival?

———

After returning from the beach that day, a salty white film coating our skin, everyone jumped in the pool. As the sun set, I felt a bit of a chill and slid into the hot tub. My nephew Joshua followed me. He watched me and my mother closely, though his attention was mostly on my sister, his mother, whose voice was beginning to rise as she debated with my brother-in-law, his uncle. They discussed Joshua's video game habits, the culture among the players, safety, and exposure. Joshua wasn't telling her about the bullying that goes on. Bringing up children in the Internet Age raised questions none of us had the answers to.

My mother stood behind me outside the tub and pressed her fingers across my throat, lifting my neck high up with her palms against the back of my head and aligning it with my spine. She lodged her thumbs under the hollows of my shoulder blades, arched them back, and raised my chest toward the sky. All my life, I've made a cave for my heart, and this position felt unnatural, but with my mother's hands securing me, it was a rush.

"Keep your shoulders back," she said, adjusting my body freely.

My mother is a massage therapist. She got her license a few years back, though she hasn't renewed it since the pandemic. It costs a couple hundred dollars, and she's already racked up student loan debt that she avoids, even though I have told her how much ignoring mine has hurt me. We share everything in this family, especially our mistakes.

"I just don't know why he's lying to me," we overheard my sister say, fearful that Joshua's instinct for privacy would be interpreted as a lack in her parenting. My sisters are adoring mothers who both seemingly overnight declared their lifelong desire for motherhood. I can't remember a conversation in our youth when either spoke of it, but I don't argue.

I wondered how Joshua felt to be spoken about, called a liar, without a say in the discussion. I was always called a liar. Joshua and I have a lot in common, which makes me so proud but also terrified to fuck it up, so I kept my mouth shut and let the grown-ups talk.

"If you speak up and say what you need to say," my mother told me, interrupting my thoughts, "all this will go away." She declared her cure for the lump in my throat, which the doctor assured me is an overproduction of hormones—all clumped together and lodged near the larynx. The same thing happens to my ovaries. My nephew turned his attention from his mother to me—staring into my eyes as they flooded. I stopped myself. I couldn't let him see me cry.

———

In our endless text threads, I realized we were afraid to say it. A group of women in constant communication, afraid to name what was killing me, killing us. We didn't call it alcoholism, addiction, or substance use disorder; it was *your alcohol stuff* or *when you stopped drinking*.

After I graduated from high school, my father sold the house and remarried. No one returned to Mendham. Our home base in New Jersey, where we'd meet every Sunday, became Karina's house in Dover. Karla and I lived in New York City together, and I went out every night—

trying to use the city's high voltage to breathe life back into my youth. It would catch up to me by the end of each week. On Sundays, a day reserved for a family dinner, I'd crawl out of a hotel suite, a loft in SoHo, a brownstone in Bed-Stuy, or a former factory in Bushwick, then hurry to meet my disappointed sister, and we'd make our homecoming in silence. Struggling to sober up on the New Jersey Transit line to Dover, I'd feel desperate to break the mood between us but wouldn't dare speak first. Eventually, she'd say, "Where did you even go last night?" I knew what she meant. What she wanted to say but couldn't: "You scared me."

We're more spread out now. Karina moved her family—husband, César, and two kids—down to Georgia from New Jersey eight years ago. The pain of separation, her choosing her family over ours, was so unbearable we strangled each other. I mean that literally. The day we fought each other, my mother received the brunt. No one was gunning for her, but she got caught in the melee. Something about it felt like payback.

Our way of loving crossed a line, even for us. I know what you're gonna say—violence is never love. I'm not calling it love; I'm saying it was pain. Balance askew, no one could hold the other. We were all in too much pain all at once, and our system of interdependence imploded. It was unsustainable. We stopped speaking for a year. I don't remember what brought us back together—which birthday or holiday it was—but one day, we talked as if it had never happened. Another thing swept under the rug.

———

Karina's new house was big enough to accommodate our entire family, so we began to travel south regularly. Once Karla had children, Karina would also travel north. With the family now spread out from central Georgia to the tri-state area, our main form of communication moved to smartphones and care packages from tía Kiki, as Karina is lovingly called, a nickname Karla's daughter, Bella, bestowed on her as a baby. As Karina settled into her life as a suburban housewife, battling a progressive autoimmune disease in isolation, she found she could be with us from a flick of her phone, sending gifts for every known occasion, sometimes to say what she found difficult to express in words. A fan of trinkets, T-shirts, and knickknacks, she keeps her shopping addiction within a reasonable price point, damage that appears less consequential than mine, and rarely buys for herself.

By the time the pandemic hit, we were already well-accustomed to family FaceTime. The calls are normally chaotic—lots of kids, barking dogs, and bad connections from Karina's country home in Georgia to urban New Jersey or New York. Our cousin overdosed at the start of quarantine, and I had called to discuss it when my nephew suddenly appeared at her side on screen.

"Addicted to drugs and alcohoooolllllll . . ." Joshua said as Karina shooed him away, shouting, "Be quiet, boy!" swapping her signature Valley Girl lilt for a newly acquired southern drawl as we lost connection.

I sometimes wonder if one of my nieces or nephews will become an addict. I feel guilty when the curiosity arises—when they ask questions and I think about how we are evading them. Karina doesn't want to discuss what she considers adult matters with the kids yet. Being a druggie is decidedly adult. During visits, I slip out to AA meetings before anyone wakes up and return with pastries from the local bakery as a cover. When they gossip about the neighbors' alcoholic antics—cops called the night before—I play along. I don't interrupt, explain, or defend. I don't tell them I'm like the neighbor. They're just too little to understand, my family says.

—

I knew my cousin about as well as I'd known my grandfather, but his death disturbed me more. There is nothing more unnatural than to bury the young. I wasn't much older and could not have saved him, but I wished I had tried. I think all addicts do when one of us dies.

Before recovery, nothing in my life was my own. There was nothing I didn't share with my partner, sisters, mother. Nowhere I could go anonymously—a place where I knew no one, and no one knew me until AA.

I told myself that my recovery was sacred and must be protected. This was true, especially in the beginning. I've always been susceptible to the opinions of others, desperate to be liked, to control the narrative, and I knew I was one harsh judgment away from a drink.

I took a vow of anonymity in AA, and that was the pass I needed to leave most people in the dark about my recovery. I didn't owe anyone an explanation. But there was another pledge called the Responsibility Statement, a promise to extend the hand of AA wherever and whenever it is sought. My cousin didn't ask me for help, but I knew we were both recovering. After I stopped drinking, my mother and I ran into my aunt. "Fíjate, Chili," my aunt began, as we all stood in an empty parking space and listened as she described a boy who'd chosen a destructive path despite the enormous privileges of American life. His rebellious decisions were inconceivable to the family. His mother and grandmother were distraught and incredulous.

No one in my family could name anything addiction-related outright—it was far too loaded—but I understood from her retelling that my cousin had survived an overdose. I felt an immediate solidarity with him and wanted to reach out. Still, I was afraid to admit to my extended family that I was an addict, too, especially after I'd listened to my aunt's opinions on the subject. I didn't have the energy to teach, challenge, or shock an elder that day. I stepped onto my side of the street, and it appeared clean to me.

———

Things had changed since I left Jersey. When I was in high school, parties were broken up by cops who responded to noise complaints. They discovered rowdy groups of us in the woods, a backyard, or a parentless home. But as the drug of choice followed a new trend toward downers, with an opioid epidemic ravaging the state, it was harder to bust kids. Local cops reported groups passed out in their parents' basements—no clink of glass rattling against their footsteps as they followed a trail of stolen bottles of alcohol, no peppery whiff of pot, no alerts or warning signs. "They just sat there . . . silent, hoodies up, and high," one cop I knew from high school said, "some dead for hours."

Coverage of the opioid epidemic is purposefully skewed to focus on the affliction of white people and wonder what could be driving good children to make poor choices. The addiction usually follows a sports injury, a careless script-happy doctor, or a fatal online purchase of Adderall to stay up late and study, not knowing that it's laced with fentanyl. These kids are billed as victims, murdered by a crooked medical system and evil drug dealers, gangbangers out to make a quick buck. They are not addicts or druggies. My cousin is a druggie, even to his own family; so am I.

Health departments will readily study the country's white population when faced with epidemics. Non-white people are rarely studied, and when they are, it's never for the same time span, effort, or expense. But they are always under the microscope of law enforcement. Around the time of my cousin's death, a local department in New Jersey had collected the stats on fatal overdoses and found that by 2021, the population it classified as "Blacks and Hispanics" accounted for nearly half of all suspected drug-related deaths in the state. The statement I found online by ODMA (Office of Drug Monitoring and Analysis, a division of the New Jersey State Police) acknowledged the role of racial injustice and systemic inequity in the increasing rates of substance use disorder in Black and brown communities—deaths rising 256 percent among Black people and 189 percent among non-Black Latinx people (described by the report as "Hispanics"), compared with a 38 percent increase among the state's white population. None of these facts seemed to matter to my family, nor did they seem aware of them.

What we all know is the story perpetuated by the very same law enforcement departments tasked to carry out the mandate against illegal (unless prescribed by a doctor) drug use, holding, and trade, which targets Black and brown people to fulfill its goal. According to the Drug Alliance Policy, 50 percent of all federal drug cases are brought against Latinx people, who make up only 19 percent of the US population. Even against the backdrop of such statistics, my cousin's death was still spoken of as an anomaly, a freak accident, a sin. It had nothing to do with us, certainly not a reflection of our values. The reality of the world never penetrates our performative bubble.

The last time I saw my cousin's grandmother, my aunt, at a family gathering, she couldn't keep track of who I was. Her eyes darted below a furrowed brow, up and down my entire person, the whites permanently yellowed as if the amber in her brown irises had been bleeding all her life. I smiled and leaned to kiss her, as is the custom expected of me. Her cheek trembled as it met mine to exchange a perfunctory peck, without a part of her lips. I understood; I inhaled the acrid evidence—the musk of needing a drink from the moment you wake up. I recognized it. My mother said she'd just pointed me out to her—she wasn't disoriented but spiteful—a ploy to snub us. I didn't argue with my mother, though I knew I'd been granted a vision of a future I had escaped. I felt lucky but also like a fraud.

They told me in AA that I talk about my family too much. If I couldn't "get honest," it meant I didn't want the help. And the statute of limitations on blaming my parents had long since expired. "Focus on yourself," they instructed.

In AA, when addiction is referred to as a family disease, people talk about how your actions have caused harm within your family. The disease of alcoholism, perhaps more than any other, infects the whole family, though the emphasis in recovery is on the individual taking personal responsibility—*find your part.* It's hard to ignore that the expression is one-sided; we discuss only the effects of the disorder on the family and deny the role of the family in alcoholism's manifestation.

I was raised with a strong skepticism of the outside world. My parents' boundaries were clear and tight, and the more we feared what was beyond their borders, the more we clung to their hips. A common dynamic for immigrant families, one the United States never failed to justify.

I revered my parents' stories. Who wouldn't? I could never have survived what they did. Thanks to them, it was different for me, but much was repeated. It wasn't easy to call out their roles in my self-destruction, but I heard a psychiatrist once tell Oprah on a podcast, "victims are violent."

Violent, oh my God, my parents will read that word and hate me. I don't know anything about violence, they'd say. Violence is earned pound for pound. Violence is being tossed in the air as a six-year-old boy, to be met not by the ground but by your father's boot, launching you across the room, like my grandfather had done to my father. When did they ever lay a hand on me?

But what did it mean to know that at various points throughout my life, my parents had wanted to die? They wanted it so badly they'd tried to do it themselves. They told me so. And for both, the thing that they claimed had stopped them was me. And that is not meant to be hurtful—what, am I crazy?—that is love. To live, to fight, to toil all for me—to take the brunt on their backs with me on their shoulders, I had to grab the nearest branch, the sturdiest one, and climb to the top of the American Dream. And from my suspended position, what is my margin of error? Is there any room for my own dreams?

Whatever you're thinking, I want you to know I love my family. We're all very close. People in AA told me I was codependent when I'd share about them. But I didn't give a fuck. Gringos never understood my family dynamic, nor could they relate. I once had friends who were sisters, close in age like me and mine, who hated each other—I couldn't think of anything sadder. On many Saturday nights, what saved me was knowing that no matter what and in whatever condition, I had to get my ass to Jersey for Sunday dinner. My commitment to my family, the way I love them and want to be with them, was the only hand that could pull me out from the undertow of a bender. A mental obsession stronger than what I was addicted to. A love stronger than my pain.

But I couldn't admit to them that I was drowning. I couldn't be honest about how much pain I was in, much less what I was doing to relieve it. I hid behind stories of glittery nightlife or self-deprecating jokes, but my mom wasn't buying it. She'd scoop me into her arms and rock me like a baby, though I was well into my thirties. "¿Qué pasa, mijita? You have everything going for you . . ." I'd break down, crying so hard I was unable to speak. "I don't know why you suffer so much."

The night I told them the truth changed everything. Coming clean and calling myself an addict changed our family irrevocably. My mother didn't cradle me. She gave me orders. I announced my day counts and job prospects and told her about the day I finally dumped my deadbeat boyfriend, but I shied away from talking about how the problem existed in our family. Much like in the rooms, it was impossible to name what was wrong without being accused of pointing fingers. "You didn't learn it from me," my parents would always interrupt if I dared to lift a corner on the carpet of our dysfunctional family history.

The fact is, I didn't grow up in a house with drinkers. I don't have an alcoholic mother or father, no bad example. Technically, I didn't learn it from them. But I didn't come up with this solution alone, either. I know I'm not the first.

———

What I feared could be misunderstood at home I often took to the rooms. After a qualification, hands would raise to admonish me, breaking the rules regarding what they call cross talk.

"Thanks for your share. But I just wanna say, that's not why we're alcoholic. I don't drink because I was molested . . . I don't drink because my mama beat me . . . or because she brought me here from Puerto Rico. I'm an alcoholic because I have an allergy," they say. "Because I have a disease."

In the book *In the Realm of Hungry Ghosts*, Dr. Gabor Maté elucidates the connection between childhood trauma and addiction. Anywhere from half to a third of drug use issues can be traced to adverse childhood events, largely perpetuated in marginalized communities due to systemic oppression. These are facts from an official report by the National Institutes of Health. But statistics don't gel with some folks' personal philosophies: taking sole responsibility seemed to be a point of pride for many addicts in the rooms and a sign of sobriety. Maté described how notions of personal responsibility prevalent in recovery lead to a lack of compassion for oneself. And if you can't extend compassion to yourself, how will you extend it to others? Self-flagellation enables our shame to hide behind a virtue signal. And I could not hide it and recover—I needed shame directly in my sights if I had any shot against it.

But I understood the allure of such black-and-white thinking. The simplicity of taking it all upon yourself, the power of grabbing hold of a *why* and owning it. The program seemed to only offer two options: you are sick or you are suffering, and because you are sick, you remain in fear of relapse. The cure was redemption, good ole USian folklore, a roadmap to repent and repair yourself for the betterment of the world— work, family, and relationships, ending with a pot of gold, or, as they say, *cash and prizes*. Clean yourself up and be of use.

These realizations came over time. I followed the steps outlined in the program. I gave my pain its proper context. I didn't see how family could be avoided. Making sense of myself through the branches of our family tree—separating me from them, just as I had disconnected the feeling from the craving—only made me love my family more.

To own the truth of your experience and still insist that all family members be given that same chance, to demand that everyone be heard, valued, and honored equally: that is radical love. I wasn't a saint for quitting drinking, but I was on a mission of service to our recovery as a family. I knew our family tree was rooted in the secrets that kept us sick. I started digging.

28

Price of Admission

For the first few years of sobriety, I was determined that nothing about my social life would change, mostly because I didn't have much of one if I wasn't partying. Nightlife, like addiction, is a commitment. If you don't keep it up, you're forgotten.

By the summer of 2017, Luis Fonsi and Daddy Yankee's "Despacito" remix featuring Justin Bieber had become the top song in the country. While it was already a hit pre-Bieber, Justin's auto-tuned Spanglish brought the song into the consciousness of many USians, qualifying a predominantly Spanish-language song as mainstream—not just digestible but desirable to the white American public.

I was at a popular lounge downtown when a DJ played the record. A white woman sitting at the neighboring banquette, partying with her daughter and friends, reached for my arm, bending my ear to her lips. "I love watching you dance," she spat. "Your people are so fun."

Interest in Latinx culture had been piqued, dubbed the Latin Wave— La ola latina—while the country stirred under the presidency of a man who had launched his campaign by calling all Mexicans drug smugglers and rapists, who made a policy of separating families at the border, and who enacted the harshest immigration policies in our country's history, a legacy in place to this day.

Some people were already cashing in. I felt like a sellout, working for a white woman at the helm of a start-up website targeting Latinx readers, but the paycheck was keeping me afloat. I rode that wave as long as I could. Inevitably fired after calling out racist practices, I dragged my ass to a meeting to lick my wounds.

There's no sign on the wall that says: don't discuss race, don't say gay, don't mention rape. But there are special interest groups—meetings created to safely discuss the parts of our humanity not considered by the founders, two privileged cisgender heterosexual white men. In their desire for legacy, they created traditions that installed and perpetuated a majority rule, which can and will police your voice if it threatens the comfort of that status quo. And that *is* up on the wall.

> Our Declaration of Unity: This we owe to AA's future; to place our common welfare first; to keep our fellowship united. For on AA unity depend our lives and the lives of those to come.

Simultaneously, the program had taught me that my authenticity guaranteed my sobriety, and a betrayal of that self-trust got me closer to a drink. So I spoke my truth. After the meeting that night, a fellow came to me. She placed one hand below mine and the other above, creating a sphere. I felt held and safe, what I so needed in that moment. Finally, she spoke. "Don't call yourself that, dear," she said.

"What?" I replied gently, ashamed of whatever awful name I'd called myself out loud.

"A woman of color, we don't say that here; there's no color. How you referred to *us* hurt me a lot . . . We are all one. There is no *us, them,* or *they,* we are all the same, no matter color. We're all children of God." She pointed to the framed plaque that listed the traditions. "Principles before personalities. You could cause a slip talking like that in here. Sounds like you need to study our traditions."

My heart pounded as a tirade of rebuttals raced through my mind and settled in my clenched stomach. "But I am," is all I managed to eke out. "I am a woman of color, and that's not an insult, nor is it a threat." Afterward, I thought for sure my non-white fellows would back me up, but still, I was shut down. "Principles over personalities," my friend said, repeating the refrain: "You know we're all sick and suffering."

End of conversation. I was beginning to understand.

———

Self-medicating for trauma is considered a key risk factor for addiction. According to the National Survey on Drug Use and Health, among Americans with mental health disorders, 9.2 million also have a substance abuse problem. Every single person in my family suffered from a variety of mental illnesses, all untreated. With costs high and access limited, Indigenous, Black, and people of color rarely make it to treatment, as they are far more likely to be criminalized for drug-related offenses. Eighty percent of people in federal prisons and almost 60 percent in state prisons for drug charges are Black or Latinx. Black people who suffer opioid overdose are half as likely as white people to receive any follow-up treatment. The few Black and "Hispanic" patients who make it into opioid treatment—which provides access to crucial medication proven to ward off cravings, preventing relapse and overdose by 50 percent—do not receive the quality or duration of care that white patients are afforded. These qualifications (access to medication, namely Buprenorphine, and duration of prescription) are the key indicators of success in clinical outcomes. And the discrepancies in treatment duration, quality, and access to these by race and ethnic group are only growing, a recent analysis by the *Journal of the American Medical Association: Psychiatry* found. For most, the only option is court-ordered NA or AA.

Racism and oppression are institutionally sanctioned forms of chronic stress with quantifiable biological effects on a targeted population. "Weathering," a term coined by Dr. Arline Geronimous, which I learned through the work of Dr. Nzinga Harrison, is the "cumulative degradation of health as a result of racism and oppression." All our painful life experiences cannot simply be forgiven, forgotten, or prayed away; our bodies have made something toxic with those feelings—something chemical, hormonal harm coursing through our bodies: cortisol.

As your blood pressure rises, the prefrontal cortex, the body's command center, is bamboozled. Meanwhile, the amygdala, revs like an engine with a full tank to crank out fear and anxiety, like exhaust from the tailpipe. It's as if our blood were a type of gasoline and stress is a match, inflaming the body. I was right about being radioactive.

For racialized people, this heightened perpetual state is directly linked to heart attacks, strokes, high blood pressure, diabetes, and substance use disorder—what killed my grandfather, what ails my mother, and what nearly killed me. While under chronic stress, you are physically not yourself, much like when you're drunk or high. You are hijacked. You're robbed of the opportunity to self-determine. The connection between the harm and the solution, the reason we reach for escape through drugs and alcohol time after time, couldn't be more straightforward or more easily understood.

In AA, all these truths were erased. It was as if the price of admission was one universal identity, the one that has perpetuated so much harm against me. Race-related trauma was labeled *terminal uniqueness* and dismissed as a false projection of my self-centered ego. The parlance of AA, an eighty-year-old organization, was the greatest weapon of protection: colloquialisms used to deny the fact of racism with the sanctimony of twelve-step esoterica. AA was about personal responsibility; collective (ir)responsibility was written many years ago, like the Constitution. "It's your ego that wants to blame parents, systems, patriarchy," I was told. "Let's stick to alcohol."

AA can prove an insidious dogma and a dangerous place for those who are vulnerable. As I came into a profound awareness of what was happening to me, the program began to stifle my progress and stand in opposition to it. According to Dr. Harrison, the medical effects of racism are two-pronged: (neuro)biological and psychological. The chronic emotional stress of knowing you need the systems to survive, while also knowing you are not safe in them, is a feature of programming installed from the time of slavery and colonization. The result is hopelessness and anger, triggering the cortisol drip once again. The cycle blocks us from the state of rest required to heal, and not all people in AA are equally at risk.

"All of those social, cultural, political inputs are compounding the psychological injury that comes from racism and oppression," Dr. Harrison explained. "At the same time, every single day, our experiences are biologically putting us at risk. The psycho-social-cultural environment is compounding that risk. And that's what gives you the outcomes that we have today." The first step toward a solution, in Dr. Harrison's assessment, happens to be the first of the twelve steps: recognize and admit you have a problem. "And so the way you do that systematically is with data. If you are not looking at that data cut by race, ethnicity, socioeconomic status, also gender identity, and sexual orientation . . . you're part of the problem. Because what you're doing is refusing to open your eyes, because if you don't see the disparity, you can't work on the disparity."

When we're beyond survival mode, that's when the most profound healing can take place. Which begs the question of my fellows: Who is entitled to heal? For the vulnerable, it's imperative to understand how a substance operates within your body, just as you must understand what part of the system is at work in your life. By naming the role of racism in the dysregulation of the nervous system and identifying how it causes you to turn to substances as a form of self-medication, you realize the false shame of moral failure. And that can inspire you to ask, *Do you want anything controlling you?* My answer was no.

29

The AA MFA

When you keep your meetings local, your chances for consistency increase. This is why you're encouraged to find and commit to a homegroup. Keeps you accountable. I crawled into AA while crashing at my ex's place in Tribeca, one of the city's most affluent and homogeneously white neighborhoods. By the time I dried out enough to realize the same damage that landed me here was also happening to me here, I was attached.

"Sounds like the flavor left the gum," an elder member said, citing a funny AAism intended to diagnose the syndrome of fatigue that plagues steppers occasionally. I loved her way of putting things, true and funny and simple enough to swallow whole, but this feeling was more than gum losing its flavor. It was more than the monotony of recovery, more than a darkened pink cloud. As I got better, I began to see that the same harm from school, jobs, and relationships was also here in the program that had saved my life, perpetuated by the people who told me they would *love me until I could love myself.* I would not be able to remain silent and stay sober. But I didn't feel prepared to face exile for speaking the truth: To whom would I turn?

What I love most about AA is the freedom of expression—I could say whatever the fuck I wanted when I had the floor. I like to joke that I got the AA MFA because it was in the rooms where I found my voice. In sharing what could compromise my sobriety each day, I saw patterns and traced them back to the source, so I could choose a little bit of liberty again and again. If I didn't want to be censored, I couldn't imagine others would either. We came to be shocked and unburdened—to peacock and perform—sharing war stories and laughter. Acceptance and compassion.

Rubbernecking reveals us as morbid voyeurs. In the wake of a tragic accident, we, the unharmed, press the pedal of our brakes, slow our cars to take stock of the damage, and search for blood, limbs, and wreckage in the broken glass. Eventually, we look through the rearview mirror, one last glimpse of the scene we've left in our dust—and reassure ourselves that we're okay, that it's not us in the body flung from the car. And we drive away.

A drunk-a-log is the addict rubbernecking. We comb through the shrapnel, the wreckage of our past safely in hindsight. We say it out loud to make it real, to be comforted by the laughter, to feel emboldened by the gasps, for a taste of what it was like. Just to remind yourself you're still in there, you'd just rather not go back.

To have a shot in hell at that high—the feeling of profound identification, the shameless recollection of what used to haunt us, the collective relief that we made it out—there can be no censorship. It's practically the last high we've got. Come as you are—just leave it at the door.

Privilege, they said, didn't exist in the rooms. We were all a group of drunks. But we'd each lived lives informed by our privilege or lack thereof, and those lives ultimately brought us into recovery. We all brought this baggage with us—but we weren't equally entitled to unpack it. Interrogating privilege edged us *closer to a drink*, they said. Passivity, forgiveness—that was freedom. We were told that acceptance was the answer to all our problems. More than that, if you were injured in the rooms, well, that was to be expected; we were all shopping in the dented can aisle. The rooms are full of the sick and suffering. For some, depending on their identity and position within the AA community, racism and misogyny could be written off as quirks, aspects of their characters you shouldn't let hurt you. In fact, the truly sober pray for those who hurt them—and place the principles of the organization before their personalities. In the alternate reality of Alcoholics Anonymous, your personality meant the pesky, inconvenient truths of your personhood. Being somebody in a program of anonymity was a privilege not afforded to people like me.

But I could write it out instead so it doesn't become a resentment. Pray for God to relieve me and keep coming back.

On the evening of June 12, 2020, an employee called 911 to report a man blocking the drive-through line at a Wendy's restaurant in southwest Atlanta. It appeared he was passed out in his car, most likely drunk. "Is he Black?" the dispatcher asked. "Yeah," the employee answered. At approximately 10:30 p.m., Officer Devin Brosnan responded to the call and found twenty-seven-year-old Rayshard Brooks asleep in his car. Brosnan awoke Brooks, who peacefully followed the officer's orders to move his vehicle to a parking space. After a few minutes of routine questioning, with full cooperation from Brooks, Brosnan called for backup. Officer Garrett Rolfe arrived within minutes and administered a field sobriety test. Brooks asked if he could walk home, where his family, especially his daughter, whose birthday they had just celebrated, was waiting for him. The officers refused and instead demanded he take a Breathalyzer test. Armed with the results, Rolfe attempted to handcuff Brooks. He resisted; they struggled. When Brooks ran in the opposite direction of the cops, Rolfe fired three shots from a distance of eighteen feet, three inches, killing Brooks.

Was Brooks simply exhausted, under excessive stress, much like the rest of us? Or was he suffering from a dependency? As an addict myself, I wondered: Were these the consequences that often befall Indigenous, Black, and people of color who struggle with addiction, now on grim display? I thought about all the stories of my white fellows who'd been pulled over while high as a kite, but who'd lived. Would this have happened if Brooks had been white?

I had a friend in my homegroup. Tall, blond, in his late twenties, he had come in on the suggestion of a posh rehab facility nearby, and despite his early-pattern balding, he was aglow, baby fresh. His story, earnest and brimming with gratitude, won him friendship and favoritism. He quickly became chair of a well-attended Saturday meeting and was chosen as one of three speakers for our annual celebration, a coveted position given to the most inspiring fellows. He worked at a well-known financial firm on Wall Street, welcomed there by a family friend after attending what people in my hometown referred to as a lesser Ivy.

Long nights and hard work in a volatile market led to even harder partying, a case of social anxiety becoming more severe—alcohol and cocaine were the antidote at first. When his use began to scare him, he called a doctor, who prescribed Xanax and Klonopin for anxiety, Adderall for work, and Ambien for sleep. He started disappearing—for days, weeks—into benders; work would send word out for him. They would contact his girlfriend, his doorman. One day, he was summoned into his boss's office, sure he would be fired. Instead, his boss asked him what was going on and how he could help. My friend wept. He confessed everything to his superior, who hugged him and reassured him it would be okay—that he would receive the best help and support available. When he was well, he would return to his job, his home, and his family—welcomed with open arms. And that's what happened.

Back home, when people called me a "dirty Mexican," I knew there was no point in correcting them. "Honduras, is that in Central America or South?" my teachers would ask me in front of the class—the makeup of my identity, father from Ecuador, mother from Honduras, held no relevance in the white suburbs where I grew up. And when you are erased, you are forgotten; when you are forgotten, you are alone; and when are you are alone, you are vulnerable.

Decades later, when Donald Trump rode his golden escalator down the center of his rusting tower in Midtown Manhattan to announce his candidacy by echoing the words of my childhood bullies, an alarm sounded in a pitch I'd tuned out the day I left Mendham. *No place was safe.*

The first ninety days sober is *everything* in the rooms. Studies show this is the approximate amount of time it takes the brain to reset from the initial influence of a drug. It's a major milestone that is enthusiastically celebrated. You get your chip; you get to say a few words in front of the group. It was one of the proudest days of my life. The idea is you cleanse the system and form a new habit. The first thirty days breaks the old pattern, the following thirty forms a new one, and the last thirty reinforces it. I loved the feeling of opening my day-counting app to see the rising hours, days, and months. At least my numbers could get high.

When I realized my ninety-day anniversary coincided with Thanksgiving and I'd be in Georgia with family, I was nervous. Georgia was a red state. On previous trips south, I'd spotted Confederate flags billowing off trucks I passed while on a grocery run, or hanging off the porch of a neighbor's house. I didn't know what to expect from the local AA, but I needed all the help I could get to reach those ninety days. My homegroup told me to find a meeting there and not let the day go by without acknowledging it. The home celebration would be waiting for me when I got back.

AA meetings in Georgia were different from those in New York City, but I got something out of each. It was a bit awkward when we closed with the Lord's Prayer, as opposed to the Serenity Prayer I was used to. Most of the fellows in Georgia got a kick out of me not knowing the words; some were more horrified. But I didn't take that personally. Over the week, although I was the only non-white person and one of few women, I got comfortable. I could recite almost the entire Lord's Prayer by my last day.

Every morning during announcements, the chair reminded everyone about the upcoming anniversary meeting, a joint celebration for all fellows in the area. My new friends hyped it up and encouraged me to come and collect a chip to bring back home.

It was dark out when I left my family watching a movie in the playroom, slipped out the garage, and got into my sister's minivan. I turned the heat and Rihanna's *ANTI* album up so high it blew the roof off that mommy mobile as I wove through roads that reminded me of the drive to high school as a teenager. My throat was raw from screaming the words to "Higher" on repeat by the time I arrived at the remote minimall complex where the meeting took place. The large hall was packed with more than a hundred men and women, all white, and raucous, a stark change from my daily experience.

I sat in the corner with my back to the wall, as I was once taught in a self-defense class, and clocked dozens of red MAGA hats. "God bless Trump!" celebrants screamed as they collected their anniversary chips to uproarious applause. My friend, a divorcée coping with the loneliness of a newly empty nest by painting the gorgeous mountainscape of the nearby Sawnee range instead of taking quarts of box wine medicinally each night, squeezed my hand as I turned to her to mouth the words, "I've gotta go." I wasn't about to announce myself in this amped crowd or celebrate my decision to stay alive with a room of people whose politics wanted me dead.

She nodded and walked me out to my sister's car, apologizing for the polarizing scene, nervously flipping her feathered blond bangs, the crisp synthetic scent of Aqua Net reminding me of alcohol.

When I got back to my sister's house, everything was dark and quiet. The plates had been cleared from the formal dining table, but the half-empty bottle of red wine was left behind—not a thought in any of my family members' minds, the object of my obsession. How the fuck did five grown adults not finish that one bottle? I fumed. Why am I the only one who would have downed it before the appetizer?

This house was full of the people I love most and who love me. Despite their support, I felt distant from them in the initial days of my new life. Now, the place I'd found that understood the one thing they could not wasn't what I thought it was. I wanted to drink. Badly. But I didn't.

Politics had made its way into my recovery at home, too. Back in New York City, I was tight with a few women my age who had all come in around the same time. We call them "running buddies" in the rooms, and the bond formed from the experience of counting days together is profound. We were in constant contact via a group chat called Sober Sisters—shooting daily spiritual affirmations back and forth, making brunch or dinner plans a few times a week, aligning our schedules to attend the same meetings, and, of course, grabbing coffee after.

The night Trump issued a Muslim ban, an executive order restricting US entry by people from Iran, Iraq, Libya, Somalia, Sudan, Syria, and Yemen, everything changed between us. Activists responded immediately across the city, rallying protesters to the local airports. I was exhausted by the chronic stress of daily instigation and the physical strain of demonstration all night. The next day, one of my Sober Sisters, herself on a visa from the United Kingdom, texted the group: "IMMIGRANTS MUST ADAPT!" It was a cut-and-paste right-wing nationalist hate speech rant. My hands trembled as I went off in the chat. The sender defended her position; one remained silent; and the other tried to mediate. "Has anyone read *The Big Book*?" the mediator asked, before reciting sanctimonious scripture about forgiveness directed toward me. Her message was that our friend was confused, and I must, in my sobriety, turn the other cheek. Soon after, a meeting was called to barter peace between us, facilitating the reconciliation of our once-fabulous foursome, but it didn't stick. I stopped going to meetings where I knew I'd run into the sender.

It took me years to shift the focus of my interrogation from the people to the system that was enabling them. The system had saved my life, too precious for me to question, and I was afraid to lose it. Besides, who was I to challenge it?

That is the question recovery demands that you answer. *Who the fuck are you?* In order to arrive at a conclusion, I had to separate the self from the system, just as I had separated the feeling from the craving at the start. I began to question everything—the book, the steps, the traditions—a colonial indoctrination so familiar, I complied. Just like they told me to as a little girl, just like they expected me to on the job, in the classroom, or at a meeting.

This time, just like booze, it stopped working.

30

It Works If You Work It

I've always been quick to obey orders. I'd been a follower among friends, a deferential girlfriend, an obedient child. I don't like being told what to do, but I want to be liked. So, when a teen—young enough to be my daughter—told me to get down on the ground, I didn't hesitate. After all, this was a rally; I was there to be of service.

The volunteer corralling a group of hundreds in front of the US Federal Courthouse at Foley Square in lower Manhattan was dressed in all black and puffed a tough exterior, though she hung her weight on the straps of her backpack, nervously gripping them until her hands appeared bloodless. When she dropped the enormous pack to demonstrate what she wanted us to do, the echo of her stainless-steel canteen against the pavement grabbed our attention more than her commands. The heavily armed police presence loomed in our nervous systems.

"Get on the ground. Kneel or lie down, preferably lie down!"

Of course, wanting to be a model protester, I took the preferable option.

As I lay my body gently down, it occurred to me I'd never considered what this would feel like. There was no way to make the position more bearable—to keep my face from kissing the ground, imprinting the debris of millions onto my cheek. I tried to keep my head off the ground, but in seconds, it felt leadened. My neck ached. I placed my palms on the pavement to rest my head against my hands, but nothing took away the pain. A paralyzing performance I knew I could interrupt. I could get up, and I would.

The coronavirus pandemic halted the world in a matter of weeks. As headlines warned of its dangers, the virus was dubbed the *great equalizer*, able to kill without distinction of race, class, or gender. People say the same about addiction.

Seventy-two hours after the official closure of all bars and restaurants, New York's alcohol delivery services surged by more than 450 percent—a statistic so staggering it certainly influenced the decision to deem liquor stores "essential businesses" that were allowed to remain open, as Governor Andrew Cuomo passed an executive order requiring 100 percent of the nonessential workforce to stay home, drowning our destabilized metropolis in a powerful depressant.

While the best way to prevent the spread of the novel coronavirus was social distancing, togetherness is essential to recovery. We all feared the worst when AA's central office closed, shutting down over five thousand meetings in the New York City area. "It's a tremendous difference," Reagan Reed, executive director of the New York Intergroup Association of Alcoholics Anonymous and a member of AA, told the *New Yorker Radio Hour*. "The way that our fellowship works is that we sit in a room together and we talk to one another face-to-face. The meetings are the cornerstone and foundation of Alcoholics Anonymous, so removing them is going to have a really big impact on people's ability to remain sober."

Effectively hobbled by necessary procedures, addiction treatment facilities and programs responded rapidly, shuttering their doors and setting up online. Adapting is a skill familiar to anyone in recovery, though an unnatural and global event like this felt unprecedented to everyone. Grateful for a solution, fellows rallied; we were there for each other with renewed fervor, transported via Zoom link to a place where we could be together. We stared into a grid of distant faces. The energy of a room could not be replicated through a screen, but we tried. Nodding our heads vigorously, we sent emoji reactions—red hearts and clapping yellow hands—and responses in the chat. My favorite AA tradition had always been holding hands at the close of the meeting and reciting the Serenity Prayer in harmony. I'd never heard it out of unison, even in groups of hundreds. On Zoom, it was always a hot mess.

No topic was off-limits at these pandemic meetings. We held space for financial fears, offered sympathy to the immunocompromised, and grieved with those who had lost people, places, and things, all over again. Whether you missed the sound of your choir singing live at church— the vibration lifting your spirit—or the relief of a full, deep breath after tolerating the heat from the sauna of your luxury gym, or the peace and quiet after escaping your children at the office, you said it out loud, however severe or trivial. Nothing was censored. And we weren't apolitical. Fellows spoke of the mask mandate, said they couldn't breathe, said that to be forced to wear a mask violated their rights.

My mother's friends began to die. Many were essential workers who lived in a tight-knit Central American community in Jersey and were exposed to the virus without access to care. One drank himself to death alone in a room he rented in a house full of people. They discovered his body days later. My mother still cannot delete his voicemail messages. Her mental health began to slip. I couldn't understand—she wasn't new to catastrophe. "You've been through so much, Mom. How could this be the scariest thing that's ever happened?" I asked her. How could wiping down bottles of Dawn dish soap with Clorox wipes from the safety of my sister's kitchen be worse than all she'd survived?

"Jessy, all that time I was in Honduras . . . I always imagined there was a safe place I could go. That's what they said, it was different here.

That idea, that fantasy, kept me alive. Your sister alive. But now, this is everywhere; there's no place to go that is safe. And Bella . . . she's so little, so innocent, she doesn't deserve that."

I remember recording that conversation. I knew it was something I'd always want to remember. The day and all that it took to unmask America to my mother.

———

Cocaine is a stimulant derived from the coca plant—thick green leaves that Indigenous peoples of the Andes region masticate to generate heat in the body. Anthropologists suggest Andean people adopted this practice to acclimate to life at high altitude. Like most drugs, its origins can be traced back millennia to a practical or spiritual purpose indicative of a people in harmony with the earth.

If you search, Google's top results will tell you that 98 percent of cocaine is produced in Colombia, Peru, and Bolivia. The coca plant requires heavy rainfall and flourishes best in a semitropical climate found on the eastern slope of the continent from Bolivia all the way up to central Ecuador, where my father is from. When I read this, I could hear my mother-in-law say *Ojo, eh*.

As I dug in a little further, a familiar story appeared: The intoxicant cocaine was isolated from the plant in the mid-1800s by German chemists. Doctors used it as an anesthetic and soon found ingesting it felt pretty far out, too. See: Sigmund Freud. Obviously, pharmaceutical companies bugged out, their eyes bulging in cartoonish dollar signs, and an enormous and unregulated production scheme took off, with Peru as the world's dominant supplier. This was around the time the United States (tired of Europe taking a piece of the action) saw fit to cut Europe out of the colonizing deal and take complete control of the region. It cast itself as the "protector of the Western Hemisphere" and came to an agreement with colonizer daddy Europe. They called it the Monroe Doctrine, named such because Monroe was the president, and they weren't in the business of being creative. That was in 1823. The arrangement was the US would fuck up this side of the hemisphere without meddling or interference and would stay out of Europe and its colonies worldwide. High five. By the turn of the twentieth century, coke was everywhere—even in your favorite soft drink. The Dutch and the Japanese had their own enterprises going strong, harvesting coca in the colonial East Indies and Taiwan, respectively.

Cocaine use, both medicinal and recreational, was getting out of control, and the drug's reputation as a miracle drug quickly transformed into a social menace. After scapegoating Black people, the government went full bore on prohibition. The Harrison Narcotics Act was passed in 1914, coke was outlawed, and the United States bullied the rest of the world to follow its lead (so much for sticking to your side). The Dutch were more amenable than the Japanese, but after the Second World War ended in 1945, US hegemony was cemented, and coca cultivation gained one exclusive route and a ripe and animating crusade against our neighbors to the south. Funny, as the United States righteously fought against the drug trade invading the southern border, it became the number one customer.

As German scientists extracted the natural stimulant from the veins of coca leaves to manufacture a synthetic drug, the American government split the narcotic into two derivatives with nothing more than a line. A smokable form of cocaine called crack was the star of President Bush's show, which I watched from the floor of my living room with my family in 1989. "One of the most deadly and addictive illegal drugs," Bush said, as my mind flashed to the image of my uncle and his wife smoking in bed.

In all the years I used cocaine, I never once thought of my uncle, though the only difference in our behavior was that between powder and smoke. It was during this time in the '80s that the authors of the Drug-Free America campaign convinced me that there was a difference, engineering a new era of enslavement through incarceration by imposing a mandatory minimum sentence for five grams of crack cocaine, while powder cocaine possession would have to reach at least five hundred grams (a hundred-to-one ratio) to even qualify for equal sentencing.

In the language of the world that introduced me to drugs, they asked, "Do you party?" No one in my family would refer to what my uncle was doing as a party. What the president described on television didn't sound like a party, and from what I observed as a child, it didn't look like a party to me either. But it was always the same party favor.

"We have to hold every drug user accountable because if there were no drug users, there would be no appetite for drugs, there'd be no market for them," Joe Biden declared following Bush's speech. "Let's take a look at what the real problem is. It's not just how many people are using drugs; as the president said, the number of people using drugs, cocaine in particular, is down in our country. That's true, but the violence associated with drugs is spewing out all over America."

Clearly, what mattered was who you were, what you used and where, who you used it with, and where you got it. The war on drugs enabled the government to accumulate the largest population of prisoners on earth in short order by spinning a tale of addiction as moral failure. Because what was more immoral than committing a crime?

Arguably, as white people became more visible as the face of drug addiction—thanks in part to the pharmaceutical industry's pushing of "safe" prescription narcotics—many people changed their tune. Even Joe Biden, who had once condemned all drug users, revised his feelings when his son was affected. "My son, like a lot of people, like a lot of people you know at home, had a drug problem," he said after Donald Trump's vulgar attempts to shame Hunter Biden during a debate in the 2020 election cycle. "He's overtaken it, he's fixed it, he's worked on it, and I'm proud of him."

The war on drugs Biden championed was not waged against drugs; it was a war on people, specific people. It has no interest or efficacy in addiction rehabilitation. What it does most effectively is spin the US narrative of good versus evil. Right and wrong. White and other. Poor and privileged.

Media and political pundits are hard at work now whipping up another drug epidemic, convincing US citizens that migrant children, mothers, and families are smuggling fentanyl across the border, en route to poison white teenagers in the suburbs, when the only thing they seek is their right to asylum. According to a recent NPR/Ipsos poll, the rhetoric is working. Most Americans believe it—even though the facts indubitably contradict it.

As the number of preventable deaths from drug overdose reaches an all-time high in the United States, corrupt politicians capitalize on tropes, race-baiting and fearmongering the user as depraved and drugs as toxic, knowing well it is the rhetoric that is toxic. It is prohibition that costs lives.

Meanwhile, solutions languish on the vine. Rather than respond with proven healthcare-based methods to treat substance use disorder, remedies are withheld from communities in need. Regulation reform could easily make drugs safe for everyone to use. Decriminalizing use would destigmatize a form of pain management that has existed throughout human history, encouraging those who seek help to do so without fear of dangerous and punitive consequences or ostracism. The drugs don't work, but how we legislate makes it worse.

Joe Biden told the world he was proud of his son and hailed his recovery as a victory. As I listened to him say those words, I sank beneath the weight of history, one that could not bear down on parent and child more differently. How could my father combat decades of messaging that convinced him we can only be derelicts, drug dealers, and addicts? The deviant image Biden conjured up in years past at the height of the war on drugs did not apply to his son, though it would always incriminate me and my community. In many ways, it still does.

I would never hear my father make the same pronouncement about me that Joe made about Hunter. Though I strived all my life to achieve an excellence that could supersede my humanity, therefore proving it, I was in a world that did not allow me to simply exist as a daughter to a father.

After Biden ascended to the presidency, he addressed the nation from Philadelphia. "America is an idea," he said, "the most powerful idea in the history of the world." He romanticized what he called an idea, invented to privilege communities like his while oppressing mine. I didn't want what Joe and Hunter have, as the edict goes in AA. I wanted to imagine who my father and I could be when we stopped believing in this idea. I had to let go of what a white father and a white son could have in this society and make from what remained something for us.

I had wanted us to build something together for as long as I could remember; it seemed like he was distant from the start. I was young when my parents confessed to me that my father missed the moment of my birth. My father blamed the nuns who he said kept him out of the room. My mother said he went to take a leak and missed the whole thing. No matter the reason, no one is to blame. And while I hated the fact it didn't come as a surprise, it felt like something I'd always known.

Can a father's love be a casualty of war? What about his pride? I worried this was true. Barriers had kept me from my father long before I ever touched a drug. But the drugs were like an electric fence. My sobriety wasn't going to prove racist stereotypes were untrue or that they didn't apply to me. There was no point in fixating on narrow falsehoods. I had to do something else. I decided to bring him into my recovery—stop assuming he couldn't handle it. I had to give him a chance to show up.

On the day of my sixth anniversary, my father came to town. Karla had bought a house near the one where we grew up, and we all gathered to help with the move. For weeks I tried to convince myself it was no big deal, no need to mention it. We would all be busy anyway.

I entered the house for the first time through the side door, the entrance that led straight to the kitchen. It reminded me of our home in Mendham. Across the hall, I could see my father as he stood at the window of the playroom, dutifully repainting the sill, an image I'd seen so many times as a little girl. Acts of service have always been the way my father expressed his love for us. It was my love language, too.

The garage alarm beeped as I opened the door, alerting the dog and triggering the most beautiful chaos. "Jessy!" my niece screamed over Jazzy's barking as they sprinted toward me and into my arms. "Do you like my new house?" she asked, beaming.

"I *love* your new house," I told her.

My father smiled, bent down to place the brush he held wet with paint in the tray on the floor, stood still, and waited for me to walk over. Each time I saw my father he felt smaller in my arms. *It's wrong to burden him*, I thought.

After a hug, he quickly returned to his project, and with his back to me he asked, "¿Cómo estás, Conchito?" A few years ago, when I was newly sober, my father started calling me "Conchito." He claims it was always my nickname, but no one in the family remembers this but him. "Mi conchito de vino," meant I was the last-born child, the youngest, *his final sip of wine.* I loved the irony of the expression, the way it winked at his humor, a hint of solidarity—we had both had to give up something.

I answered his question honestly. I told him how six years ago on this day I stopped sipping once and for all. We laughed. "Está bien, mija," he said, "eso me hace feliz." I asked if we could add this date to the family calendar, along with our birthdays, Mother's and Father's Day. If we could not just acknowledge it but celebrate it, that would mean a lot to me.

"OK, mija, lo hago," he said wiping my tears. "No tienes que tener pena."

He was right. There was no reason for me to be ashamed.

31

Off the Ropes

CNN News ran twenty-four seven as we doomscrolled on our phones. Popular influencers fled to their second homes, wealthy celebrities boasted negative test results online and sang songs out of key. Black markets boomed—caches of masks, toilet paper, and hand sanitizer stockpiled in suburban garages like bodies, all for profit.

Strict guidelines were broadcast daily, with New York as the epicenter. Our population accounted for half the cases in the United States. Rules for sheltering in place depended on who you were and where you lived. During our daily walks, police could be seen congenially distributing masks to white parkgoers in Hudson River Park near Tribeca. Then we'd catch a video online of a violent escalation in Bed-Stuy—a couple of folks who sat chatting on their stoop soon assaulted and arrested—as social distancing violations were enforced at the discretion of the police. And then, a mortar round of murder flooded American media.

Confined to our homes, glued to our screens, there was no way to miss the news or to deny an uprising that captured the world's attention.

Not without actively turning away, willfully shutting it down. From room to room, glaring disparities were brought to light. It was no longer plausibly deniable that people were not treated equally; we were neither suffering nor susceptible in the same way. But no one said a word on the news or in the AA meetings I went to. How were they so inured to police brutality? Yet they could be triggered by the so-called "trauma" of protests they referred to as "riots," the destruction of property, a line that should not be crossed, echoing police. Language from the war on drugs playbook.

While at first I felt rescued by our community, soon I was being pushed to the brink. I didn't want a drink or a drug; I wanted a riot. Though to fight at AA put me at risk, silence was a relapse. Moving into these real and fraught waters had always risked surveillance. I chalked up people's willingness to correct me to my age or time in the rooms, and if I referenced my positionality as a woman of color, I was told not to get stuck in that muck, in those ideas, those limiting beliefs—my fears and paranoia were but projections of my "self-centered ego." Outside issues were to remain out of the group to preserve and uphold the creators' institutionalized ideas. Who was I to use the program as I needed when to do so "endangered" so many? No one considered that to not speak, or to try to be silenced, endangered me, too.

The most precious privilege of being white is you are never forced to consider what your existence in a community means to the other people around you. I didn't expect my fellows to acknowledge their privilege, but I would no longer allow it to be weaponized against me. Nor would I listen to moralizing judgment and false assertions of victimhood without a rebuttal. I wanted an equal platform without the threat of harassment, censorship, or policing. Fellows denied I'd been shouldered into the margins; no one told me what to say or not to say. But they never failed to throw their weight around or let me know when I was outside program lines, exposing another enduring tradition of AA: white supremacy.

How could I debate them when the rules were right there up on the wall? I couldn't plead ignorance when the bylaws are clearly stated at the convening of each meeting. What is an appropriate response when the traditions can be copied and pasted from AA.org and directly messaged to me via Zoom chat? "AA does not align nor does it wish to engage in political . . ."

Who was this denial benefiting? Who was it hurting? Did it help any of us to stay sober, if you can even be sober at this level of denial? It felt completely dishonest not to talk about how racialized trauma affected our recovery. *Don't say BLM.* I was told elders of Black AA suffered far worse and did not complain. Who was I to whine?

———

The targeted attack on Black life was not new. But within the cauldron of an international pandemic and subsequent economic depression, the murders of Ahmaud Arbery, Breonna Taylor, Nina Pop, George Floyd, and Tony McDade caused long-standing tension to boil over.

The symbolic gesture I participated in at that rally lasted nine minutes—the time it took Officer Derek Chauvin to kill George Floyd with his knee. Nine minutes is an eternity. I allowed myself to descend fully into the experiential act of empathy. I was overcome. We shouted their names: AHMAUD, BREONNA, GEORGE, NINA, TONY, TRAVIS, ERIC, DAVID, TAMIR, DARIUS, TRAYVON, AIYANA, CHRISTOPHER, CAMERON, MIKE, AMIR, and on and on. With my head facing east, I could make out an inscription on the frieze of the neoclassical courthouse: "The true administration of justice is the firmest pillar of a good government." Our bodies strewn in protest below were proof of its lie.

We opened our eyes to a SWAT team surrounding the perimeter of the courthouse. They weren't there when we began. The organizers, a group of young Black people, aware of the change, began directing the crowd north up Centre Street. Freddy and I followed the march hand in hand and split off at Spring Street, heading west, toward home. I collapsed in bed. Freddy held me. But I couldn't stop trembling.

I'd gotten up to make us dinner when my friend texted the login for a meeting at our homegroup and asked me to show face. Two of only a handful of Black and brown members, we made a point to support each other unconditionally. I told him I'd be there and promised myself I was just going to listen.

I knew what I could expect from that room, but I held out hope. For nearly an hour I listened to the lament of senseless property damage devaluing their neighborhoods, their fear of violent so-called rioters blocking safe passage to the gym, the noise of the movement robbing their sleep—"Why can't they just follow the rules? I follow the rules," one young woman complained. Not one acknowledged the violence outside our doors, the swell of revolution poised to meet it. No one. Each fellow's myopic share seized the last sip of air in the room.

I embraced the right to protest, one protected by the First Amendment, as an exercise in the unapologetic expression and preservation of self, magnified through mass mobilization. It is recovery in action. Through public, coordinated, and lawful marches that spread worldwide, the Black liberation movement demonstrated the potential for great structural reform. The uprising within disenfranchised communities resonated further than ever, inspiring the world to believe in liberation from all oppressive inventions of hierarchy—race, gender, and class. No organization or institution was exempt from self-examination, least of all AA.

The need to be seen and heard is intrinsically human, as essential as food, water, and air. It is crucial to recovery. The program designed protocols to address these needs. One is the burning desire: a pause reserved toward the close of the meeting to ensure all who feel they need to speak have had the opportunity. It is extended to anyone who feels their silence could lead them to a drink or drug, to hurt themselves or others, so we dedicate time to hand it to the group, and we promise to hold it.

Despite being tucked into my reading chair, I could not steady my body's tremor. My hand quivered as I reached toward the keyboard, barely able to click the raise-hand function. I knew when I spoke that night, when I took the burning desire, it would be the last time I ever attended a meeting at my homegroup. Months shy of my anniversary, I would lose the people who had helped me get sober over the past four years, the same people who also perpetuated the culture operating as a gateway to my addiction.

I heard the words of my therapist: "Don't get in the ring"—wise caution in boundary work—but I'd been put in the ring. This was the fucking ring. And it was my recovery that had enabled me to change my lifelong course from flight to fight. Sobriety can be clinically measured by a patient's ability to align their actions with their belief system. We build integrity. Brick by brick. Self-rejection and conformity threatened my life. I couldn't stay and recover. I could not be voiceless and love myself.

———

The next morning, my stomach lurched beneath my ribs. Cramps sent sharp darts of pain up my spine. Tension pressed down above my eyebrows, fire sizzled behind my dry eyes, a streak of film crusted down my temple. I'd been crying in my sleep. For a minute, I wondered if I'd slipped a drink last night. I felt hungover. All it took was one night, a few hours, for me to question my strength. But recovery isn't linear; it's a practice. I was about to learn it couldn't be climbed like steps. It was a circle that flowed in a cycle, just like the seasons, just like life.

"What do you think it means that I just want to give up?" I asked Freddy.

"It means you're a human being," he replied.

A statement satisfying enough to feel like the momentary fix I craved, when I turned my head. Behind the wall of glass belonging to our favorite restaurant, one we weren't sure would make it through the shelter-in-place order, sat rows of top-shelf tequila bottles below the neon pink script of a fluorescent sign beckoning passersby. Beckoning me. I'd come for its specialty, cornmeal pancakes, a brunch item available only on weekends. I hoped they would cure my emotional hangover. But my comfort food was now rendered by the fermentation of my drama into cold Frisbees that no amount of syrup could possibly salvage.

In the glass, I saw the reflection of a man seated at the table behind us. Blue eyes stared back from below the brim of his baseball cap, cheeks flushed; he held a phone to his ear, answering for his whereabouts to the person on the other end. "No, I just came around the corner . . ." he said. "Needed the guacamole." He sat alone, though the table appeared to hold drinks for a party of three. Not a crumb of food. He hung up hurriedly, chugged the drinks, and asked for the check.

"There's no way two white guys invented this shit," Freddy said, validating my feelings of betrayal by and disappointment in the program upon which I'd become dependent. It felt good to laugh. He raised his phone and began to type as I turned to see if the clandestine drinker was still there, but he was gone.

Freddy can find literally anything on the internet, and being Nawa, he knows well that stakes of claim by white men can always be traced to stolen land. After my burning desire tirade, my friend texted that one of the group's founding members would reach out, but he never did. Freddy sent me an article in The Fix clarifying the record as to the true genesis of group therapy, describing how the foundation of the program we now know as AA was established. It was the story of Handsome Lake.

———

Have you ever had an epiphany and tried to keep it to yourself? Epiphanies are a total high.

The Fix was the tip of the iceberg. My research led me to the true

202 | JESSICA HOPPE

history of the recovery movement, a Native American network of support groups established nearly two hundred years before the founding of AA. Centuries of Indigenous knowledge affirmed my desire for my recovery to amount to more than just endless hours of abstinence or a fistful of AA chips, but a deeper understanding of my relationship with myself and my purpose on this earth. By reading the work of Eduardo Duran, an Apache/Tewa/Lakota author and clinical psychologist, I learned a culturally competent and decolonized approach to recovery that includes the spiritual needs of oppressed people (specifically Native Americans), a practice that naturally empowers us to demand social justice. The denial of harm prevalent in Western methods compromises healing. Awareness of oppression, past and present, is the key to liberation for the individual, the family, and the greater community.

I came to many conclusions later in life: time lost, for which I mostly blamed myself. But this delay wasn't all a consequence of my ignorance. Instead, it was much like the revisionist version of our national history—separating people from their story, thereby dislocating them from themselves. This was about population mind control.

If you believe you're a liar, if you believe you are broken, if you believe you are sick or a criminal, if you believe you are powerless, what is the result? Who benefits from the vulnerability of your bent neck, from the collapse to your knees, from your surrender?

What if the first step is to correct the record? What if we name how we got here—the source, the actors, and the experiences still in our bodies, now turned to fire in our blood, fog in our heads, splinters in our hearts? What if we reject what we were told, the internalization of a fatal flaw or weakness, the false fear of a demon at our backs, counting push-ups in the corner, and instead tell the truth?

What if I said, *It's not your fault*? What if I asked, *Do you know what's happening to you?*

Within the very first pages of *The Red Road to Wellbriety*, alcoholism is identified as a symptom, an "alien disease" strategically spread as a weapon of genocide. During the mid-eighteenth century, Native Americans launched a coordinated resistance through religious movements and cultural revitalization. Thus began the tradition of storytelling as the cornerstone of recovery, and the earliest interpretation of the twelve steps was recorded through oral transmission. In 1799, the Gai'wiio (Good Message) of Ganioda'yo (Handsome Lake) became known as the Code of Handsome Lake.

Caribbean slave plantations supplied cheap molasses to the newly independent colonies that became the United States, and rum distilleries cropped up along the Atlantic coast of North America. A spike in commerce led to a sharp escalation of binge drinking among "the rootless American colonists, who lacked one unifying culture or authority." It terrorized the country in a wave of unrest soon answered by the Second Great Awakening at the end of the eighteenth century, a passionate religious revival that broke with prevailing conventions of formality to popularize an accessible practice of Christianity.

Slave revolts in the Caribbean in 1793 signaled an opportunity for the abolitionist movement to take hold in the new United States as the use of alcohol as a tool of enslavement and oppression was exposed, though the government fervently denied it. In a famous letter to Handsome Lake, Thomas Jefferson justified the sale of whiskey, writing, "But these nations have done to you only what they do among themselves. They have sold what individuals wish to buy, leaving everyone to be the guardian of his own health and happiness." Here, Jefferson trafficked in the US victim-blaming strategy that would be echoed throughout centuries. He added, "Spirituous liquors are not in themselves bad, they are often found to be an excellent medicine for the sick; it is the improper and intemperate use of them, by those in health, which makes them injurious. But as you find that your people cannot refrain from an ill use of them, I greatly applaud your resolution not to use them at all."

While white observers thoroughly documented what they considered depraved behavior by Native Americans while under the influence, Indigenous leaders worked to rehabilitate and fortify Native peoples. Zuanah (Quanah Parker) established the farthest-reaching religious movement for North American Natives at the turn of the nineteenth century, home to the practice of peyotism, and Squ-sacht-un (John Slocum) and Whe-bul-eht-sah (Mary Thompson) worked to institute the Indian Shaker Church.

The language of good versus evil in the portrayal of addiction as demonic possession emerged across cultures, and the divide in the dominant narrative was strictly drawn across racial lines, excluding Black people from the temperance movement. Efforts to establish independent spaces to support abstinence were burned to the ground. On March 30, 1846, Frederick Douglass told the story to an audience in Paisley, Scotland. In an address called "Temperance and Anti-Slavery," Douglass identified, like Handsome Lake, the trick of spirits as justification for enslavement and ruin. "As I desire, therefore, their freedom from physical chains, so I desire their emancipation from intemperance because I believe it would be the means—a great and glorious means—toward helping to break their physical chains and letting them go free."

Of the approximately 10.7 million people abducted from Africa, only 10 percent landed in North America. Well over 90 percent of enslaved people were held captive in Brazil, Caribbean territories claimed by Europeans, and Spanish colonies in Central and South America. Slavery was abolished across most of Latin America during the early to mid-nineteenth century, with the United States following in 1865 and abolition arriving decades later (in the 1880s) in Cuba and Brazil. Oligarchs continued cataloging their colonization in a supposed taxonomy of admixtures, known as the casta system, a veritable hierarchy of humanity based on skin tone and phenotype. They colluded with colonizers masquerading as businessmen from the United States to steal large swaths of the Honduran coast, install plantations, and indenture African, Indigenous, and mixed-race people and the poor, like my grandfather, effectively upholding the legacy of slavery and colonial rule. Desalmado, as he was, disconnected from his soul by powerful external forces, my grandfather sought to bridge the existential gap with a shortcut—a catholicon, spirits.

While working to understand my history, I followed each branch of interconnection to the source of my autonomy. The objectivity of history disproved the illusion of being defective, a lie I had internalized and projected onto my grandfather, as well. Instead, I identified what Duran called the "soul wound," and drew the connection between us through the intergenerational trauma that we shared to the revelation of recovery: consciousness. I don't have to beware of my so-called evil or accept that I am the inheritor of some wicked providence. I don't have to demonize a neutral substance. I get to choose, free from shame. My agency is restored. My soul is found.

32

The Tenth Tradition

After finishing a Pilates session via YouTube from my kitchen, I rolled up my mat and logged on. Almost five years sober and months into Zoom AA, I was set to autopilot. With my mic muted and camera off, I went about my morning routine, half listening. "I just wanted to identify as a person of color in recovery," the stranger said, his voice soft yet confident, emanating from a distant Zoom tile, from God knows where geographically and through me like a lightning bolt. Now I was listening intently, my chest rising and falling slowly, deeply. It was the first time I'd heard anyone say those precise and necessary words. Until then, I hadn't realized how much I needed to hear them. "I'm brown," he continued. "I want to see someone like me. It makes me feel less intimidated." I sat down at my computer and turned my camera on. We were the only two brown faces in the room.

———

There is no single determinant for addiction. A constellation of factors—biological, psychological, spiritual, social—must be activated in a person. Therefore, each person's recovery will be unique. But the one constant that has been proven to promote healing is social networks, and the most effective way to install a successful support system is through mutual aid. The largest and internationally recognized mutual aid group is AA, though its efficacy has been debated nearly as often as it has been proved.

The purpose of mutual aid is to fulfill a need that has been underserved or abandoned by the governing body. A community forms by its own volition to make resources available in a reciprocal, mutually beneficial ecosystem through shared responsibilities and a collective promise to care.

Alcoholics Anonymous was structured within the framework of mutual aid in the 1930s by two rich white men: Bill Wilson, a stockbroker in New York, and Bob Smith, a Protestant doctor from Akron, Ohio. As far as suffering alcoholics go, even during a period of intense stigma toward alcoholism, Wilson was fortunate: he had access to several exclusive and expensive treatments, with endless shots at bat. When he met Dr. Bob, Wilson had maintained a period of sobriety within the Oxford Group, evangelical Christians who believed drunks could be saved by faith, though he was struggling when he reached out to another alcoholic. During his first meeting with Dr. Bob, Wilson sensed the power of connection and its impact on his desire to drink. He knew service, a key principle he'd learned from the Oxford Group, was also central. Together, they created the twelve steps of Alcoholics Anonymous, a system of individual reform based on three agreements: that you are powerless over alcohol; that as such, you give your will and power over to a God as you understand Him; and that you help other alcoholics who want to do the same. Later, as their strategy gathered steam, they codified these beliefs into a code of conduct called the Twelve Traditions, which came to be known as the AA Bill of Rights and would be used by each self-governing AA group.

In Tradition Ten, Bill and Bob tell the story of the Washingtonians, a group of six teetotalers in Baltimore, Maryland, who gathered to share their experiences with alcohol and support each other in the face of societal condemnation—this was the 1840s, the height of the moralizing temperance movement. Their membership surpassed a hundred thousand before their unfortunate demise, which according to Bill and Bob, began with the fight over abolition, instigating violent public debates. They would not allow history to repeat itself and vowed to keep their mission singular, stating for the record, "Alcoholics Anonymous has no opinion on outside issues; hence the A.A. name ought never be drawn into public controversy."

Today, the culture of white supremacy is easily (and often) perpetuated by any AA member by simply referencing Tradition Ten. This issue was brought forth at a general sharing session in 1986 by the first Black trustee, Garrett T., who offered his personal experience in Washington, DC, where Black members were openly unwelcome at white meetings. It was asserted that in adhering to its traditions, AA had failed to address racism responsibly but rather let it happen.

The AA tradition is the American tradition. And the Constitution was written by rich white men who believed they were the only people who counted as fully human. Women were property, and an enslaved person was only three-fifths of a person. One hundred years from the demise of the Washingtonians to the inception of AA wasn't enough time to forfeit this entitlement. Rather, the founders of AA legitimized a legacy of permission alive and well today.

The collective critical consciousness surrounding white supremacy requires that we call it out, especially where it exists within ourselves. There cannot be a place dedicated to wellness where its existence is denied, where some are forced to suppress themselves.

Handsome Lake's legacy continues from within the Wellbriety movement, a philosophy rooted in ancestral teachings. That is the place you begin—elders, traditions, and culture operate as the anchor to secure your sobriety. The discovery of Handsome Lake and the Indigenous history of sobriety rocketed me to the fourth dimension Bill W. described in *The Big Book*. I wanted to learn more.

The director of White Bison Wellbriety Training Institute, Kateri Coyhis, agreed to speak to me over the phone. I recall her asking for a moment to clarify before beginning the interview. She told me she had enormous gratitude for Alcoholics Anonymous, and I was relieved because so did I. "Recovery is not a one-size-fits-all," she said. "But we all need to work together, not against each other."

As human beings, we are *of* this earth, not *in* it. Coyhis and her staff believe a particular environment must be created to allow healing to enter and flourish. "We use traditional medicines to create a safe space before every meeting," she told me, painting a vivid picture. "We burn sage, sweetgrass, cedar, corn pollen, or whatever medicines are available in the area. And we realize the talking circle is harder to do virtually, but we will utilize the talking circle. The way the elders describe when you're sitting in a circle is that you're in harmony with the entire universe." Establishing a healing sanctuary promotes a culture of nonjudgment. "People feel more open and moved to share," Coyhis said. "As far as healing is concerned, I've never seen anything like it. It's something really magical for people. It connects them. You face each other."

When we ended our call, I repeated that phrase in my mind all day. *We face each other.* It seemed to be the thing AA refused to do. The story of Handsome Lake helped me realize the gift of addiction, although it seems like a curse at first—healing anoints us. We become the healers just by telling our stories. To me, this act is accountability. This is the promise of recovery—if we face ourselves, we gain the courage to face each other. We do not abandon ourselves, so we will not abandon our community.

My plan was to study at the institute, but the pandemic made that impossible. I was uncertain about where I would be able to best practice my recovery with others. I wasn't the kind of AA fellow who carried big credentials—I no longer had a sponsor, I didn't sponsor others, I couldn't bear to read *The Big Book* again, and I did the steps only once, in my first year. I never revisited them, never really gave them much thought after completing them. The whole process took a year, and I sort of gave up on making amends. It seemed to make everyone I approached seriously uncomfortable. But I have committed to the practice of living amends. I'm fully aware of the harm I am capable of. I have found the courage to see it and reverse course whenever I am able. To apologize quickly when I transgress. In my second year, I took a position as a volunteer conducting AA meetings at a detox hospital on Saturday nights and in Rikers Island Jail's women's facilities once. It was probably the most sober I ever felt. And because of the stories I heard and the safe space I helped create in some of the darkest and most dangerous places, I knew I needed meetings to combat isolation.

Once I found the courage to break anonymity, I felt I had to address the legacy of white supremacy in AA, beginning with the erasure and appropriation of Indigenous teachings. As I wrote about this in an article, a severe case of arthritis paralyzed both my wrists. I couldn't reach parts of my body in the shower, turn my doorknob, or type on my keyboard without tremendous pain. I started to doubt myself, and my progress slowed. I was afraid, but I did it anyway. I typed into my email subject line a title suggestion so honest it made me wince, took a deep breath, and sent it to my editor.

Soon after publishing the piece, I visited my niece in New Jersey to decompress. My friend shot me an invite to a Zoom meeting in Oakland, California, titled "Race and Recovery." I asked for the name of the organizer(s), anxious to link up with anyone in the discussion. My friend wasn't sure, but we agreed to meet there. The format began with a five-minute meditation, followed by a reading. I listened as strangers began to read my words out loud—forming a healing circle around me through a grid of anonymous faces.

"OMG!! Are you going to stay incognito," my friend texted as I listened carefully to the sound of revolution.

Anti-racism work is its own form of recovery, and I had to start with myself. But this reawakening was happening worldwide, connecting me to fellows I needed to be in community with, a path to recovery I knew I could not miss. Members all over the country who identified as Indigenous, Black, and people of color assembled to organize marathon meetings open to all topics deemed outside issues by AA standards, creating space exclusively for people of color. From there, dozens of independent meetings and affinity groups formed—queer and nonbinary people of color, all recovery meetings open to anyone who could identify with the struggle of addiction—food, sex, codependency—reclaiming the culturally rooted medicine we've always known existed.

———

In October 2015, the author and intellectual bell hooks held a discussion titled "Moving from Pain to Power" at the New School in New York City, alongside writers Marci Blackman and Darnell L. Moore. From 2013 through 2015, hooks held a residency at the Eugene Lang College of Liberal Arts and, throughout her time there, facilitated conversations with Cornel West, Gloria Steinem, and Laverne Cox, among others. Years later, I watched the talks on YouTube, dimming the blue light of my handheld screen to listen late at night on my headphones as my boyfriend slept. "Healing does not take place in isolation," hooks told her audience. "We cannot move from pain to power in isolation." Still, she acknowledged that not all will be in harmony in each other's ideas of transformation, as differences in needs and opinions can be threatening.

As a child, I always ran in the face of fear, hid from danger. The isolation I'd imposed on myself as an adult well into recovery could no longer be my solution. It wasn't sustainable. When hooks went on to describe decolonization as wholeness, which is the measure of healing and the goal of all forms of recovery, I was shocked to hear praise for Alcoholics Anonymous within that framework.

She cited the example of her brother, "a recovering addict for twenty-five years," and in telling his story, she masterfully contextualized my dilemma.

"I still think that the recovery movement, Bill Wilson, everything, is still one of the great movements in our society," hooks said, crediting AA and NA for providing a therapeutic practice free of cost to disadvantaged communities. "But the thing that I take from the idea that you are always vulnerable to addiction is that we're always vulnerable."

She teaches us that we, particularly people of color, are most vulnerable to a narrative. And that insidious story is everywhere—church, classroom, AA—and willfully drilled into our psyches, where we turn it on ourselves. I wasn't wrong for going to AA. I wasn't stupid for loving it or ignorant because I stayed and felt like I belonged. And I wasn't wrong now to question it. In fact, I had to.

Despite his abstinence from drugs, hooks's brother suffered from chronic discontent. "He really beats himself up for not having money," she said. "And I say to him, Ken, look at the blessing of your life. How many working-class Black men can come back from addiction? Can be born again in recovery?"

———

Heroes of Early Black AA is the seminal text of the history of Black activism, advocacy, and membership in Alcoholics Anonymous. Published in 2017, written by AA historian and scholar Glenn F. Chesnut, it's a sobering tome that does not shy away from the horrors of the time in our country, nor its reality in the rooms—and all it took to establish Black AA. It's also a rousing collection of stories from Black members, their messages of hope and gratitude, and their unique perspectives on how to stay sober.

The authors and various contributors are direct and honest about the facts, yet the tone regarding the founder, Bill W., is reverential, as it is in all AA literature. From the archives, Bill W. is given a lot of credit as a progressive-leaning figure who (in the 1940s) allowed two Black alcoholics into a meeting in New York. After they'd heard Bill W. speak while committed at an institution, they approached him to ask for his permission to come to a meeting following their release. Bill W. said yes. Soon after, on October 22, 1943, he wrote to Joe D. to explain with regret that AA could not be integrated. Bill W. described the reason as a "stark fact" that "whites refuse to mingle with blacks socially." He continued, "Nor can they be coerced or persuaded to do so, even alcoholics! I know, because I once tried here in New York and got so much slapped down that I realized no amount of insistence would do any good." Black alcoholics were on their own.

Two years later, on October 20, 1945, a letter was sent to the New York AA office. It was written by Torrence S., secretary of the new and first-ever segregated Black AA group. The group began with five members in St. Louis, Missouri, on January 24, 1945, and was named "AA-1 Group." And though the members were ecstatic at this enormous accomplishment, it had come as a compromise with the local white groups, who had banned Black people from their rooms. Therefore, the AA-1 Group asked the central office and Grapevine to "withhold publicity about our group that may occasion controversial discussions of racial problems within A.A." Just as Bill W. upheld the culture of white supremacy from the Washingtonian era, the founders of the Black AA movement feared the same violent consequences Frederick Douglass had spoken of a century before.

It is what the Black AA movement created that hooks spoke of and praised, though it was in no way beyond critique. She understood in observing her brother, sober for a quarter century, that he remained addicted to a "scale of evaluation" set by the standards of imperialism, white supremacism, capitalism, and patriarchy perpetuated by the philosophy of AA, derived from the American Dream.

"A culture of domination always wants us to think of power as outside of ourselves. But power is always conceived as power over something and not as what is my power within? And so I feel that part of our colonization of Black people, brown people, Asian people is we often internalize that sense of powerlessness because we feel like what's my power in relationship to the world? I don't have any. And so, I think that we often embrace death," hooks said.

We begin each meeting at my new homegroup by reading a passage from *Heroes*. We recently started to read the story of Brownie, a pioneer of the movement, described by the author as an existentialist who believed that "life is lived towards death." He (like hooks's brother) also remained dissatisfied in sobriety. He described a state of hostility, hatred, and misery, though he worked the program as best he knew how. He found serenity five years into his sobriety, at the Second International AA Convention held locally in St. Louis in the summer of 1955. He was able to hear Bill W. himself and poignantly described observing people from all walks of life enraptured by joy and gratitude. But his proselytizing gets problematic: he told a tale of watching people with various disabilities enjoying themselves. The sight of a man without arms or legs particularly struck him. "I cast my eyes down upon a man that didn't have no legs, and no arms, and this man were laughing. And I said to myself, 'What the hell is he laughing about? Wherever this man goes, somebody got to push him there. Whatever this man do, somebody got to help to do whatever he have to do.' I sat there and begin to feel my arms, begin to feel my legs, begin to feel my eyes, and said to myself, 'Who in the hell say this AA program won't work!' Then that's when I began to practice the principles and work the program."

The pity he felt for others surpassed the pity he felt for himself. A troubling lesson to read.

Brownie dedicated himself from that point on to eliminating hatred from his life and from the life of any alcoholic. "Racial prejudice and hatred are just another version of the old death wish, the old evil desire to hurt and destroy and put down other people. The spirituality of AA teaches us to put aside that old death wish, the old enjoyment of suffering. We alcoholics cross a great divide when we finally decide that we want to live. If we fall back into racial hatred and fear and the constant rehearsal of old resentments, we turn back into that old land of death and suffering and hatred, the land (ultimately) of despair and hopelessness. Alcoholics have no other choice—to hate is to die." I agreed that anger can be corrosive. When forced to repress anger—as I had been— it can mutate into hatred. By naming the pain inflicted by racist systems and their role in our addiction, I learned how to transmute that anger into something that felt like freedom.

When our discussion began, we addressed the harm of ableist content—taking into consideration the colonial indoctrination that would influence that work and the context of the time. We must turn the page. We claimed our power, stood on the shoulders of our ancestors, and discussed the text honestly—we critiqued and refuted, we gave praise and thanks.

"To hate is to die," one fellow repeated from the reading, admitting their uncertainty and fear. "I don't think I can forgive," they continued, surveying the loss of their tribe as a result of colonial genocide, still felt keenly after so many generations. We parsed anger from hate and the pain of being denied our righteous anger and breaking free of it. We discussed what moved us, what repelled us, and admitted what we knew we wouldn't be able to do. We empowered each other to build upon the legacy of our elders and divest from the value system into which we'd been indoctrinated—not only in AA but within a wider culture. We would decide for ourselves what language, principles, steps, and modules helped us recover, soothe pain, and intercept self-harm. I had lost faith in the program because my anger was denied and I had constantly been redirected. I was told, "You've stepped on toes, you've broken the rules." And even when you try to comply, which is a form of assimilation, it's never enough.

"Finding my people," as some like to say in recovery, wasn't a matter of simply finding people of color. I knew many. It was about connecting with those who rooted their recovery in a politic of liberation. People who demand to know why we have been erased from the history books, why the story for so many begins with Bill and Bob, and to correct the record, elevating the names of our sober ancestors—and inscribing ours into that rich history.

33

We Need More Stories of Recovery

The video I made in 2020 tearfully outing myself on my social media platform was not the first outing. In the early days of the pandemic, Freddy and I were free agents, hustling for bylines, brainstorming ideas twenty-four seven, pitching constantly. Freddy had lost his weekly Al-Anon meeting, as I had lost AA. He had a contact at a new men's journal dedicated to the health and wellness of men of color. I thought they'd like a piece about his work in Al-Anon. I was right. He got the assignment, which I knew would require talking about his partner, mc, the alcoholic. I wasn't the central figure, but it would be out there, and people could ask questions.

Freddy was hesitant to go there, but I pushed him. I wanted him to succeed, and I believed sincerely in the message and that his was the right voice to contribute to the conversation—so then why did I feel uncomfortable? It wasn't until I began to write this chapter that I realized I hadn't been the one to out myself—I had made him do it for me. Once Freddy's pieces were published, they received a warm and enthusiastic response. No one gave a second thought to my small mention—it wasn't about me. But the authentic identity I passively denied from behind a supposed virtue of anonymity backed my ass into a corner. It was time to embrace my true self, and that included being a person in recovery. Not just to my few close friends, other AA fellows, and immediate family. I wanted to celebrate the aspect of myself that had unlocked my captivity. I had grown out of the idea that it was safe to be part of a club; the edge of a secret society had flopped. Substance use disorder is a common mode of pain relief. And we are all in pain. Likewise, we all attach to what helps us soothe that pain. But because of our system of criminality and moral judgment regarding drugs, substance use disorder can result in critical consequences quickly, particularly for people of color, who have become accustomed to moralizing drug use along racial lines. We call it stigma, a form of public shaming, something you can't just get over or not take personally. The effects of stigma are tangible and quantifiable—there are penalties.

Within the echo chambers of sobriety circles and wellness spaces, it might appear as if recovery is moving toward the mainstream, but not everyone can publicly claim sobriety with the same bravado. People's voyeuristic appetite for media stories sensationalizing addiction drives a steady supply of salacious content but minimal depictions of recovery, much less recovery of Black, Indigenous, and people of color, though we are frequently cast to portray drug abuse, trafficking, and trauma.

I wanted more stories of our recovery.

I relied heavily on AA not only because it spoke to me but also because it was accessible. I didn't have insurance and couldn't afford to pay for rehab, in- or out-patient. I knew AA wasn't going to be the cure—no one claimed it was the panacea—but I didn't know where else to go. The commercialized sobriety movement I found online, marketing abstinence as the key to great skin, rapid weight loss, and professional achievement, was the same cash and prizes model that AA was built on, the same dream America promised, and it held no substantial meaning. Nor did it apply to me.

In the wake of George Floyd's murder, I heard a white woman respond to the media coverage of his drug use by saying she could relate because there is no identity more stigmatized than that of an addict. What got George Floyd killed that day was being a Black man in the hands of militarized police. It was proven in the autopsy that drugs played no role. His identity as a drug user made his murder justifiable for some. A Black addict is a criminal; a white woman in recovery is a girl boss. They are not the same. And that is by design. The so-called quit lit genre is dominated by white authors, not because people of color are incapable, ignorant, or in denial. It is because, throughout history, Indigenous, Black, and people of color have been forcefully excluded and erased. But their work exists.

Chaney Allen was working in rehabilitation in the early '70s in California when she noticed the need for culturally competent recovery care. The few resources she received in public service, such as brochures and pamphlets, were ineffective. Allen was known for her grassroots, community-powered tactics and the development of groundbreaking techniques in treating people of color in recovery, particularly Black women and women of color. In 1976, aware of the need in her community for literature they could identify with, Allen self-published *I'm Black and I'm Drunk*, quickly selling five hundred copies within the first two months. With the help of a friend who had a printing press in his kitchen, she reprinted it and published it in 1978 as *I'm Black and I'm Sober*, the first autobiography of a Black woman in recovery. "We Blacks must start documenting somewhere, sometime, in order to help others," Allen, who founded the California Black Commission on Alcoholism and the California Women's Commission on Alcoholism, wrote in the author's note.

A few years later, in 1983, Allen, a frequent national speaker, gave a radio interview on a program titled *In Black America* for KUT radio (Austin, Texas) hosted by John L. Hanson. "I didn't know I was an alcoholic for years," she began, her story echoing my own. "I'd never seen a person in my life in '62 who said they were an alcoholic. I knew nothing about any program. I didn't know what to do. I didn't know what was wrong. Except I knew I had to be going insane."

On August 30, 1968, Allen was directed to the program, where she not only maintained sobriety but also found alignment with her purpose.

Though the interviewer applauded her good work, he still questioned how a preacher's daughter, one raised with *good Christian values*, could become an *abuser of alcohol*. "As a Black [person], I was taught, and Blacks are always taught usually that alcoholism is a sin. Or, as they told me, there was no place in heaven for the wayward woman, the drunkard, the divorcee, the adulteress; I was guilty of everything; I was all wrong," Allen replied, explaining that condemnation is what keeps many like her from admitting they need help. Allen believed in the disease model, which allowed her to set aside shame and ask what she could do about the condition. She followed those steps. Identification was central to her repeated message: "the wound to be healed must be revealed."

Despite the obvious chaos, the spiral toward rock bottom, the news of addiction can come as a shock. Allen guided many through the path to identification and understood that it's different for everyone. From her work at the women's center, she observed not only the inequity of the services provided but also the targeted attack on lives. "What it takes for one woman to survive, it doesn't take that for the other one. We're talking about different needs now."

Allen called out the gross disparities she witnessed while working for treatment facilities in poor communities, where the populations they were meant to serve—the poor, and poor women of color in particular— were blocked from assistance through mandatory procedures the facilities knew well they could not follow. "Unfortunately those are the poor ladies that's almost written out on our programs, they're almost forgotten. As I worked there in the ghetto, that burned me up too." Meanwhile, those with the resources required to meet the programs' criteria (namely time, transportation, and money) wouldn't be caught dead at such cheap facilities. This waste was intentional.

Still, Allen knew that what kept women of color from treatment most of all was the story. "Three stigmas: female, alcoholic, and Black," Allen said. "Every strike is against you." She believed in the importance of being seen and surrounded by others who look like you and acknowledge and understand your unique experience. "A woman will stay hidden, but when they can see another woman come out, they don't have to feel so ashamed anymore."

Throughout Allen's career, she made immeasurable progress across the recovery movement. Still, she especially wanted to champion Black women, whom she described as the impetus behind writing and publishing her book and carrying its message widely. "I hope, and I'm trying to be a model for my Black women. If I'm not ashamed to pull the cover off myself, come on out and admit it. We need that to keep us from having to feel ashamed because, for years, they had us thinking that it was men's and white folk's disease, and I'm sorry, alcohol is not prejudiced towards anybody. So that's that."

34

Claiming an Identity They Taught
Me to Despise

I've always been told I look like a Jessica or that I'm a *total* Jessica. I never quite knew what people meant by that. Recently, while I shopped for my father, I found a greeting card produced by Shoebox, a humor genre at Hallmark. Two parrots sit perched on a branch that runs perpendicular across the front of the card, two superimposed images affixed onto a solid lavender background. Thought bubbles float above each parrot's head. The bird on the left chirps, "Polly want a cracker!" The one on the right sports mirrored sunglasses and a feathered mohawk and replies, "Jessica want a margarita!" Inside, the double-sided neon-yellow cardstock reads, "Party like a Jessica on your birthday," in a spindly violet script, as if handwriting could be tipsy.

I held the pastel hand grenade, a bit shocked, mostly amused, accustomed to being told who I am. I took a photo of it with my phone and wondered who I could text it to, to have a laugh at my expense. Then, I thought about posting it on social media to take a crack at myself publicly. But I never did either. Instead, I bought the card. It sat at the bottom of my purse until I stuffed it into a drawer in my desk.

As my parents age, they tend to repeat certain stories. My father repeats stories as reinforcement. He wants to state the record and for me, the writer, to retell it accurately. He is like a boy as he dictates, a child desperate for safety. All that's needed to provide that safety is for me to agree. There is no way to keep myself safe when I do it. But if I don't, he will abandon me.

My mother repeats stories, lately one in particular, for validation. She has not suppressed her truth or diminished her voice—she has been silenced and dismissed. She is like a girl, her words rapid and breathless, like when my niece arrives home from school eager to tell us about her day. No one ever listened to my mother like we listen to Bella, and she deserves to be heard, understood. My mother needs to hear it's okay. But her okay comes at the expense of mine. The answer she needs for closure is the beginning of my questions.

My mother lost me for the first time thirty-five years ago. She'd lost track of my sisters before that. My sister Karla went missing after the babysitter, court-ordered to appear downtown, took her to the courthouse without my mother's knowledge or consent. Another time, while living with my grandmother, my mother returned from school to an empty crib. Frantic, she searched for my sister Karina until she heard her voice behind the locked bathroom door. My grandmother and her husband were naked in the tub with the baby girl. He just wanted to give the baby a bath, my grandmother said. No hay nada de malo.

My mother vowed never to let me out of her sight. No babysitters, not even—especially not—family. But school was harmless, good for me even, although she was sad to be left alone all day. She found a gig to keep busy and ran late for pickup at the bus stop one day. When she arrived, she found an empty house and peeled off in her car to chase the bus. I wasn't on it. She sped to the school; I wasn't there either. Panic-stricken, she returned home to scour the house. She found me far back in the corner of the closet, buried beneath one of the tattered T-shirts she used as nightgowns; I'd cried myself to sleep.

The story is not about the child she pictures hidden in a hole in the wall like a mouse. It is about the child's mother who believes that if I listen, she will be forgiven, and if I forgive her, she will forgive herself. I tell her I don't remember, and I don't, but I feel the pain of the memory now, in the present, because, in so many ways, I never stopped hiding. But I'd rather she believe the pain doesn't exist—it can't if I don't recall it. She shouldn't worry. There is nothing to forgive. I'm fine. I abandoned that child, too.

The magic of repetition is in its power to engender familiarity. Familiar feels safe, making you more apt to agree—you can remember, engage, and participate in a story, fact, or figure. I've heard that story about myself so many times, yet I know the memory is not mine. I and my mother are the only two people who know it happened. She is the narrator, and her narration has become my memory. That doesn't mean my version of the story doesn't exist. Manifested in fear and contextualized by my actions, my story played out in a shameless willingness throughout my life to do anything to not be abandoned, a belief that abandonment is something you bring upon yourself and can, therefore, prevent.

———

Even if you know nothing about AA, you've heard the opener: "Hi, my name is Jessica, and I'm an alcoholic." That is the entrance fee; it's the buy-in, the handshake. If you can admit this much, you can stay. You've earned your seat; you've got a shot.

The whole room, having witnessed your humility, will repeat your name, rote. Without pause or hesitation, they reply: "Hi, Jessica." Some will ad-lib *welcome*. The ritual is soothing and straightforward and is repeated whenever a person speaks. A holy chorus like the prayers recited at a Catholic church, the kind I always wanted to memorize, not because I believed in them but because I was willing to pretend if it meant I could be a part of something. Because I needed a friend like I needed drugs.

At first, I'd forget—skipping the intro, I'd barrel into my manic thoughts, desperate to be heard—inevitably, someone would interrupt and walk me back to the starting line. *What's your name?* they'd shout over me until I stopped talking. I'd laugh shyly and begin again, obeying the ritual. That's when I realized I believed what I'd been taught about alcoholics and addicts, and didn't want the word associated with me. But I wanted to stay. I wanted to be a part of this group and with these people. I wanted to make sense of myself. I took the blame; this was my ego, I thought. So, I started saying it until I believed it. Like I said, I've always been quick to take orders. What I later learned was that I resented these orders.

Identity is as intrinsic to recovery as group conscience is to AA. Group conscience is determined by a vote. Majority rules. From a statistical perspective, the AA population remained composed of its target audience—89 percent white and 62 percent male-identified, according to its latest report, from 2014.

Still, you are taught that you are one of many, a part of something, and your ego will not only threaten your own sobriety but also has the power to affect others. The alienation I experienced at AA was my doing, I was told. When you abide by the traditions, you don't get hurt. You can only be damaged when you allow it. Shrinking myself in the way I'd been required to do since childhood, pretending that pain didn't exist, would kill me. And to experience this in my place of worship, a place I had come to trust, felt like abandonment.

From the cache of individual stories, you identify with the feelings; you look for the similarities, not the differences. You stick with the winners and set your sights on someone who has what you want. Following the steps leads to cash and prizes—a life beyond your wildest dreams.

Within the framework of a reward system, there are winners and losers, strong and weak—as a friend of mine often remarked, some are thicker and some are sicker.

The illness model implies a pathology. Unlike leukemia or breast cancer, where a foreign object has invaded perfectly healthy blood cells and tissue for some unknown reason, this illness has been inside you, and the fortitude you lack has caused it to take hold. But admitting my flaw in a cocoon of shared identity gave me the deepest sense of belonging I'd experienced. A safe pursuit to exhilaration. We aren't bad people trying to be good, I told my parents; we're sick people trying to get well, a disease model popularized to garner compassion and mitigate stigma. And it works. Anonymity is called the spiritual foundation of Alcoholics Anonymous. What a perfect justification for my silence. What a perfect place for an *other* to hide. I couldn't afford to take any steps back from the mark. So I kept hiding.

"To claim all of the self is an act of courage," wrote Alice Walker in praise of Michelle Cliff's work, a quote that appears on the back of her book, *Claiming an Identity They Taught Me to Despise*. "And is there a limit to what we may claim? The missing link affirmed, connects us to the whole." What we deny is precisely what keeps us from being whole. And the search for wholeness is a daily practice. I asked myself: Who told me to deny my truth? My family. And who instructed my family in how it was safe to exist in this world? Is what they say true? What happens to us if I refuse to lie about who I am?

Bruce Alexander's dislocation theory didn't warn solely of the dislocation from self but also of estrangement from others, which leads to a loss of meaning and purpose. I was determined to reconnect to myself, to recall the embryonic instinct to just be, and to develop the maturity to embody that, in the face of rejection, with integrity. The dislocation from my group forced me to ground my center inside myself. I had to understand the ideas that governed the machinery that demanded my silence, passivity, and forgiveness. Liberation is wholeness. Decolonization is wholeness. Healing is wholeness. And I had to admit I wasn't a victim; I wasn't sick. I was human.

The Latinx community is eager to overcorrect harmful stereotypes by centering redemptive or respectable stories. This tendency is harmful. As a circumstance worthy of understanding, complexity, and support, addiction is an aspect of humanity denied to people of color. How we became addicted and how we saved our lives are not the same.

Fifty years since President Richard Nixon declared a war on drugs on June 17, 1971, the time of my parents' migration to the United States, it is clear that the legacy of drug war policies continues to kill Indigenous, Black, and people of color—upholding a procedure of criminalization for the poor, Black, and brown and a procedure of rehabilitation for the wealthy and white. These systemic inequities perpetuate a narrative that drug use among white people is recreational, while drug use among people of color is criminal. The conditions caused by the traumas of migration, assimilation, colonialism, and marginalization are never correlated, never properly linked to substance use disorder: instead, they're pathologized and reduced to stereotypes.

Understanding the true role of our country's government in spreading this epidemic of addiction to poor communities of color—those denied fair access to resources and care, both medicinal and therapeutic—was crucial to me. It helped me shift the focus of blame for my condition from myself and my family to the truly responsible, and to work consistently with my family to identify and understand this. As the tide of sobriety ebbed and flowed through my life, all was revealed, and I became prepared to finally face the dysfunction from the personal to the political.

It took me a while to realize, and even longer to admit, that I had a problem with drugs and alcohol. The only people in my family who suffered similarly wound up dead, deported, or in jail, and it has taken consistent effort to undo the programming attached to those outcomes.

I thought when I found the courage to be myself—completely—that acceptance would be the sign that I was finally worthy. The world would reflect my goodness like a mirror. I learned that finding the courage to take a stand would be a sign of my health because freedom would not be bestowed upon me. I would have to take it. By force.

The abandonment I'd learned as a child began with myself. I was too little to grasp the effect, too weak to face the pain. This cycle of behavior became apparent to me as I lost the fantasy of favor in my homegroup, when I showed them who I was and demanded of the program exactly what it asked of me: progress not perfection. It wasn't part of AA engagement rules—it was a direct affront—but I knew it was a sign of my recovery.

———

It had been three years since I had stepped into a room. Since I had even considered going back to in-person or admitted the longing I held to take a seat among fellows again—to share in creating the inscrutable magic of our sacred space.

During announcements at my online homegroup meeting, a friend, dismayed at the lack of diversity at the meeting she was assigned to chair, asked if any New York City locals could come support her. "Help me integrate the space, y'all," she joked.

As I walked west on Houston toward St. Anthony's on Sullivan Street, I passed the outdoor market where I used to stop every morning on my way to a meeting. Vendors drive in from Jersey, Connecticut, and Pennsylvania, vans chock-full of woven baskets, pashminas, vintage jackets, and gemstones of all shapes and sizes, to try to sell them to rich Manhattanites but mostly tourists from the sidewalk. I could never resist a judicious pass of the jewelry but never much cared for the crystals.

One day early in my sobriety, something called to me from the very back table. Elevated on a rack sat a large rock, generic and gray, sliced wide open like a melon, its glistening mineral flesh reflecting the sunlight in a kaleidoscope of color. I got closer to run my fingers along its jagged teeth and read the laminated note underneath.

AMETHYST: HELPS WITH RECOVERY. HELPS KEEP SOBER MIND.

The amethyst is one of many varieties of quartz, its color said to be derived from wine. A myth animated by the story of a nymph named Ametis, who when stalked by Bacchus, the god of wine, rejected his advances and called upon the virgin goddess Diana for help. Diana turned her into a crystal to guard her chastity. Angered and rebuffed, Bacchus poured wine on the limpid quartz in a drunken rage, endowing the stone with its signature hue, cementing the sorcery of the stone to ward off drunkenness as Ametis had the brute, Bacchus.

While there are many versions of the story, the etymology of its name *a-methustos* means "not drunken," and belief in its powers can be traced to the ancient Egyptians, Romans, and Greeks who drank from chalices forged with amethysts, who held the gem beneath their tongues to prevent inebriation as they imbibed. Alongside sardonyx, amethyst placed on a drunkard's navel was said to dispel poisoning. The totem cloaked the wearer in a protective field, guarding against Earth's negative energies and imbuing a sound mind, quick wit, and a temperate spirit.

Since getting sober, I had witnessed the mysterious ways faith is rewarded. And I was happy to admit that sobriety had changed my life. Suddenly I wanted something powerful to protect it, something tangible, something I could hold and carry with me: a magical amulet that promised to reverse poisoning and ward off intoxication. A lapidarian symbol, one etched in stone, of my vow to honor myself. In my desire, I accepted without shame or doubt that I'm the kind of person who could use some help. And it helped to have something to believe in. A place to go where others believed too.

Farther east on Houston and one block south is a jewelry store I wandered into sometime after. The selection is a mix of fine and costume jewelry—the good stuff is kept behind glass—ornate cases along the walls and throughout the floor cover the single-room shop. One in the back near the register holds rare vintage, always my preference, and that's where I saw it: a lavender geode from the mid-century carved into the shape of a liver, held by a fist of sterling silver talons bent and sprouting below the pendant, all floating within a square border like a painting. What a fashionista might call a statement piece, what a witch would recognize as a talisman. The antique chain had no clasp, so I bowed slightly as the shopkeeper placed it over my head as if it were my coronation. The weight of the piece fell into the depression of my chest, over my heart. I placed my hand over both and said a prayer for us.

Years later I tucked the protective crystal into my cleavage and returned to the rooms. The bitter scent of coffee flared my nostrils as I stepped down into the dimly lit basement. It had been brewing since the first meeting at 7 a.m. I still poured myself a cup. The walls were covered in chipped wooden frames—the fat Old English script shouting the slogans in red—ONE DAY AT A TIME. FIRST THINGS FIRST. EASY DOES IT.

The meeting was small and intimate. No raised hands, we went around in a circle. My tongue struggled to meet my lips, I took a sip of coffee to wet my throat and began with the story of the amethyst, the historical meaning and the personal implication for me. I admitted I was nervous to return, to share truthfully; my heart pounded as I spoke. But I'd followed the suggestion of a friend, the instinct to be useful, and I'd been nourished far more than anyone I might hope to be of service to.

Once each person had spoken, we stood and joined hands. One man concerned with passing germs abstained and remained seated, placing me between two young newcomers. The palm to my left felt clammy to the touch. A former athlete turned broker dressed in all black athleisure barely raised his arm above his thigh. I reached and grabbed his hand assuredly and smiled. To my right a genial girl ninety days in, with the chip she'd just been presented in her pocket, held mine limply and bounced on her heels. I squeezed gently three times, to say to her "I got you."

We held a moment of silence for those still suffering inside and outside of the rooms and closed with the Serenity Prayer. The rush of touch, the harmony of shared faith, the practice of the ritual generated a spark gathering charge from each fellow as it coursed through my entire body, the hole within overflowing with love. This was the feeling of grace. This is how it felt to embody recovery—to stand in communion with an imperfect group of strangers who would never gather together for any other reason. And also to stand in solidarity with my friend and in defiance of an oppressive status quo. I raised my head, tears streaming, and recited the words of Angela Davis: "I'm no longer accepting the things I cannot change. I'm changing the things I cannot accept." This is my Serenity Prayer.

35

Myth of the Model Minority

A tiny pot of white rice boils on the stove for my niece, Bella. She's six. Two cups of brown rice steam on the counter for the rest of us. We eat rice with every meal but can no longer afford to have bleached rice—carbs must be complex these days. Mom's sugar is always high.

On Sundays, I cook for my whole family. My mother and I have reversed roles—I am now the head chef and she, my sous. Of my mother's three daughters, I was the only one who embraced domesticity, the only one who loves cooking as much as we all enjoy eating. She claims my cooking is the best, and she tries to mimic my recipes, ones foreign to her that I picked up from a casalinga while living in Italy with my ex-husband, but it just never tastes the same. She warned me about Italian men. "Por lo menos aprendiste la cocina," she said when I returned to New York without him, joking that at least I'd learned to cook Italian food before the divorce.

There are no secrets to my cooking, no mysterious ingredients or superior technique. It's my love that she can taste, a meal prepared for once without the grease of her own labor. When I say her cooking is the best, she replies, "Qué va," undermining her lifelong work as a mother, homemaker, chef. But none of the Hoppe women have a taste for our own love.

On this day, I was busy cooking dinner for extended family, fourteen in total. When I sold my book, Karina came up from Georgia to visit with the kids. New life was bursting through a dark pandemic, and we were determined to celebrate it all—the book, my fortieth birthday, and the arrival of my nephew Leo, Karla's rainbow (*rainbow, rainbow*) baby. We were ecstatic.

With Jessy chicken, a simple roast chicken that had become my niece's favorite, in the oven, I stood at the counter to chop a fresh salad. I felt the elation of popularity among preteens and teen-teens as they excitedly asked me about publishing. They did not hold back—so I gave them the truth. They wanted to know if they'd be in it, what it was about, and—most of all—how much money I would make. It was hard to believe I had the answers to these questions. This was our information now forever. What I learned was theirs, too. And it was important for them to know the story I would tell. The one I dedicated to them.

Their eyes widened as I told them I am recovering from substance use disorder. They turned to find their mother's eyes, then my mother's. I gave them a brief and technical explanation of what happened to me, what I did to get better, and what I continue to do every day. I told them it was nothing to be scared or ashamed of. We would no longer sweep our issues under the rug, gossip, or make fun of people who need help. If and when it came up again in our family, we'd handle it as if it were a toothache.

My confession does nothing to prevent the disorder from arising, but by offering myself as an example, I could initiate a new conversation. They have someone to come to if they ever have questions, I said. They can see there are other fates for those afflicted besides death and disgrace—I can be a realistic vision of a person who looked like them in recovery. Four heads nodded at me and smiled. I handed them plates to set the table.

As we all took our seats, my nephew Joshua asked, "What's it called?" wondering about the title of my book.

"*First in the Family.*"

"But you're last . . ." he said before his mother's reaction caused him to laugh shyly as if he'd hurt my feelings. He hadn't—he instinctually understood my intention.

I am the last born, the youngest daughter, the observer. I've watched this family carefully all my life—taken my cues from their pain, navigating in the wake of our misfortunes. Hindsight bestowed in birth order.

My nephew is right; I'm not the first person to get sober; my uncle went to AA in his twenties after an ultimatum from his wife. He stayed for five years in Honduras and fell off when he got to the States. There are probably more, but I wouldn't know because we don't talk about it. No one would ever admit it. I'm not the family pioneer of sobriety. I'm just the one who is willing to come forward. I'm correcting the family record and writing a new chapter, with many *to be continued*s.

Recovery is a process of narration, a story we write to remember all we've forgotten, to challenge what has been denied and erased and stolen. Owning your true story can make you whole, and wholeness is the definition of healing. Were we violent? Yes. Did we use drugs, sex, food to manage our pain? Yes. Did we abandon each other, harm each other? Yes. Did anyone know what was happening to us? No.

The American Dream is not my story; it was my gateway—forcing me to compensate for my humanity with exceptionalism, convinced it was my responsibility to pay back the sacrifices of those who brought me through achievements they'd been denied—that discovery was my awakening. But I still dream. I have big, radical, fantastic dreams. They're about my family. I dream of what we can reclaim and continue to build together. How profoundly we will love each other outside the shadows.

I am first in the family. I am also the next, the last, and will be first again. There have been firsts before me and there will be lasts after. Until all that is left to claim are our choices in life because that is more than enough.

I wanted to tell my nephew that firsts in a family are like batons passed in a relay, an equal effort, each building upon the other. It's not about setting the bar higher; we prop each other up. We end the cycles to clear the path, and each does our part; the only destination is back home to ourselves, where we will always find each other. One day, he'll understand the baton he carries and what he will do. Though he will not have to do it alone. Or in silence or secrecy. So when he told me I couldn't be first because I am last, I said:

"I hope so."

Acknowledgments

———————

This book would not exist without the unfailing support of my family, indomitable team, and the grace of the recovery community. My guardian angel, Claire: thank you for saving my life and for asking the question that changed it. To the brave women who came forward, who told me the truth that set me free, a blessing I consider the first miracle of my sobriety, thank you. And to every person at Planned Parenthood who cared for me. I'm forever grateful.

Papá, es mi deseo que el mundo entero sepa cuánto te adoro. Que sepan lo que heredé de ti. Que cada persona que lea este libro aprenda de tu lucha, conozca tu corazón y te vea como yo te veo, un héroe. Admiro tu esfuerzo y humildad. Tu humanidad. Estoy más que orgullosa de ser tu hija. Te amo.

Mom, I've idolized you since the day I was born. I always will. I could never repay all that you gave me, though nothing could stop me from trying. Thank you for sharing the stories you lived to tell. You are miraculous and I love you.

Beatriz, abuela, jamás dejaste de desear y por eso yo sigo haciéndolo.

Karina and Karla, our sisterhood is my life force. Thank you for always protecting me. What a blessing it is to be your baby sister. Kiki, thank you for being my hands when I was little; I am here to be yours. Ku, *you are the wind beneath my wings.* Cesar and Ariel: thank you for being my brothers and for loving my sisters. My nieces and nephews, Emma, Joshua, Bella, Leo: it is the honor of my life to be your tía. Jewel and Zahir: I love you.

Hans, when I'm afraid, I remember your final words, *God works in mysterious ways.* May our stories help others. Maria, forever young, forever beautiful, forever missed. I love you, prima. Thank you for playing music for me when I felt lost. I wish you were here.

Freddy, amor de mi vida, my favorite poet, best reader and researcher, "I have the utmost respect for you." Your words changed my life. Your respect shattered any doubt. Your love answered my prayer. Te amo. Fifi, hijita, gatita, had I known how literally you would embody it, I might not have named you after a storm. But you are ours, and you make us a family.

To my agent, Johanna Castillo, mi paisana, my right hand. No one could have championed me or this project the way you have. Te lo agradezco de todo corazón. Gracias también, Victoria Mallorga Hernandez. I appreciate all that you do. Many thanks to Carisa Hays, who put this book in the hands of anyone who would listen and thus to those who need it most.

Thank you to everyone at Flatiron who made *First in the Family* possible: Megan Lynch, Katherine Turro, Joanne Raymond, Marlena Bittner, and Brittany Leddy.

To my editor, Nadxieli Nieto, you held the door open for me. It changed my life. Thank you for understanding what needed to be said and encouraging me to say it with my whole chest. Kukuwa Ashun, I appreciate you. Frances Sayers, Jane Haxby, Joaquin Badajoz, thank you for continuously working with me to improve this book and stretch as a writer.

First in the Family's path to publication was blessed by many hands. First conceptualized under the guidance of Valerie Boyd. Thank you for saying "You have a book!" with such certainty. I will never forget. Jenn Baker, your tireless advocacy so often unlocked the gatekept. Yahdon Isreal, thank you for putting your name right in the subject line. Sarita Gonzalez, eres la madrina de FITF. Gracias, amiga. To my crew of Centam & Isthmian writers, you nurtured this project from seed to tree. This is for us.

For early reads, feedback, and most of all your friendship, thank you Nico Montano, Travis Gutiérrez Senger, Sabrina Senger, and Allison Markin Powell. The book is better because of you. Lupita Aquino, Javier Zamora, Lilliam Rivera, Michelle Malonzo, and Carl Erik Fisher, thank you for reading first and seeing the value in the work in progress.

Hanif Abdurraqib: I don't know a more generous writer or genuine person. Thank you. Leslie Jamison, years ago you affirmed that what I felt was true. I'm eternally grateful. It was my first step toward this book. Claire Potter, my friend, editor, mind reader: there is no book without you. Gratitude is not enough.

To my beloved recovery community, thank you for taking care of me, for buying me coffee, for letting me win the dance competition at my first sober holiday party, and for helping me get honest, even if it changed us. I'm alive thanks to you. And to Shine Your Light: you have rocketed me to the fourth dimension. You have healed, affirmed, and loved every part of me and now I really, truly love myself.

And to the reader: your story matters. Thank you for reading mine.

The AA MFA Reading List

The Writers Who Are My Teachers, the Voices That Gave Me Permission, the Stories That Affirmed My Own

Recovery

Alexander, Bruce K. *The Globalization of Addiction: A Study in Poverty of the Spirit*. New York: Oxford University Press, 2008.

Duran, Eduardo. *Healing the Soul Wound: Counseling with American Indians and Other Native Peoples*. New York: Teachers College Press, 2006.

Evangelista, Patricia. *Some People Need Killing: A Memoir of Murder in My Country*. New York: Random House, 2023.

Fisher, Carl Erik. *The Urge: Our History of Addiction*. New York: Penguin Random House, 2022.

Fong, Benjamin Y. *Quick Fixes: Drugs in America from Prohibition to the 21st-Century Binge*. New York: Verso, 2023.

Geronimus, Arline T. *Weathering: The Extraordinary Stress of Ordinary Life in an Unjust Society*. New York: Little, Brown Spark, 2024.

Ghosh, Amitav. *Smoke and Ashes: Opium's Hidden Histories*. New York: Farrar, Straus and Giroux, 2024.

Hansen, John G., Teresa A. Booker, and John E. Charlton, eds. *Walking with Indigenous Philosophy: Justice and Addiction Recovery*. Vernon, British Columbia: JCharlton Publishing, 2014.

Harrison, Nzinga, and Lynya Floyd. *Un-Addiction: 6 Mind-Changing Conversations That Could Save a Life*. New York: Union Square, 2024.

Hassan, Shira. *Saving Our Own Lives: A Liberatory Practice of Harm Reduction*. Chicago: Haymarket Books, 2022.

Leland, Joy. *Firewater Myths: North American Indian Drinking and Alcohol Addiction*. New Brunswick, NJ: Rutgers Center of Alcohol Studies, 1976.

Maté, Gabor. *In the Realm of Hungry Ghosts: Close Encounters with Addiction.* Berkeley: North Atlantic Books, 2010.

Ramsey, Donovan X. *When Crack Was King: A People's History of a Misunderstood Era.* New York: One World, 2023.

Vakharia, Sheila P. *The Harm Reduction Gap: Helping Individuals Left Behind by Conventional Drug Prevention and Abstinence-Only Addiction Treatment.* New York: Routledge, 2024.

White Bison, Inc. *The Red Road to Wellbriety: In the Native American Way.* Colorado Springs: White Bison, 2002.

Medicine

Buqué, Dr. Mariel. *Break the Cycle: A Guide to Healing Intergenerational Trauma.* New York: Dutton 2024.

Herman, Judith Lewis. *Trauma and Recovery: The Aftermath of Violence—from Domestic Abuse to Political Terror.* New York: Basic Books, 1992.

Marya, Rupa, and Raj Patel. *Inflamed: Deep Medicine and the Anatomy of Injustice.* Farrar, Straus and Giroux, 2021.

Maté, Gabor. *Scattered Minds: A New Look at the Origins and Healing of Attention Deficit Disorder.* London: Vermilion, 1999.

Maté, Gabor, and Daniel Maté. *The Myth of Normal: Trauma, Illness and Healing in a Toxic Culture.* New York: Avery, 2022.

Menakem, Resmaa. *My Grandmother's Hands: Racialized Trauma and the Pathway to Mending Our Hearts and Bodies.* Las Vegas: Central Recovery Press, 2017.

O'Rourke, Meghan. *The Invisible Kingdom: Reimagining Chronic Illness.* New York: Riverhead Books, 2022.

Perry, Bruce D., and Oprah Winfrey. *What Happened to You? Conversations on Trauma, Resilience, and Healing.* New York: Flatiron Books, 2021.

Wolynn, Mark. *It Didn't Start with You: How Inherited Family Trauma Shapes Who We Are and How to End the Cycle.* New York: Penguin Life, 2016.

Generosity

Abdurraqib, Hanif. *There's Always This Year: On Basketball and Ascension.* New York: Random House, 2024.

Allen, Chaney. *I'm Black and I'm Sober: A Minister's Daughter Tells Her Story About Fighting the Disease of Alcoholism—and Winning.* Minneapolis: CompCare Publications, 1978.

Angelou, Maya. *I Know Why the Caged Bird Sings.* New York: Random House, 1969.

Broom, Sarah M. *The Yellow House.* New York: Grove Press, 2019.

Cha, Theresa Hak Kyung. *Dictee.* Berkeley: University of California Press, 2001.

Chee, Alexander. *How to Write an Autobiographical Novel: Essays.* New York: Mariner Books, 2018.

Chung, Nicole. *A Living Remedy: A Memoir.* New York: Ecco, 2023.

Cliff, Michelle. *Claiming an Identity They Taught Me to Despise.* Watertown, MA: Persephone Press, 1980.

Clifton, Lucille. *Generations: A Memoir.* New York: The New York Review of Books, 2021.

Coel, Michaela. *Misfits: A Personal Manifesto.* New York: Henry Holt, 2021.

Contreras, Ingrid Rojas. *The Man Who Could Move Clouds: A Memoir.* New York: Doubleday, 2022.

Díaz, Jaquira. *Ordinary Girls: A Memoir.* Chapel Hill: Algonquin Books, 2019.

Ditlevsen, Tove. *The Copenhagen Trilogy: Childhood—Youth—Dependency*. New York: Farrar, Straus and Giroux, 2021.

Ford, Ashley C. *Somebody's Daughter: A Memoir*. New York: Flatiron Books, 2021.

Gonsalez, Marcos. *Pedro's Theory: Reimagining the Promised Land*. Brooklyn: Melville House, 2021.

Guerrero, Jean. *Crux: A Cross-Border Memoir*. New York: One World, 2018.

Gurba, Myriam. *Creep: Accusations and Confessions*. New York: Avid Reader Press, 2023.

Gurba, Myriam. *Mean*. Brooklyn: Coffee House Press, 2017.

Harjo, Joy. *Crazy Brave: A Memoir*. New York: W. W. Norton, 2012.

Hong, Cathy Park. *Minor Feelings: An Asian American Reckoning*. New York: One World, 2020.

Hudes, Quiara Alegría. *My Broken Language: A Memoir*. New York: One World, 2021.

Jamison, Leslie. *The Empathy Exams: Essays*. Minneapolis: Graywolf Press, 2014.

Jamison, Leslie. *The Recovering: Intoxication and Its Aftermath*. New York: Little, Brown, 2018.

Jefferson, Margo. *Constructing a Nervous System: A Memoir*. New York: Vintage Books, 2023.

Jones, Chloé Cooper. *Easy Beauty*. New York: Avid Reader Press, 2022.

Jones, Saeed. *How We Fight for Our Lives: A Memoir*. New York: Simon and Schuster, 2019.

Laymon, Kiese. *Heavy: An American Memoir*. New York: Scribner, 2018.

Laymon, Kiese. *How to Slowly Kill Yourself and Others in America: Essays*. New York: Scribner, 2013.

Lorde, Audre. *Zami: A New Spelling of My Name—A Biomythography*. Berkeley: Crossing Press, 1982.

Machado, Carmen Maria. *In the Dream House: A Memoir*. Minneapolis: Graywolf Press, 2019.

Miller, Chanel. *Know My Name: A Memoir*. New York: Viking, 2019.

Myers, Leah. *Thinning Blood: A Memoir of Family, Myth, and Identity*. New York: W. W. Norton, 2023.

Nguyen, Viet Thanh. *A Man of Two Faces: A Memoir, a History, a Memorial*. New York: Grove Press, 2023.

Ortiz, Wendy C. *Excavation: A Memoir*. Portland: Future Tense Books, 2014.

Owusu, Nadia. *Aftershocks: A Memoir*. New York: Simon and Schuster, 2021.

Smith, Tracy K. *Ordinary Light: A Memoir*. New York: Vintage Books, 2016.

Taffa, Deborah Jackson *Whiskey Tender: A Memoir*. New York: Harper, 2024.

Talusan, Grace. *The Body Papers: A Memoir*. Brooklyn: Restless Books, 2019.

Trethewey, Natasha. *Memorial Drive: A Daughter's Memoir*. New York: Ecco, 2020.

Ward, Jesmyn. *Men We Reaped: A Memoir*. New York: Bloomsbury, 2013.

Washuta, Elissa. *White Magic: Essays*. Portland, OR: Tin House, 2021.

Yuknavitch, Lidia. *The Chronology of Water: A Memoir*. Portland, OR: Hawthorne Books and Literary Arts, 2010.

Zamora, Javier. *Solito: A Memoir*. New York: Hogarth, 2022.

Liberation

Cárdenas, Maritza E. *Constituting Central American-Americans: Transnational Identities and the Politics of Dislocation*. New Brunswick, NJ: Rutgers University Press, 2018.

Churchwell, Sarah. *Behold America: A History of America First and the American Dream*. New York: Bloomsbury Publishing, 2019.

Davis, Angela Y. *Freedom Is a Constant Struggle: Ferguson, Palestine, and the Foundations of a Movement*. Chicago: Haymarket Books, 2016.

Euraque, Darío A. *Reinterpreting the Banana Republic: Region and State in Honduras, 1870–1972.* Chapel Hill: University of North Carolina Press, 1996.

Fanon, Frantz. *The Wretched of the Earth*, trans. Richard Philcox. New York: Grove Press, 2021.

Galeano, Eduardo. *Open Veins of Latin America: Five Centuries of the Pillage of a Continent.* New York: Monthly Review Press, 1973.

Goodwin, Michele. *Policing the Womb: Invisible Women and the Criminalization of Motherhood.* New York: Cambridge University Press, 2020.

Graeber, David. *Debt: The First 5,000 Years.* Brooklyn: Melville House, 2011.

Hamad, Ruby. *White Tears Brown Scars: How White Feminism Betrays Women of Color.* New York: Catapult, 2020.

Hernández, Tanya Katerí. *Racial Innocence: Unmasking Latino Anti-Black Bias and the Struggle for Equality.* Boston: Beacon Press, 2022.

Muñoz, José Esteban. *The Sense of Brown.* Durham: Duke University Press, 2020.

Portillo Villeda, Suyapa G. *Roots of Resistance: A Story of Gender, Race, and Labor on the North Coast of Honduras.* Austin: University of Texas Press, 2021.

Róisín, Fariha. *Who Is Wellness For? An Examination of Wellness Culture and Who It Leaves Behind.* New York: Harper Wave, 2022.

Roy, Arundhati. *War Talk.* Cambridge, MA: South End Press, 2003.

Said, Edward W. *Culture and Imperialism.* New York: Vintage Books, 1994.

Poetry

Abdurraqib, Hanif. *A Fortune for Your Disaster: Poems.* Portland, OR: Tin House Books, 2019.

Akbar, Kaveh. *Portrait of the Alcoholic.* Little Rock, AK: Sibling Rivalry Press, 2017.

Alyan, Hala. *The Moon That Turns You Back.* New York: Ecco, 2024.

Amezcua, Eloisa. *Fighting Is Like a Wife.* Minneapolis: Coffee House Press, 2022.

Ampuero, María Fernanda, *Human Sacrifices.* Translated by Frances Riddle. New York: The Feminist Press, 2023.

Diaz, Natalie. *Postcolonial Love Poem.* Minneapolis: Graywolf Press, 2022.

Guzmán, Roy G. *Catrachos: Poems.* Minneapolis: Graywolf Press, 2020.

Jones, Saeed. *Alive at the End of the World: Poems.* Minneapolis: Coffee House Press, 2022.

Limón, Ada. *Bright Dead Things.* Minneapolis: Milkweed Editions, 2015.

Limón, Ada. *The Hurting Kind.* Minneapolis: Milkweed Editions, 2022.

Maldonado, Sheila. *that's what you get.* New York: Brooklyn Arts Press, 2021.

Phillips, Carl. *Then the War: And Selected Poems 2007–2020.* New York: Farrar, Straus and Giroux, 2022.

Scenters-Zapico, Natalie. *Lima::Limón.* Port Townsend, WA: Copper Canyon Press, 2019.

Shire, Warsan. *Bless the Daughter Raised by a Voice in Her Head: Poems.* New York: Random House, 2022.

Shuck, Kim. *Deer Trails.* San Francisco: City Light Books, 2019.

Smith, Danez. *Homie: Poems.* Minneapolis: Graywolf Press, 2020.

Toha, Mosab Abu. *Things You May Find Hidden in My Ear.* San Francisco: City Light Books, 2022.

Tran, Paul. *All the Flowers Kneeling.* New York: Penguin Poets, 2022.

Walker, Alice. *Hard Times Require Furious Dancing: New Poems.* Novato, CA: New World Library, 2010.

Zamora, Javier. *Unaccompanied.* Port Townsend, WA: Copper Canyon Press, 2017.

Imagination

Akbar, Kaveh. *Martyr!* New York: Knopf, 2024.

Asghar, Fatimah. *When We Were Sisters.* New York: One World, 2022.

Baldwin, James. *Early Novels and Stories.* New York: The Library of America, 1998.

Baldwin, James. *Later Novels.* New York: The Library of America, 2015.

Cruz, Angie. *How Not to Drown in a Glass of Water.* New York: Flatiron Books, 2022.

Fragoza, Caribbean. *Eat the Mouth That Feeds You.* San Francisco: City Lights Books, 2021.

Machado, Carmen Maria. *Her Body and Other Parties.* Minneapolis: Graywolf Press, 2017.

Morrison, Toni. *Beloved.* New York: Knopf, 1987.

Morrison, Toni. *The Bluest Eye.* New York: Holt, Rinehart and Winston, 1970.

Naga, Noor. *If an Egyptian Cannot Speak English.* Minneapolis: Graywolf Press, 2022.

Orange, Tommy. *There There.* New York: Vintage Books, 2019.

Orange, Tommy. *Wandering Stars.* New York: Knopf, 2024.

Philyaw, Deesha. *The Secret Lives of Church Ladies.* Morgantown: West Virginia University Press, 2020.

Torres, Justin. *Blackouts.* New York: Farrar, Straus and Giroux, 2023.

Torres, Justin. *We the Animals.* New York: Houghton Mifflin Harcourt, 2011.

Varela, Alejandro. *The People Who Report More Stress.* New York: Astra House, 2023.

Varela, Alejandro. *The Town of Babylon.* New York: Astra House, 2022.

Vuong, Ocean. *On Earth We're Briefly Gorgeous.* New York: Penguin Press, 2019.

Wisdom

Allen, Paula Gunn. *The Sacred Hoop: Recovering the Feminine in American Indian Traditions.* Boston: Beacon Press, 1986.

Febos, Melissa. *Body Work: The Radical Power of Personal Narrative.* New York: Catapult, 2022.

Febos, Melissa. *Girlhood.* New York: Bloomsbury, 2021.

hooks, bell. *All About Love: New Visions.* New York: William Morrow, 2018.

Kimmerer, Robin Wall. *Braiding Sweetgrass: Indigenous Wisdom, Scientific Knowledge, and the Teachings of Plants.* Minneapolis: Milkweed Editions, 2013.

Longenbach, James. *The Art of the Poetic Line.* St. Paul: Graywolf Press, 2008.

Luger, Chelsea, and Thosh Collins. *The Seven Circles: Indigenous Teachings for Living Well.* New York: Harper One, 2022.

Mehl-Madrona, Lewis. *Healing the Mind Through the Power of Story: The Promise of Narrative Psychiatry.* Rochester, VT: Bear, 2010.

Morrison, Toni. *The Source of Self-Regard: Selected Essays, Speeches, and Meditations.* New York: Knopf, 2019.

Rilke, Rainer Maria. *Letters to a Young Poet / The Possibility of Being,* trans. Joan M. Burnham. New York: MJF Books, 2002.

Ruiz, Don Miguel. *The Four Agreements: A Practical Guide to Personal Freedom* (A Toltec Wisdom Book). San Rafael, CA: Amber-Allen, 1997.

Notes

1. Dream On

13   **The vapor released during distillation:** Nick Hines, "Why Is Liquor Called 'Spirits'?" Vinepair, March 7, 2017, https://vinepair.com/articles/why-liquor-called-spirits/.

13   **dislocation theory of addiction:** Bruce K. Alexander, *The Globalization of Addiction: A Study in Poverty of the Spirit* (New York: Oxford University Press, 2008), 1–84.

13   **"Dislocation, in other words":** Bruce K. Alexander, "Dislocation Theory of Addiction: Speech Highlights," Granite Recovery Centers, July 26, 2018, YouTube video, 11:25, https://www.youtu.be/05FPW4vwinA.

13   **Our collective psychospiritual wound:** Alexander, https://www.youtu.be/05FPW4vwinA.

14   **Handsome Lake, a Seneca chief:** "1799: Haudenosaunee Prophet Calls for Peace," *Native Voices: Native Peoples' Concepts of Health and Illness*, National Library of Medicine, https://www.nlm.nih.gov/nativevoices/timeline/247.html.

14   **alcoholic beverages were brewed widely:** Lucia Henderson, "Blood, Water, Vomit, and Wine: Pulque in Maya and Aztec Belief," in *Mesoamerican Voices* 3, ed. Joel Palka (Chicago: Beaker Press, 2008), 53–76, https://www.academia.edu/3811531/Blood_Water_Vomit_and_Wine_Pulque_in_Maya_and_Aztec_Belief.

14   **Colonization—the violent dislocation of land and culture:** "Our Native Elders Speak," in *The Red Road to Wellbriety: In the Native American Way* (Colorado Springs: White Bison, 2002), h-l.

14   **distilled liquor, namely whiskey:** Carl Erik Fisher, *The Urge: Our History of Addiction* (New York: Penguin Press, 2022), 33. See also Peter C. Mancall, *Deadly Medicine: Indians and Alcohol in Early America* (Ithaca, NY: Cornell University Press, 1995), 85–130; Samson Occom, "A Sermon Preached at the Execution of Moses Paul, an Indian," in *Early American Writings*, ed. Carla Mulford (New York: Oxford University Press, 2002), 867–82, https://web.english.upenn.edu/~cavitch/pdf-library/Occom_NarrativeandSermon.pdf.

14   **According to historians:** Christopher Finan, *Drunks: An American History* (Boston: Beacon Press, 2017), 6–17.

14   **and the first sobriety movement:** "Introduction," *The Red Road to Wellbriety*, d.

14 **Handsome Lake became a prophet:** "1799: Haudenosaunee Prophet Calls for Peace," https://www.nlm.nih.gov/nativevoices/timeline/247.html.

14 **His teachings, known as Gai'wiio:** "Introduction," *The Red Road to Wellbriety*, e.

14 **"No one leaves home":** Warsan Shire, "Home," *Bless the Daughter Raised by a Voice in Her Head* (New York: Random House, 2022), 24.

15 **"adverse childhood experiences":** Jingzhen He, Xinyu Yan, Rufang Wang, Juyou Zhao, Jun Liu, Changwei Zhou, and Yumei Zeng, "Does Childhood Adversity Lead to Drug Addiction in Adulthood? A Study of Serial Mediators Based on Resilience and Depression," *Frontiers in Psychiatry* 13 (2022): 871459, https://doi.org/10.3389/fpsyt.2022.871459.

2. Location, Location, Location

17 **Unemployment skyrocketed throughout 1981:** Michael A. Urquhart and Marillyn A. Hewson, "Unemployment Continued to Rise in 1982 as the Recession Deepened," *Monthly Labor Review*, February 1983, 3, https://www.bls.gov/opub/mlr/1983/02/art1full.pdf.

3. Workhorse

24 **officially listed on both:** "Schiff's History," Schiff Nature Preserve, 2023, https://www.schiffnaturepreserve.org/schiff-natural-lands-trust.cfm.

25 **Union School, built in 1851:** "Union School 1851," Mendham in Morris County, New Jersey—The American Northeast (Mid-Atlantic), Historical Marker Database, https://www.hmdb.org/m.?.m=16981.

25 **The one-room schoolhouse, one of five:** "School Days, School Days, Dear Old Golden Rule Days," *The General Store: Newsletter of the Ralston Historical Association*, Summer 2019, 2, www.ralstonmuseum.org/sitebuildercontent/sitebuilderfiles/219rhanewsletter.pdf.

7. Traviesa

48 **The annual two-week-long celebration:** Nicole Canún, "Action-Packed, Colorful Celebration of La Ceiba Carnaval in Honduras," *Spanish Academy* (blog), July 25, 2021, https://www.spanish.academy/blog/action-packed-colorful-celebration-of-la-ceiba-carnaval-in-honduras/.

49 **The tradition originated as a pilgrimage:** Isabel García, "El Madrid de San Isidro: una ruta entre milagros, chulapos y rosquillas tontas y listas," *El Mundo*, May 13, 2023, https://www.elmundo.es/viajes/espana/2023/05/13/6458ff8efc6c8396718b45a1.html.

49 **the festivities now known as the Honduran Mardi Gras:** Canún, https://www.spanish.academy/blog/action-packed-colorful-celebration-of-la-ceiba-carnaval-in-honduras/.

8. D(rug) A(buse) R(esistance) E(ducation)

56 **rather than being in school, were giving birth:** George H. W. Bush, "President George H. W. Bush Addresses the Nation on His National Drug Policy," September 5, 1989, National Archives Identifer 54630, in Series: Moving Images Relating to U.S. Domestic and International Activities, 34:41, at 15:54, https://catalog.archives.gov/id/54630.

57 **Nixon's age of "law and order":** Richard M. Nixon, "Drugs Our Second Civil War: Cut the Chain of Greed, Poverty, Self-Indulgence," *Los Angeles Times*, April 12, 1990, https://www.latimes.com/archives/la-xpm-1990-04-12-me-1267-story.html.

57 **one the government was prepared to spend billions:** Krissy Clark, "30 Years Ago, George H. W. Bush Held Up a Baggie of Crack on Live TV. Where'd He Get It?" *Marketplace*, March 21, 2019, https://www.marketplace.org/2019/03/21/george-hw-bush-baggie-crack/.

57 **"Americans have a right to safety":** Bush, https://catalog.archives.gov/id/54630.

57 **"beyond our borders":** Bush, https://catalog.archives.gov/id/54630.

59 **Statistics show:** Abby Budiman, "Key Findings About U.S. Immigrants," Pew Research Center, August 20, 2020, https://www.pewresearch.org/short-reads/2020/08/20/key-findings-about-u-s-immigrants/.

60 **"a dealer or an addict":** Bush, https://catalog.archives.gov/id/54630.

60 **"Families must set the first example":** Bush, https://catalog.archives.gov/id/54630.

60 **While still a Texas governor:** Jonathan Weisman, "Bush Says He's Been Drug-Free 25 Years," *Baltimore Sun*, August 20, 1999, https://www.baltimoresun.com/news/bs-xpm-1999-08-20–9908200196-story.html.

60 **ICE arrested more than sixty-seven thousand:** "Drug War Stats," Drug Alliance Policy, https://drugpolicy.org/issues/drug-war-statistics.

60 **The government has been able to expel:** Grace Meng, *A Price Too High: US Families Torn Apart by Deportations for Drug Offenses* (Human Rights Watch, 2015) http://www.hrw.org/node/135529.

60 **Simple (pot) possession escalated:** Jason A. Cade, "The Plea Bargain Crisis for Noncitizens in Misdemeanor Court," *Cardozo Law Review* 34 (2013): 1754; Jenny Roberts, "Why Misdemeanors Matter: Defining Effective Advocacy in the Lower Criminal Courts," *UC Davis Law Review* 45 (2011): 277.

11. Sick as Our Secrets

74 **similar to Valium but ten times stronger:** "Rohypnol," Drugs.com, https://www.drugs.com/illicit/rohypnol.html.

74 **Its effects magnify:** "Rohypnol," Foundation for a Drug-Free World, https://www.drugfreeworld.org/drugfacts/prescription/rohypnol.html.

74 **The most common symptoms:** "Rohypnol," https://www.drugs.com/illicit/rohypnol.html.

74 **It is a potent tranquilizer:** "Rohypnol," https://www.drugfreeworld.org/drugfacts/prescription/rohypnol.html.

15. Red Flags, Green Light

94 **During the nineteenth century, references to pot:** Matt Thompson, "The Mysterious History of 'Marijuana,'" *Code Switch: Word Watch*, NPR, July 22, 2013, https://www.npr.org/sections/codeswitch/2013/07/14/201981025/the-mysterious-history-of-marijuana.

94 **But after the political upheaval in Mexico:** Eric Schlosser, "Reefer Madness," *Atlantic*, August 1994, https://www.theatlantic.com/magazine/archive/1994/08/reefer-madness/303476/.

94 **Cannabis was banned in Mexico in 1920:** Isaac Campos, *Home Grown: Marijuana and the Origins of Mexico's War on Drugs* (Chapel Hill: University of North Carolina Press, 2012), 19.

94 **Mexicans would cross the border:** Olivia B. Waxman, "The Surprising Link between U.S. Marijuana Law and the History of Immigration," *Time*, April 20, 2019, https://time.com/5572691/420-marijuana-mexican-immigration/.

95 **Most immigrants did not smoke pot:** Waxman, https://time.com/5572691/420-marijuana-mexican-immigration/.

95 **"I wish I could show you":** "Additional Statement of H. J. Anslinger, Commissioner of Narcotics," The Marihuana Tax Act of 1937: Transcripts of Congressional Hearings, Drug Library, https://www.druglibrary.org/schaffer/hemp/taxact/t10a.htm. See also Floyd Baskette, *Alamosa Daily Courier*, September 4, 1936, https://www.druglibrary.org/schaffer/hemp/taxact/t10a.htm.

97   **All parts of the moon are exposed:** "Moon in Motion," NASA Science, https://moon.nasa
     .gov/moon-in-motion/moon-phases/.

97   **On August 18, 2016, the full sturgeon moon:** "The Next Full Moon Is the Sturgeon Moon,"
     NASA Science, August 13, 2016, https://moon.nasa.gov/news/20/the-next-full-moon-is-the
     -sturgeon-moon/.

16. Unreliable Narrator

102 **Delirium is described:** Susan Bernstein, "Delirium Tremens," WebMD, September 3, 2022,
     https://www.webmd.com/mental-health/addiction/delirium-tremens.

20. Inheritance

120 **William Sydney Porter, known as O. Henry:** North Carolina History Project, s.v. "O.
     Henry (1862–1910)," by Jonathan Martin, https://northcarolinahistory.org/encyclopedia
     /o-henry-1862-1910 /. See also NCpedia, s.v. "William Sidney Porter (O. Henry)," by Christy E.
     Allen, https://www.ncpedia.org/biography/porter-william-sidney; Wikipedia, s.v. "O. Henry,"
     last modified October 13, 2023, https://en.wikipedia.org/wiki/O._Henry.

120 **book of short stories:** O. Henry, *Cabbages and Kings* (1904). See also https://en.wikipedia
     .org/wiki/O._Henry.

120 **Economists, journalists, and political pundits:** Dario A. Euraque, "Cliché and Caricature:
     Why January 6 Was Not Like a Banana Republic," *Perspectives on History*, May 12, 2021,
     https://www.historians.org/research-and-publications/perspectives-on-history/may-2021
     /clich%c3%a9-and-caricature-why-january-6-was-not-like-a-banana-republic. See also Dario
     A. Euraque, *Reinterpreting the Banana Republic: Region and State in Honduras, 1870–1972*
     (Chapel Hill: University of North Carolina Press, 1996), 77–89.

120 **The term *banana republic* tells the story:** Euraque, historians.org/research-and
     -publications/perspectives-on-history/may-2021/clich%c3%a9-and-caricature-why-january
     -6-was-not-like-a-banana-republic. See also Euraque, *Reinterpreting the Banana Republic*.

120 **O. Henry was actually in Honduras:** "Short Story Writer O. Henry Is Released from Prison,"
     This Day in History: July 24, 1901, History.com, November 13, 2009, www.history.com/this
     -day-in-history/o-henry-is-released-from-prison. See also en.wikipedia.org/wiki/O._Henry.

121 **He published fourteen stories under pseudonyms:** Eugene Current-Garcia, *O. Henry:
     A Study of the Short Fiction* (New York: Twayne Publishers, 1993), 123. See also https://en
     .wikipedia.org/wiki/O._Henry.

121 **O. Henry died at forty-seven:** Charles T. Brown, "O. Henry the Pharmacist," *Military Med-
     icine* 132, no. 10 (October 1967): 823–25, https://doi.org/10.1093/milmed/132.10.823.

121 **"decades of Dictators":** Kevin Strand, "Hondurans Campaign for Democracy, 1944," Global
     Nonviolent Action Database (Swarthmore College), February 25, 2012, https://nvdatabase
     .swarthmore.edu/content/hondurans-campaign-democracy-1944. See also Euraque, *Reinter-
     preting the Banana Republic*, 61–62, 68.

121 **The northern coast of Honduras:** Suyapa G. Portillo Villeda, *Roots of Resistance: A Story of
     Gender, Race, and Labor on the North Coast of Honduras* (Austin: University of Texas Press,
     2021), 87.

21. Concepción

129 **"Panama Disease":** Suyapa G. Portillo Villeda, *Roots of Resistance: A Story of Gender, Race,
     and Labor on the North Coast of Honduras* (Austin: University of Texas Press, 2021), 239.

129 **Unlike in neighboring countries, Honduran workers:** Portillo Villeda, *Roots of Resistance*, 188.

129 **Two US-based and -backed companies:** Dario A. Euraque, *Reinterpreting the Banana Republic: Region and State in Honduras, 1870–1972* (Chapel Hill: University of North Carolina Press, 1996), 6–7, 28, 43–44, 48.

130 **bosses at these companies:** Daniel Bradburd and William Jankowiak, "Drugs, Desire, and European Economic Expansion," in *Drugs, Labor, and Colonial Expansion*, ed. William Jankowiak and Daniel Bradburd (Tucson: University of Arizona Press, 2003), 3–4.

130 **While on the job:** Portillo Villeda, *Roots of Resistance*, 137.

130 **Women reported that drunkenness often led:** Portillo Villeda, *Roots of Resistance*, 139.

130 **workable defense against:** Portillo Villeda, *Roots of Resistance*, 139.

22. Abandono

132 **On April 26, 1954:** Suyapa G. Portillo Villeda, *Roots of Resistance: A Story of Gender, Race, and Labor on the North Coast of Honduras* (Austin: University of Texas Press, 2021), 294.

132 **a document known as the Rolston Letter:** Portillo Villeda, *Roots of Resistance*, 138.

133 **In other words, let's soak them:** Daniel Bradburd and William Jankowiak, "Drugs, Desire, and European Economic Expansion," in *Drugs, Labor, and Colonial Expansion*, ed. William Jankowiak and Daniel Bradburd (Tucson: University of Arizona Press, 2003), 3–4.

133 **Rolston's plan in 1920:** Portillo Villeda, *Roots of Resistance*, 138.

133 **The letter's legitimacy:** Portillo Villeda, *Roots of Resistance*, 138, 293.

135 **The process of ripening is called senescence:** "What Is Ethylene?," Be Fresh Technology, 2018, http://www.befreshtech.com/en/what-is-ethylene/

25. Land of the Free

150 **Honduras is one of six countries:** Amy Braunschweiger and Margaret Wurth, "Life or Death Choices for Women Living under Honduras' Abortion Ban," Human Rights Watch, June 6, 2019, www.hrw.org/news/2019/06/06/life-or-death-choices-women-living-under -honduras-abortion-ban.

152 **The World Health Organization:** "The End of Roe v. Wade: Leaked Opinion Shows Supreme Court Is Set to Overturn Abortion Rights," Democracy Now!, May 3, 2022, YouTube video, 21:38, at 9:32, https://youtu.be/XHS9yJ7mV0I. See also *Clinical Practice Handbook for Safe Abortion* (Geneva: World Health Organization, 2014), https://www.ncbi.nlm.nih.gov /books/NBK190095/.

27. Family Disease

168 **a local department in New Jersey:** "NJ CARES Data by Race: The Opioid Epidemic's Impact on Communities of Color," State of New Jersey Department of Law & Public Safety, January 1, 2015–October 15, 2021, https://www.njoag.gov/programs/nj-cares/nj-cares-data -by-race/.

168 **ODMA:** "NJ CARES Data by Race," https://www.njoag.gov/programs/nj-cares/nj-cares-data -by-race/.

169 **50 percent of all federal drug cases:** "Latinxs and the Drug War," Drug Policy Alliance, accessed May 2023, https://drugpolicy.org/latinxs-and-drug-war.

169 **only 19 percent:** "Quick Facts," US Census Bureau, accessed February 2024, https://www .census.gov/quickfacts/fact/table/US/RHI725222.

172 **In the book *In the Realm of Hungry Ghosts*:** Gabor Maté and Daniel Maté, *The Myth of Normal: Trauma, Illness and Healing in a Toxic Culture* (New York: Avery, 2022), 30; Gabor Maté, *In the Realm of Hungry Ghosts: Close Encounters with Addiction* (Berkeley, CA: North Atlantic Books, 2008), page xix–xxxv.

172 **Anywhere from half to a third of drug use issues:** Jingzhen He, Xinyu Yan, Rufang Wang, Juyou Zhao, Jun Liu, Changwei Zhou, and Yumei Zeng, "Does Childhood Adversity Lead to Drug Addiction in Adulthood? A Study of Serial Mediators Based on Resilience and Depression," *Frontiers in Psychiatry* 13 (2022): 871459, https://doi.org/10.3389/fpsyt.2022.871459.

172 **Maté described how notions of personal responsibility:** Gabor Maté and Daniel Maté, *The Myth of Normal: Trauma, Illness and Healing in a Toxic Culture*, 30.

28. Price of Admission

174 **calling all Mexicans drug smugglers:** Adam Gabbatt, "Donald Trump's Tirade on Mexico's 'Drugs and Rapists' Outrages US Latinos," *Guardian*, June 16, 2015, https://www.theguardian.com/us-news/2015/jun/16/donald-trump-mexico-presidential-speech-latino-hispanic.

176 **they are far more likely to be criminalized:** "Race and the Drug War," Drug Policy Alliance, accessed May 2023, https://drugpolicy.org/issues/race-and-drug-war.

176 **Eighty percent of people in federal prisons:** "Race and the Drug War," https://drugpolicy.org/issues/race-and-drug-war. See also Betsy Pearl, "Ending the War on Drugs: By the Numbers," Center for American Progress, June 27, 2018, https://www.americanprogress.org/article/ending-war-drugs-numbers/.

176 **Black people who suffer opioid overdose:** Nzinga Harrison, "Racism Is an Addiction," June 2020, in *In Recovery*, produced by Claire Jones, podcast, MP3 audio, 01:01:34, Lemonada Media, https://lemonadamedia.com/podcast/racism-is-an-addiction/.

176 **overdose by 50 percent:** Matthias Pierce, Sheila M. Bird, Matthew Hickman, John Marsden, Graham Dunn, Andrew Jones, and Tim Millar, "Impact of Treatment for Opioid Dependence on Fatal Drug-Related Poisoning: A National Cohort Study in England," *Addiction* 111, no. 2 (February 2016): 298–308, https://doi.org/10.1111/add.13193. See also Emily Baumgaertner, "Medication Treatment for Addiction Is Shorter for Black and Hispanic Patients, Study Finds," *New York Times*, November 9, 2022, https://www.nytimes.com/2022/11/09/health/opioid-addiction-treatment-racial-disparities.html.

176 **do not receive the quality or duration of care:** Huiru Dong, Erin J. Stringfellow, W. Alton Russell, and Mohammad S. Jalali, "Racial and Ethnic Disparities in Buprenorphine Treatment Duration in the US," *JAMA Psychiatry* 80, no. 1 (2023): 93–95, https://doi.org/10.1001/jamapsychiatry.2022.3673. See also Baumgaertner, https://www.nytimes.com/2022/11/09/health/opioid-addiction-treatment-racial-disparities.html.

176 **These qualifications:** Dong et al., https://doi.org/10.1001/jamapsychiatry.2022.3673.

176 **And the discrepancies in treatment:** Dong et al., https://doi.org/10.1001/jamapsychiatry.2022.3673. See also Baumgaertner, https://www.nytimes.com/2022/11/09/health/opioid-addiction-treatment-racial-disparities.html.

177 **Racism and oppression are institutionally sanctioned:** Harrison, https://lemonadamedia.com/podcast/racism-is-an-addiction/.

177 **"cumulative degradation of health":** Harrison, https://lemonadamedia.com/podcast/racism-is-an-addiction/.

177 **For racialized people, this heightened:** Harrison, https://lemonadamedia.com/podcast/racism-is-an-addiction/.

178 **According to Dr. Harrison, the medical effects:** Harrison, https://lemonadamedia.com
    /podcast/racism-is-an-addiction/.

178 **"All of those social, cultural, political inputs":** Harrison, https://lemonadamedia.com
    /podcast/racism-is-an-addiction/.

178 **"At the same time":** Harrison, https://lemonadamedia.com/podcast/racism-is-an-addiction/.

178 **"And so the way you do that systematically":** Harrison, https://lemonadamedia.com/podcast
    /racism-is-an-addiction/.

29. The AA MFA

181 **On the evening of June 12, 2020:** Malachy Browne, Caroline Kim, Muyi Xiao, and Barbara
    Marcolini, "The Killing of Rayshard Brooks: How a 41-Minute Police Encounter Sud-
    denly Turned Fatal," *New York Times*, June 22, 2020, https://www.nytimes.com/video/us
    /100000007198581/rayshard-brooks-killing-garrett-rolfe.html.

30. It Works If You Work It

188 **New York's alcohol delivery services surged:** David Gauvey Herbert, "New York's Booze
    Deliveries Are Skyrocketing," *New York Magazine*, March 18, 2020, https://www.grubstreet
    .com/2020/03/nyc-liquor-delivery-apps-massive-business-spikes.html.

188 **"It's a tremendous difference":** Reagan Reed, interview by Rhiannon Corby, "Alcoholics
    Anonymous Goes Remote," March 31, 2020, in *New Yorker Radio Hour*, podcast, 19:05,
    https://www.npr.org/podcasts/458929150/the-new-yorker-radio-hour.

188 **"The way that our fellowship works":** Reed, https://www.npr.org/podcasts/458929150/the
    -new-yorker-radio-hour.

190 **Anthropologists suggest Andean people:** V. Casikar, E. Mujica, M. Mongelli, J. Aliaga, N.
    Lopez, C. Smith, and F. Bartholomew, "Does Chewing Coca Leaves Influence Physiology at
    High Altitude?" *Indian Journal of Clinical Biochemistry* 25 (July 2010): 311–14, https://doi
    .org/10.1007/s12291-010-0059-1.

190 **The intoxicant cocaine was isolated:** Andrzej Grzybowski, "Historia kokainy w medycynie
    i jej znaczenie dla odkrycia różnych form znieczulenia" (The history of cocaine in medicine
    and its importance to the discovery of the different forms of anesthesia), *Klinika Oczna* 109
    (2007): 101–5.

190 **"protector of the Western Hemisphere":** "Message of President James Monroe at the Com-
    mencement of the First Session of the 18th Congress (the Monroe Doctrine)," December 2,
    1823; Presidential Messages of the 18th Congress, ca. December 2, 1823, to March 3, 1825;
    Record Group 46; Records of the United States Senate, 1789–1990; National Archives, https:
    //www.archives.gov/milestone-documents/monroe-doctrine.

191 **By the turn of the twentieth century:** Cecil Adams, "Why Does South America Grow All
    the Coca?" *Salt Lake City Weekly*, May 16, 2018, https://www.cityweekly.net/utah/why-does
    -south-america-grow-all-the-coca/Content?oid=8896326; Paul Gootenberg, "Cocaine: The
    Hidden Histories," introduction to *Cocaine: Global Histories*, ed. Paul Gootenberg (London:
    Routledge, 2014), 40–44, 46–48; Marcel de Kort, "Doctors, Diplomats, and Businessmen:
    Conflicting Interests in the Netherlands and Dutch East Indies, 1860–1950," in *Cocaine*,
    310–63; and Steven B. Karch, MD, "Japan and the Cocaine Industry of Southeast Asia,
    1864–1944," in *Cocaine*, 364–402.

191 **Cocaine use, both medicinal and recreational:** Joseph F. Spillane, "Making a Modern

Drug: The Manufacture, Sale, and Control of Cocaine in the United States, 1880–1920," in Gootenberg, *Cocaine: Global Histories*, 68–70, 82–98.

191 **and the drug's reputation:** Gootenberg, "Cocaine: The Hidden Histories," in Gootenberg, *Cocaine: Global Histories*, 42.

191 **the government went full bore on prohibition:** Carl Erik Fisher, *The Urge: Our History of Addiction* (New York: Penguin Press, 2022), 137, 127; Spillane, "Making a Modern Drug," in Gootenberg, *Cocaine: Global Histories*, 94–98.

191 **and the United States bullied the rest:** Gootenberg, "Cocaine: The Hidden Histories," in Gootenberg, *Cocaine: Global Histories*, 42.

191 **The Dutch were more amenable:** Adams, https://www.cityweekly.net/utah/why-does-south-america-grow-all-the-coca/Content?oid=8896326. See also Gootenberg, "Cocaine: The Hidden Histories," in Gootenberg, *Cocaine: Global Histories*, 41–43, 46–48; Spillane, "Making a Modern Drug," in Gootenburg, *Cocaine*, 94–98; Marcel de Kort, "Doctors, Diplomats, and Businessmen," in *Cocaine*, 310–63; and Steven B. Karch, MD, "Japan and the Cocaine Industry of Southeast Asia, 1864–1944," in *Cocaine*, 364–402.

191 **Funny, as the United States righteously fought:** Adams, https://www.cityweekly.net/utah/why-does-south-america-grow-all-the-coca/Content?oid=8896326. See also Joseph F. Spillane, "Making a Modern Drug," 67–97; Mary Roldan, "Columbia: Cocaine and the 'Miracle' of Modernity in Medellin," 404–46; and Luis Astorga, "Cocaine in Mexico: A prelude to 'Los Narcos,'" 447–67, all in Gootenberg, *Cocaine*.

192 **for five grams of crack cocaine:** Deborah J. Vagins and Jesselyn McCurdy, *Cracks in the System: Twenty Years of the Unjust Federal Crack Cocaine Law* (ACLU, October 2006), https://www.aclu.org/sites/default/files/pdfs/drugpolicy/cracksinsystem_20061025.pdf. See also Fisher, *The Urge*, 256.

192 **"We have to hold every drug user accountable":** Joseph Biden Jr., "Democratic Response to Drug Policy Address," C-SPAN, video, 11:00, September 5, 1989, https://www.c-span.org/video/?8997-1/democratic-response-drug-policy-address.

192 **The war on drugs enabled the government:** Fisher, *The Urge*, 256.

192 **thanks in part to the pharmaceutical:** Fisher, *The Urge*, 255.

192 **"My son, like a lot of people":** Brian Mann, "Experts Say Attack on Hunter Biden's Addiction Deepens Stigma for Millions," *Morning Edition*, NPR, October 16, 2020, https://www.npr.org/2020/10/16/923647389/experts-say-attack-on-hunter-bidens-addiction-deepens-stigma-for-millions.

193 **It has no interest:** Fisher, *The Urge*, 255–57.

193 **According to a recent NPR/Ipsos poll:** Joel Rose, "Many Americans Falsely Think Migrants Are Bringing Most of the Fentanyl Entering U.S.," *All Things Considered*, NPR, August 18, 2022, https://www.npr.org/2022/08/18/1118271910/many-americans-falsely-think-migrants-are-bringing-most-of-the-fentanyl-entering.

194 **"America is an idea":** "Full Transcript of President Biden's Speech in Philadelphia," *New York Times*, September 1, 2022, https://www.nytimes.com/2022/09/01/us/politics/biden-speech-transcript.html.

31. Off the Ropes

201 **being Nawa:** "Cuna Náhuat: Proyecto de inmersión lingüística para salvar el idioma originario náhuat-pipil," Colectivo El Salvador Elkartasuna, https://www.elsalvadorelkartasuna.eus/zertan-ari-gara-que-hacemos/cuna-nahuat/.

202 **established nearly two hundred years:** "Introduction," *The Red Road to Wellbriety: In the Native American Way* (Colorado Springs: White Bison, 2002), d.

202 **deeper understanding of my relationship to myself:** Eduardo Duran, *Healing the Soul Wound: Counseling with American Indians and Other Native Peoples*, Multicultural Foundations of Psychology and Counseling series (New York: Teachers College Press, 2006), 66.

202 **culturally competent and decolonized approach:** Duran, *Healing the Soul Wound*, 9–10.

202 **awareness of oppression:** Duran, *Healing the Soul Wound*, 9–10.

203 **an "alien disease":** "Introduction," *The Red Road to Wellbriety*, d.

203 **During the mid-eighteenth century:** "Introduction," *The Red Road to Wellbriety*, d–e.

203 **Caribbean slave plantations supplied:** Carl Erik Fisher, *The Urge: Our History of Addiction* (New York: Penguin Press, 2022), 50.

203 **a wave of unrest soon answered:** Fisher, *The Urge*, 78–79.

203 **In a famous letter:** Thomas Jefferson, "To Brother Handsome Lake," Jefferson's Indian Addresses, November 3, 1802, Avalon Project Documents in Law, History and Diplomacy, Yale Law School Lillian Goldman Law Library, 2008, https://avalon.law.yale.edu/19th_century/jeffind2.asp.

203 **"But these nations have done to you":** Jefferson, https://avalon.law.yale.edu/19th_century/jeffind2.asp.

203 **"Spirituous liquors":** Jefferson, https://avalon.law.yale.edu/19th_century/jeffind2.asp.

204 **Zuanah (Quanah Parker) established:** "Introduction," *The Red Road to Wellbriety*, e.

204 **excluding Black people from the temperance:** Frederick Douglass, "Temperance and Anti-Slavery: An Address Delivered in Paisley, Scotland on March 30, 1846," *Renfrewshire Advertiser*, April 11, 1846, in *The Frederick Douglass Papers: Series One—Speeches, Debates, and Interviews*, ed. John Blassingame et al., vol. 1 (New Haven, CT: Yale University Press, 1979), 205.

204 **On March 30, 1846, Frederick Douglass:** Douglass, "Temperance and Anti-Slavery."

204 **"As I desire, therefore, their freedom":** Douglass, "Temperance and Anti-Slavery."

204 **Of the approximately 10.7 million people:** Tanya Katerí Hernández, *Racial Innocence: Unmasking Latino Anti-Black Bias and the Struggle for Equality* (Boston: Beacon Press Books, 2022), 13.

204 **supposed taxonomy of admixtures:** Hernández, *Racial Innocence*, 5–6.

205 **objectivity of history:** Duran, *Healing the Soul Wound*, 51.

205 **"soul wound":** Duran, *Healing the Soul Wound*, 65.

205 **consciousness:** Duran, *Healing the Soul Wound*, 66.

32. The Tenth Tradition

207 **efficacy has been debated:** John F. Kelly, Alexandra Abry, Marica Ferri, and Keith Humphreys, "Alcoholics Anonymous and 12-Step Facilitation Treatments for Alcohol Use Disorder: A Distillation of a 2020 Cochrane Review for Clinicians and Policy Makers," *Alcohol and Alcoholism* 55, no. 6 (November 2020): 641–51, https://doi.org/10.1093/alcalc/agaa050. See also Lance Dodes and Zachary Dodes, "The Problem," and "Does AA Work?," in *The Sober Truth: Debunking the Bad Science Behind 12-Step Programs and the Rehab Industry* (Boston: Beacon Press, 2014).

207 **even during a period of intense stigma:** Carl Erik Fisher, *The Urge: Our History of Addiction* (New York: Penguin Press, 2022), 152–53.

207 **When he met Dr. Bob:** Fisher, *The Urge*, 154–55.

207 **He knew service, a key principle:** Fisher, *The Urge*, 153–55. See also T. Willard Hunter, "AA's Roots in the Oxford Group—Mel B.," Silkworth.net, https://silkworth.net/alcoholics -anonymous/aas-roots-in-the-oxford-group-mel-b/.

207 **Together, they created the twelve steps:** Fisher, *The Urge*, 155–56.

208 **In Tradition Ten:** "Tradition Ten," in *Twelve Steps and Twelve Traditions* (New York: A.A. Grapevine and Alcoholics Anonymous Publishing, 1953), https://www.aa.org/twelve-steps -twelve-traditions.

208 **Washingtonians, a group of six:** Richard Ewell Brown, "Washingtonians," A.A. Grapevine, December 1948, https://silkworth.net/alcoholics-anonymous/washingtonians-by-richard -ewell-brown-december-1948/. See also Wikipedia, s.v. "Washingtonian Movement," last modified September 27, 2023, https://en.wikipedia.org/wiki/Washingtonian_movement.

208 **"Alcoholics Anonymous has no opinion":** "Tradition Ten," https://www.aa.org/twelve -steps-twelve-traditions.

208 **This issue was brought forth:** James C. and Michael Herbert, "African American Alcoholics (Part 2)," *The Recovery Guide* (blog), May 6, 2016, https://recoveryguide.net/african-american -alcoholics-part-2/.

211 **hooks held a residency:** Emma Donelly-Higgins, "New School Mourns Death of Former Scholar-in-Residence bell hooks," New School Free Press, December 22, 2021, https:// www.newschoolfreepress.com/2021/12/22/new-school-mourns-death-of-former-scholar-in -residence-bell-hooks/.

211 **"Healing does not take place in isolation":** bell hooks, "Moving from Pain to Power," panel discussion with Marci Blackman and Darnell Moore, Eugene Lang College of Liberal Arts at The New School, New York, October 7, 2015, YouTube video posted October 12, 2015, 1:30:40, https://www.youtube.com/watch?v=cpKuLl-GC0M.

212 **"I still think that the recovery movement":** hooks, https://www.youtube.com/watch?v =cpKuLl-GC0M.

212 **"He really beats himself up":** hooks, https://www.youtube.com/watch?v=cpKuLl-GC0M.

213 **allowed two Black alcoholics:** Glenn F. Chesnut, *Heroes of Early Black AA: Their Stories and Their Messages* (South Bend, IN: Hindsfoot Foundation, 2017), 3–9.

213 **he wrote to Joe D.:** Chesnut, *Heroes of Early Black AA*, 3–9.

213 **on October 20, 1945:** Chesnut, *Heroes of Early Black AA*, 3–9.

214 **Brownie, a pioneer of the movement:** Chesnut, *Heroes of Early Black AA*, 219–38.

214 **five years into his sobriety:** Chesnut, *Heroes of Early Black AA*, 219–38.

214 **"I cast my eyes down upon a man":** Chesnut, *Heroes of Early Black AA*, 219–38.

215 **"Racial prejudice and hatred":** Chesnut, *Heroes of Early Black AA*, 219–38.

33. We Need More Stories of Recovery

219 **"We Blacks must start documenting":** Chaney Allen, *I'm Black and I'm Sober: A Minister's Daughter Tells Her Story about Fighting the Disease of Alcoholism—and Winning* (Minneapolis: CompCare Publications, 1978), ix.

219 **"I didn't know":** Chaney Allen, interview by John Hanson, "In Black America; Ms. Chaney Allen," October 1, 1983, KUT radio (Austin, Texas), American Archive of Public Broadcasting (GBH and the Library of Congress), Boston and Washington, DC, audio, 25:38, https: //americanarchive.org/catalog/cpb-aacip-529-cj87h1ft89.

220 **"As a Black [person]"**: Allen interview, https://americanarchive.org/catalog/cpb-aacip-529 -cj87h1ft89.

220 **"the wound to be healed must be revealed"**: Allen interview, https://americanarchive.org /catalog/cpb-aacip-529-cj87h1ft89.

220 **"What it takes"**: Allen interview, https://americanarchive.org/catalog/cpb-aacip-529-cj87h1ft89.

220 **"Unfortunately those are the poor ladies"**: Allen interview, https://americanarchive.org /catalog/cpb-aacip-529-cj87h1ft89.

221 **"Three stigmas: female, alcoholic, and Black"**: Allen interview, https://americanarchive .org/catalog/cpb-aacip-529-cj87h1ft89.

221 **"I hope, and I'm trying to be a model"**: Allen interview, https://americanarchive.org/catalog /cpb-aacip-529-cj87h1ft89.

34. Claiming an Identity They Taught Me to Despise

225 **From a statistical perspective:** "Alcoholics Anonymous 2014 Membership Survey," AA General Service Conference, 2014, https://www.aa.org/sites/default/files/literature/assets/p -48_membershipsurvey.pdf.

229 **one of many varieties:** Lance Grande and Allison Augustyn, *Gems and Gemstones: Timeless Natural Beauty of the Mineral World* (Chicago: University of Chicago Press, 2009), 323.

229 **A myth animated:** Claude Lecouteux, *A Lapidary of Sacred Stones: Their Magical and Medicinal Powers Based on the Earliest Sources*, trans. Jon E. Graham (Rochester: Inner Traditions, 2012), 47. See also "Gemstone Lore: Amethyst—The Story of Bacchus," *Gemporia*, August 5, 2019, https://www.gemporia.com/en-us/gemology-hub/article/1492/gemstone-lore -amethyst-the-story-of-bacchus/#:~:text=Bacchus%20was%20pursuing%20Amethyste%20 and,to%20protect%20her%20from%20Bacchus.

229 **the etymology of its name:** Grande and Augustyn, *Gems and Gemstones*, 87.

229 **the belief in its powers:** Grande and Augustyn, *Gems and Gemstones*, 323–24.

229 **Alongside sardonyx:** Lecouteux, *A Lapidary of Sacred Stones*, 47.

About the Author

JESSICA HOPPE is a Honduran Ecuadorian writer and the creator of @NuevaYorka. She has been featured on ABC News and Pa'lante! Max. Her work has appeared in the *Latino Book Review*, the *New York Times*, *Vogue*, and elsewhere. Hoppe is a board member of Time of Butterflies, a nonprofit supporting families through domestic abuse recovery, and is an organizer with the CentAm & Isthmian Writers group. She lives in New York City.